JOLSON

JOLSON

MICHAEL FREEDLAND

𝖘𝖉

STEIN AND DAY/*Publishers*/New York

Stein and Day/*Publishers*/ New York
First published in 1972
Copyright © 1972 by Michael Freedland
Library of Congress Catalog Card No. 72-83094
All rights reserved
Designed by David Miller
Printed in the United States of America
Stein and Day/*Publishers*/7 East 48 Street, New York, N.Y. 10017
ISBN 0-8128-1523-8

To Sara,
who has the gift of
making music out
of a marriage

CONTENTS

	Acknowledgments	11
1	Let Me Sing and I'm Happy	15
2	A Cantor for the Sabbath	18
3	Is It True What They Say About Dixie?	36
4	Give My Regards to Broadway	54
5	I'm Sitting on Top of the World	80
6	April Showers	105
7	California, Here I Come	116
8	Almost Like Being in Love	133
9	What'll I Do?	148
10	All Alone	161
11	Don't Forget the Boys	168
12	That Wonderful Girl of Mine	189
13	Me and My Shadow	196
14	There's a Rainbow 'Round My Shoulder	215
15	'N' Everything	230
16	When I Leave the World Behind	244
17	You Ain't Heard Nothin' Yet	248
	Index	251

ILLUSTRATIONS

Following page 96
Jolson in 1913
Jolson on Broadway, 1911 and 1916
Jolson the minstrel
The typical minstrel line-up
Jolson with Ruby Keeler in 1928
Jolson with his wife Erle in 1945
Jolson with Warren G. Harding
Jolson the racegoer
Scandinavian ad for *The Jazz Singer*

Following page 180
Singing Kol Nidre in *Hollywood Cavalcade,* 1939
Jolson with Jack Dempsey
Jolson with Charlie Chaplin
Jolson in blackface
Larry Parks in the title role in *The Jolson Story*
The two Jolsons: Larry Parks and Al Jolson
The radio star and his guests
Jolson with Asa, Jr., 1949
Jolson in Korea, 1950
Jolson receiving a UN tribute

ACKNOWLEDGMENTS

THIS BOOK was nearly two decades in the making. The idea first took shape in 1952, when the first scraps of notes were made for a definitive biography of the singer with whom I had plagued family and friends for so long. But it was almost eighteen years before those notes were appraised seriously and the real work of research begun, thanks to a man whose knowledge of Al Jolson is matched only by his encyclopedic familiarity with the cinema—Dennis Sykes. It was Dennis Sykes who made useful and constructive suggestions regarding source material and provided so much background knowledge; it can be fairly said that without his help this book would never have been. His colleague in the International Al Jolson Society, Leslie Kaye, who can recite dates and events in show business history with the ease of the learned student he is, was invaluable, too. To those who provided interviews on which the book was based I give my thanks, too—Jack Benny, George Burns, George Jessel, Morris Stoloff, Sidney Skolsky, Jonie Taps, Ralph Reader, Bessie Love, Fred Kelly, Eli Levy of Columbia Pictures, Abe Lastfogel, Stephen Longstreet, Larry Adler, Ben Lyon, Cesar Romero, and to those wonderful veterans of the world of show business in the Lambs and Friars Clubs of New York and Los Angeles and the Hillcrest Country Club of Beverly Hills. My great admiration goes to the librarians of the Theatrical Library at Lincoln Center, New York, and of the library of the Academy of Motion Picture Arts and Sciences in Los Angeles. My thanks too, to Ivor Davis of the *Daily Express*, London, and to the thousands of newspapermen and women who through the years documented the career of this giant of show business—particularly those on the staffs of the *New York Times* and *Variety*.

I thank my friend Maurice Davis, who—despite the number of years he had to put up with my collection of Jolson records—allowed his secretary, Eileen Hayes, to type much of the manuscript. And I thank Eileen, too—together with that band of wonderful ladies who helped me complete the typing: Beryl Whiteman, Sandra Chippeck, Serena Scott, and my wife, who has been the greatest inspiration of all. Nor do I forget the couple who bought me my very first Jolson record, "I'm Just Wild About Harry,"—back in May 1950 and fired my imagination for this book and indeed my whole career. They are my parents, to whom special thanks.

Michael Freedland

JOLSON

1

LET ME SING AND I'M HAPPY

ON THE NIGHT of October 23, 1950, they turned out the lights of Broadway. The traffic that normally thunders in and out of Times Square was brought to a halt.

At the Friars Club in Los Angeles, Harry Cohn, the iron dictator of Columbia Pictures, burst into tears. In a restaurant nearby, Barnie Dean, one of the principal gag writers for Bing Crosby and Bob Hope, couldn't control his weeping on reading the telegram he had just received.

Al Jolson was dead. Not just a singer. Not just an entertainer. Not just a friend. But Al Jolson.

When people talk about the giants of the entertainment industry, the name Al Jolson can't be considered just one among many; he heads any list. The all-time colossus of show business. He was thought by many to be an egomaniac; he frequently referred to himself as the World's Greatest Entertainer. Nobody argued.

Jolson wasn't everybody's favorite. Many of his contemporaries disliked him. Many more were jealous of him. But no one has ever challenged his supremacy.

Jolson could turn a tired, hungry New York audience into a congregation of true believers. It has been said that he didn't play to an audience, he made love to it. For forty years he consummated that love openly, demanding as much in return as he gave. He was rarely disappointed.

When his star appeared to fall in middle age, he sought a magic ingredient to take him to the top again. He found it in a motion picture called *The Jolson Story,* which became his memorial, as he knew it would.

15

Could a man like Jolson ever be happy when he was not singing? The answer lies in the "other woman" cited by three wives in divorce actions against him—his audience. Jolson was happy only when he had a song to sing and someone to listen to him singing it.

George Burns said of him: "It was easy enough to make Jolson happy at home. You just had to cheer him for breakfast, applaud wildly for lunch, and give him a standing ovation for dinner."

Jack Benny compares Jolson's ability as an entertainer to that of Judy Garland: "But Jolson was still the greatest." George Jessel compares him to Frank Sinatra. Jonie Taps, an executive at Columbia Pictures, agrees: "Jolson has been equaled by one man only—Frank Sinatra."

Others in show business who knew Jolson well had different words to describe him: "electric," "like a cyclone."

The cyclone called Jolson could be said to be the biggest single influence in entertainment history. Even today, young unknowns still make their debuts singing Jolson songs or saying that Al Jolson was the one entertainer they admire above all others. His records are still avidly bought. His films still attract audiences. His songs are still played on the radio. He was the man who gave George Gershwin his first big break and who sang the first songs by an ambitious youngster called Irving Berlin.

He did everything that other show people have done since—sang in small towns as well as on Broadway, sang on the screen, on radio, on television, and on long-playing records, and sang to troops—only he did it first.

Jolson was the great Jewish entertainer. He wasn't observant, rarely went to a synagogue, but there was something Jewish about the way he put his heart, his soul, and his ambitions into his songs.

"In 1910," said Jessel in his eulogy at Jolson's funeral, "the Jews who had emigrated from Europe were a sad lot. Their humor came out of their own troubles. Men of thirty-five seemed to take on the attitude of their fathers and grandfathers and were old before their time, and when they sang they sang with a lament in their hearts. But then there finally came on the stage a man vibrant and pulsating with youth, authority, and courage, who marched on the stage, head held high and with the look of a Roman emperor. He had a gaiety that was militant, uninhibited, and unafraid."

16

That man was Jolson. Born in Russia, he sang of Dixie and a Swanee River he never saw until he was forty. He once said: "I've got so much dough that fourteen guys couldn't spend it in their lifetimes. But I'd rather die than quit this business."

This is his story.

2

A CANTOR FOR THE SABBATH

THERE IS an old tale in Jewish folklore about the cantor in the synagogue who yearned to be an opera singer. The man who spent his days singing to God really wanted to chant other melodies to an altogether different audience.

In Srednik, a tiny cluster of wooden buildings in Russian Lithuania, Cantor Moses Yoelson stood before the Holy Ark in the little synagogue where he led prayers and occasionally allowed his mind to wander in that direction.

For four generations his ancestors had been cantors in places like Srednik, little Fiddler-on-the-Roof hamlets which the villagers knew as *shtetels*, where everyone knew every other person's business and where the biggest scandal imaginable was for one of their number to move away to an unknown place, or, worse still, to marry an outsider of a strange religion. But in those days, when the tsars ruled with an iron hand and there was the constant fear of the sound of horses' hooves heralding cossacks about to pillage and rape in a new pogrom, scandal did not happen very often.

It was even rarer for a cantor in a synagogue, the poor but always respected functionary who was never out of work, to even think of another calling. But Moses Yoelson loved music and sang the traditional melodies with a splendid baritone—and he did think. Occasionally, someone would return to the Pale of Settlement, the band of shtetels like Srednik which were the only places in which Jews were usually allowed to live, with tales of what they heard at the St. Petersburg Opera.

Moses would listen spellbound and wonder what it would be like to sing *Boris Godunov*. Could he ever try his luck in that foreign world?

18

He thought—and then dismissed the idea from his mind. And his father, grandfather, great-grandfather, and great-great-grandfather rested a little easier in their graves.

Tsar Alexander was a tyrant who dearly would have loved to find a solution to the "Jewish problem." Russia's Jews were a useful scapegoat for his country's constant ills. When financial problems beset him or when the country was in political turmoil, Jews made convenient targets for the blame. Jews could also be called up into the armed forces, and with a country the size of Russia to control, this was nothing to overlook.

Strangely, for a government system so autocratic, there was one streak of humanity. The law insisted that every fourteen-year-old boy go into the army for twenty years. All, that is, except the eldest son in the family. That escape clause led to the mass emigration that soon took millions of Jews to the United States and England.

The Jews had been trained from time immemorial to honor the laws of the countries in which they lived. Old, yellowed Hebrew prayer books are still in use with prayers in Russian script for the health and well-being of the same tsar whom they feared so much. But the religious among them—and few were not religious in those days—had to weigh national loyalty against the realities of the situation. The Ten Commandments, which so clearly outlawed the taking of life, were infringed on by the tsar's soldiers every day of the week.

The Jews also knew that once a young man went into uniform, there was a very real risk that he would never be seen again. So families would scrape together a purse of rubles with which to bribe the local petty officials, and so formally disown their children. They gave them new names, and created new phony families to which their younger sons could belong, so that these children would escape the draft.

The rabbis did it too. So did the family of a certain Hirsch Hesselson, a cantor—or *chazan,* as the Yiddish-speaking people of his village knew him. He managed to scrape together enough money with which to bribe two separate officials on behalf of two of his sons. The two Hesselson boys took the name Yoelson. There were new papers and new families for both. They became sons of fathers who had met mysterious deaths.

The boys could not stay at the Hesselson home. But that was no great problem. It was time for them to start thinking of earning a living and it was quite usual for boys to leave home when their first jobs beckoned.

Moses Yoelson went to stay with an uncle in what then seemed the large town of Keidani, which boasted five hundred houses! It was near Kovna, the state capital, and for the country folk that seemed to increase its size and standing.

Moses Hesselson's (now Yoelson's) uncle was impressed with the boy's voice and suggested that he take part in the High Holiday services at the local synagogue. But first there had to be auditions.

The elders of the congregation looked sternly at young Moses. One looked at the way he wore his hat: the Orthodox Jews never went without head covering. Another examined his beard, for the length of facial growth was in itself an indication of piety. But the decision on his voice was left to the synagogue's president, who sat next to the Ark containing the Holy Scrolls of the Law. He was the only one with real power in a community where the synagogue was the hub around which all else revolved. The president was Reb Asa Cantor.

As he heard the young chazan sing Kol Nidre, the dirge recited in synagogues at the holiest service of the year on the eve of the Day of Atonement, his mind wandered to other things.

He admired the way this young man, who seemed to want the job so desperately, could reach the high notes, hold them, and then, without warning, make his voice plunge to his badly worn leather boots. But more than that, Reb Cantor looked approvingly at Moses' straight back and the fine features of his face.

He could have the job, Reb Cantor hold him, but only on a trial basis. His main task would be to kill chickens according to traditional kosher dietary laws. Later, he would have to learn to circumcise baby boys to initiate them into the faith. As Moses wrapped his prayer shawl and placed it neatly in its red velvet bag, he realized that singing in the synagogue was the only "glamorous" part of the job. Reb Cantor patted the young man on the back and invited him home to lunch.

Moses had never seen such a spread. On a white tablecloth was a bowl of hot soup. From the oven came the smell of *cholent*, the meat-and-vegetable mixture which had been simmering since sundown the previous evening so as not to break the injunction against cooking on the Sabbath.

Most exciting of all, there, in a neatly ironed white dress, was Reb Cantor's daughter Naomi. Her face had a fresh natural look that set Moses' pulse racing. She was the prettiest girl he had ever seen.

Within two weeks of that meeting, Moses and Naomi stood under a canopy outside the synagogue. A glass broken under the young man's left foot symbolized the fact that they were now man and wife.

Everyone in the town came to congratulate the young bride and bridegroom. The men danced together. The women, all in their best clothes and their Sabbath wigs, stood behind rope barriers and clapped.

The elders of Keidani clapped loudest of all. For they knew that the marriage contract included the provision that Moses and his bride had to live in Reb Cantor's house for one year. For one year they would have a chazan to be proud of.

Before the year was up, the Yoelsons' first baby was born, a girl they called Rose. With a family to support, Moses abandoned his secret ambition to sing in the opera. He decided to become a rabbi, a position with much more respect owing to it than that of a mere cantor. The local rabbi heard him study, examined him on the Talmud, and awarded him his diploma.

But the value of these diplomas varied according to the respect in which the man awarding it was held. The Keidani rabbi could not have had too good a reputation. Moses Yoelson was lucky to be accepted as a chazan with a beautiful voice. More often, he was the singing shochet—the ritual animal slaughter; or the *mohel*—the man who performed circumcisions.

But in Srednik, there was only one synagogue and it could afford only one officiant. A man who was both rabbi and cantor as well as a shochet and mohel, was just what they were looking for. Word spread to Keidani of Srednik's need.

Moses was asked to attend for an audition. But although they liked his voice, the community's leaders—the local butcher, the tailor, and the milkman—thought he was too young. And, of course, not a potential son-in-law. Indeed, he had a baby daughter to support, and a wife who appeared to be pregnant again.

Asa Cantor clinched the deal on his son-in-law's behalf with a donation of one hundred rubles to the local *mikvah*, the communal bathhouse which Jewish law dictates all married women should visit once a month to purify themselves.

21

In Srednik, in a tiny wooden house, Naomi gave birth to another daughter, but the child was not strong enough to survive the cold Lithuanian winter. Within a few months of her second child's death, Naomi was again pregnant. Their third daughter, Etta, was strong and robust.

When their fourth child was born a year later, Chazan Yoelson seemed content. He now had the son who was to carry on the family tradition and be the sixth of the line to conduct services in the synagogue. They called the child Hirsch.

Life was hard in Srednik. Without Naomi's father to provide for their needs, they had to learn how to run a home on their own resources. When the community was prosperous, Moses and his family prospered—there were chickens to kill. When the villagers were poor, the Yoelsons went hungry with them.

Five years after Moses' marriage to Naomi, Asa Cantor died. For seven days, Naomi sat on a low stool in the living room of their tiny house while neighbors visited her with words of consolation. It was a particularly hard time, for Naomi was going to have another child.

When the baby turned out to another boy, both Naomi and Moses were delighted. Not only would there be another chazan in the family, but this one could be named after his grandfather. He was the new Asa.

When the birth actually occurred, no one now knows. It could have been any time between 1880 and 1888. It could have been in January or July. In the Russian Pale of Settlement in the 1880s, no one thought of birth certificates. (Years later that baby Asa was to decide that the year was 1886 and the day May 26. He liked the idea of a spring birthday.) The Yoelsons were a happy family. In those days, most religious Jewish families were. They never asked for wealth, because they realized they were unlikely to get any. The wealth they did have was in their children, and they were content enough.

More than that, they felt they had a double bonus. A double religion, almost. They had Judaism, which they hallowed with a deep, sincere sanctity, and they had their music, which for the Yoelsons was inextricably linked with prayer.

As soon as his sons could utter their first words, Moses Yoelson set about training their voices so that one day they would be great cantors. He propped open their mouths with little matchsticks so that they made the right sounds, and at home they practiced their singing as much as they did the blessings they were required to recite before eating a piece of bread or drinking a cup of milk.

Moses' proudest moment was when they joined him in the synagogue for the first time. Later on, the two boys stood at his side on the dais from which the congregation's prayers were led.

To the people of Srednik, the Yoelsons became a family choir. From the ladies' gallery above, the high voices of Naomi and her daughters Rose and Etta could be heard joining in the familiar melodies.

Judaism is by its very nature a family religion. Religious practices were carried on in the home as much as in the synagogue. Everything the Yoelsons did seemed to have a religious purpose behind it. And for that purpose, there was music, too.

Sabbath lunches were punctuated with the singing of joyous family table hymns. On that day the poorest shack became a palace.

No work was ever done from sundown on Friday until sundown on Saturday. In anticipation of that day, the children were scrubbed, the tiny wooden home was cleaned as thoroughly as Naomi's physical strength would allow, and hemlock was strewn on the floor to give an aromatic fresh scent. All made the day seem special.

As the hours went by, the scent mixed with the cozy aroma of the chicken soup. There was also the beautifully polished Sabbath samovar, in which the tea became stronger and stronger as the day progressed. But no one objected. The samovar had to remain heated all day, lest the strict prohibition against making fire be broken.

At the New Year, the family went to the crowded synagogue, and waited eagerly for Moses to sound the *shofar*—the ritual blowing of the ram's horn, a call to the faithful to spend the next twelve months in devotion to God.

Nine days later, on Yom Kippur, the day-long fast of atonement, they watched admiringly as the handsome figure of Moses Yoelson, dressed completely in white, sang the traditional mournful prayers.

Passover was the happiest time of the year. All the family sat around the long table laden with unleavened bread (*matzoh*), bitter herbs, eggs, and salt water, all of which symbolized the departure of the children of Israel from Egypt, sang the happy songs of freedom, and read the allegorical tales of the plight of a people always escaping some new calamity.

At Chanuka, the eight-day festival of the Maccabees, they all gathered around the eight-branched *menorah*, or candelabra, to sing the happy songs of the season.

On ordinary weekdays, there were the traditional foods that they all took for granted, the rich horseradish sauce mixed with beetroot, and the gefilte fish made from carp which the day before had been swimming around the tin sink in the Yoelson kitchen.

The Yoelsons' home was their strength. Naomi, in particular, was the heart of that strength. When Asa was no more than about five or six, her strength and family leadership were put to their strongest test.

Cossacks rampaged through neighboring villages in the Pale of Settlement. The Jews of Srednik quaked in their small houses. The majority in the shtetel, they had a synagogue, whereas the local Russians had to use a room over the tavern for their Orthodox Church. The Jews had a whole street of shops, whereas all the Russian trade seemed to center in that one tavern. But if the Jews were in the numerical majority, the Christians had the power.

For one thing, the town was owned by a local nobleman, for whom the whole population would turn out whenever his carriage passed by. And for another, the Orthodox priest was believed to be influential with the local constable and, rumor had it, the constable had friends in high places in St. Petersburg.

Young Jewish men vanished overnight. Some of them turned up in Siberia. But others, it was learned later, had arrived in America.

The Yoelsons talked about this, too. When the children were tucked in at night, Moses and Naomi went over and over the same question: Dare they risk this new life? Moses had an uncle in America. By all accounts the pavements in this new land really were covered in gold and everyone did live in a palace.

Naomi made the decision. Jewish law rules that it is the mother who has the power to influence her children more than the father, and in the Yoelson family she was the strong one. Her word counted.

She decided that Moses should go to this new world they had heard so much about and prepare the way for the rest of the family to follow. She did not admit to her husband that there were times when she felt so ill that she had no idea whether she would live to see him again.

Once the decision that he should leave for America was made, the question of how he was to get there had to be faced. The Russians were no happier about Jewish men leaving their country than they were about having them there in the first place.

Hayim Yossi, their neighbor and closest friend, had the answer. Yossi was a local wood merchant who loved children. Because he had none of his own, he particularly loved the Yoelson youngsters and it was because of the children that he had let out half his house to the family.

When Moses told him of his decision to emigrate, Yossi promised to take care of the family while he was away. He also devised a plan to get the chazan out of Russia. He blackened the younger man's face, gave him a bundle of old clothes to put on, and pointed to the raft lying on the shore of the river Neiman, separating Srednik, and with it Lithuania, from East Prussia.

With Moses Yoelson acting as one of Yossi's workmen, the two could float together across the river. No questions would be asked because wood was Yossi's business.

Moses kissed Naomi and the children and made his way to the riverbank. When Yossi returned, he simply told the customs man that his workman had gotten drunk and fallen overboard.

For four years, letters from Moses trickled into the Yoelson home. Naomi felt weaker but told no one. The children continued to play, to talk in Yiddish to each other—they knew no other language—and to go to school at the local *cheder*, or Hebrew school.

From his letters they gathered that Moses was finding life hard; America was not the promised land he had been led to expect. But finally they received a letter from New York, inviting the rest of the family to join him. He had a job as cantor at a synagogue in Newburgh and sent along enough money for their journey.

They traveled to New York via Liverpool, England. By the time the family arrived in New York, Chazan Yoelson had a new job, in a synagogue in Washington, D.C.

For Moses Yoelson, Washington was little different from Srednik. He had adjusted himself to being in a minority in a big city instead of one of a majority in a tiny hamlet. But life went on.

He was delighted to have his family around him. But his work was his life and he regarded domestic upsets as his wife's responsibility. For Moses, the important things were his books and his singing in the

25

synagogue. The girls were growing up now and seemed to be enjoying taking their place in running the home. But the boys were restless.

America was a bustling, exciting place. The streets were not paved with gold—but they were paved, and that was remarkable. Men and women walked arm in arm with each other, something Orthodox Russian Jews would no more think of doing than they would of eating a plate of ham.

They came face to face with the first Negroes they had ever seen and heard their singing. When Hirsch and Asa came home singing about the Swanee River, Chazan Yoelson was shocked. But Naomi was there to pacify him. If the boys wanted to sing, she told him, they should go ahead; they were strengthening their voices for the day when they would join him as synagogue cantors.

She didn't always tell Moses when she spanked the boys for being late for her hot chicken soup or when they failed to wash their hands before sampling the Sabbath *hallah*, the home-baked loaf that played such a large part in the home religious ritual.

The boys took their punishments bravely. They were mischievous, but somehow they knew they were usually no naughtier than other boys their age.

She made sure the boys had violin lessons. Asa seemed to like them especially. Their father believed it was a mere frippery. He told them they had a God-given talent—their voices—which they must never forsake for any other kind of music. He gave them singing lessons when they were supposed to be practicing their violins. The cantor pointed out that each note was a praise to the Lord.

Hirsch sang pleasantly, but not especially well. With little Asa, though, Moses realized there was something special. He knew how to breathe properly; he realized instinctively that singing came from his stomach, not simply from his throat.

Moses was delighted with his younger son's progress, and in their music there seemed for a time to be a remarkable rapport between father and son. The youngster seemed to understand why his father made strange faces, why he lifted up his hands to indicate fluctuations of the voice and dropped them to show that another tone was needed.

Moses was still angry when Asa wanted to rush out to play, but he put it down to the new surroundings which he was sure they would soon get used to. The Yoelsons, he liked to feel, were a happy family.

Shortly after Hirsch's bar mitzvah—the confirmation ceremony that spiritually marks the coming of age of the thirteen-year-old Jewish boy—everything changed.

Naomi's illness struck again. Moses took the children into her bedroom. Only the day before she had been playing with them, helping the girls with their cooking, checking the boys' Hebrew grammar, and learning with them the mysteries of this strange new English language. Now, as she lay in bed, her face was deathly pale.

Chazan Yoelson walked desolately to his synagogue office in East Street West just before the doctor arrived at the Yoelson home. He had no real idea how ill his wife was. Hirsch was told to fetch his father. They walked into her bedroom just as the sheet was being lifted over Naomi's face.

Al Jolson always remembered his mother's funeral as the time that he first had to think of being an individual and not simply one of a group. He was probably only nine or ten as he stood in a bitterly cold wind by her graveside, a pair of gray woolen socks shielding his hands from the frost.

Somehow, that frighteningly abrupt confrontation with reality was for this small boy the beginning of it all. If his mother had lived, he might now be remembered in some circles as one of America's most interesting cantors. Not a great one, but one with a joy in his singing. It is fair to assume that had she not died when they were so young, neither he nor Hirsch would have seriously thought of going into show business.

Because their father had been away from home for four long years, he was understandably more distant than the mother they had loved and respected and who had always been with them. If Moses had been a little more appreciative of the traumatic experience through which they were going, life might have been happier. As it was, he shouted at the boys and they accepted the punishment as a tax to be paid for the fun they sought from life.

They joined a street gang after Asa had proved he could knock down any kid bold enough to call him a greenhorn. They sold papers on street corners in competition with each other.

Hirsch was the first to discover the magic of money jingling in his pockets after selling the latest news from a street corner. Asa thought it was such a good idea that he got his own pitch on the opposite corner, and any news that Hirsch called out, Asa exaggerated. If Hirsch shouted: "Read all about it. Ten people killed in shipwreck," Asa would answer back, "Twenty people lost in wreck. Read all about it."

They had an apartment above a shop that sold hay for horses. When Moses heard them whistling on the stairs, he knew his boys had returned. Whistling was foreign to him and he hated it, but even this he was powerless to stop.

In the local public school, Asa and Hirsch were bright pupils. But even though he was three years younger, Asa would try to find ways of getting his brother to play hookey with him. He would say he didn't feel well, or that he had left their father ill in their flat and had to get back to his bedside.

Once in the street, the younger boy would egg on the older one to stand on the pavement and sing the ballad of the day for a penny or two. They must have been a fine pair, two young immigrants still wearing the fringes of the ritual shawl all Jewish boys were supposed to have, singing "My Old Kentucky Home."

When their father heard about this, it meant another swipe across the ears. But it seemed to make no difference. His boys were just "loafers"—one of the few American words Cantor Yoelson had picked up from his surroundings.

Rose had by now taken on the mantle of mother. She cooked for them the way her mother had taught her, but the boys complained that the *lokshen*—the homemade noodles essential to the best chicken soup—were not as tasty as they had once been.

When Etta chastised them for leaving their bedroom messy, the boys just laughed and went out to fight with the other boys on the block.

Their father grew more uncompromisingly Orthodox in his ways and spent more time—when he was not killing chickens or circumcising babies—in his synagogue work or with his books. He no longer dreamed of being an opera singer, but he would have liked to become a great rabbi. He now knew this was not to be. Nor could he pride himself on being a successful father.

Perhaps, he thought, it would be better if he married again. He remembered the daughter of Perri Yoels, his wife's cousin back in the old country. Would she marry him? She wrote back accepting by return mail.

28

Her name was Hessi—Ida, as she later Americanized it. But instead of acting as a bridge between their new life and the old family traditions, Hessi only served to drive an even bigger wedge between father and sons.

In later years, the boys both grew very fond of her. Hessi was not very much older than themselves, and she was good and kind. But when she first joined their household, the boys simply resented her as an intruder.

At the age of fifteen, Hirsch gave himself a new name. He was to be called Harry. He convinced Asa that unless he changed his name too, he would not be able to hold his head up, so Asa became Al—Al Yoelson.

The signal for the real change in their lives came one day when Harry was walking near the Capitol building, singing one of the latest vaudeville tunes. A politician sitting on a park bench told him he did not feel well and asked the youngster to call him a cab. As he helped the elderly gentleman to the horse-drawn vehicle, Harry felt a coin pressed into his hand. A gold ten-dollar piece.

To Harry it represented riches beyond all his dreams. He used the money to take the train to New York, while Al paced up and down at home, quarreled with his father, shouted at his sisters, and brushed aside the kindly advice Hessi tried to offer. He was determined to join his brother, whom he considered brave, adventurous, and totally sensible. He had no idea where he could find Harry, but he did have enough sense to find out where most of the newspaper sellers hung out: on the Bowery.

Once he got to New York, Al, too, sold papers, shined shoes, did anything that could raise a cent or two. He was probably about twelve and, as he said many years later, "you get awfully hungry when you're twelve years old."

He was walking along Broadway one day when he saw a theatre for the first time in his life. He could not afford the price of a ticket. Nor did he know the trick of sneaking in through the side entrance. But there was a magic about the colorful marquees, the posters, and the theatre people he saw walking up and down the district—a magic that made an immediate impact he could not really understand.

All he did know was that he was being drawn to the theatre by a powerful force. As he walked down Broadway, he heard the sound of singing coming from the alleyway at the side of one of the big showplaces. If he was very quiet, he thought, he could edge his way toward the stage and hear a little more. What he heard led to an event that affected the future of show business for half a century.

A tall, stately blond singer was rehearsing a new song. A stagehand came by and told Al her name: Fay Templeton. The song had a gay, throbbing lilt to it. It was "Rosie, You Are My Posie."

"Funny," Al thought, "that should be a song for a man, not a girl." When Miss Templeton had finished singing, and had told the rehearsal pianist to pack away his music, Al couldn't get out of his mind the breathtaking sight of a real theatre.

When he did eventually leave, and walked back to the Bowery, the song remained in his head. He couldn't forget it: "Rosie, you are my posie . . . you are my heart's bouquet . . . come out, here in the moonlight . . . my blushin' Rosie . . . my posie sweet. . . ."

He walked and walked. And he got hungrier and hungrier. When he reached a small grimy-looking restaurant on the Bowery called McGirk's, he couldn't take his eyes from the window. There, inside, were plates of steaming hot food being handed over the heads of the patrons.

Eventually, he plucked up courage to approach the owner of the joint. "Would you give me something to eat if I sing for you?" he asked.

The proprietor was a kindly man who had seen hungry boys before. He smiled and agreed. And through the noisy, smoke-laden atmosphere of McGirk's came the sound of Al Yoelson singing "Rosie, You Are My Posie."

By the time he had finished, a hush had descended on the diners. It was the first indoor public performance by a boy who was to become a show business legend, singing what was to become one of his best-loved songs.

Al got his dinner—the first food he had ever eaten that was not kosher. But it didn't bother him. What mattered now was that he was getting into show business.

On the Bowery he bumped into Harry, who was living in a home for newsboys. A kind Jewish woman had given Al a pair of worn, overlarge shoes, and the two youngsters felt sure they were on the threshold of a great career.

Still, they never seemed to have enough to eat. Eventually, they swallowed their pride and went to visit an uncle living in Yonkers, where they found that their elder sister Etta had beaten them to it and was living and working there after a row with Hessi.

Etta put Al on the train back to Washington; she did not trust him to take the fare and go by himself. Even so, he still got off at Baltimore, where he was arrested by the Gerry Society, a police morals squad that had a description of Harry and picked Al up, mistaking him for his brother.

The events that followed became legends. The police, still mistaking him for Harry, took him to the St. Mary's Industrial Home for Boys in Baltimore's city center, run by Roman Catholic monks.

The idea of a boy from a strict Orthodox Jewish background suddenly thrust in the midst of a Catholic institution like St. Mary's is comical enough by itself, but in later years this episode was fully developed and embroidered, not least of all by Al himself.

There have been stories of his being chosen to sing in the church choir—*The Jolson Story* made a great play of this—but it seems unlikely. He was not at the home long enough to learn the hymns he would have been required to sing.

Babe Ruth, who meant to American baseball roughly what Jolson meant to show business, spoke often of meeting Al there for the first time. A gangling Negro dancer called Bill "Bojangles" Robinson, another Broadway sensation of the twenties, said the same thing. St. Mary's was the only home Ruth and Robinson ever had as boys. But it was never home to Jolson.

Al himself complicated history still further with a story he told so often that he almost believed it. He told an interviewer in 1930, "I ran away again and Papa caught me. I ran away again. He caught me. I could go on saying that for five minutes and it would be true." Of that part of the story there can be little doubt.

But he went on, "One day he told me I was just a 'bummer' and he was going to lock me up. He took me to Baltimore and put me in St. Mary's. My good papa—and I like to kid him about it now and he likes it—told the priests what a lowlife I had turned out to be and asked that Catholic lickings be tried where Jewish lickings had failed."

It hardly seems likely that a man whose own religious outlook would have prevented him from ever entering a church would consider allowing his son to live in that environment.

But there is another part of Al's own account of those days that seems likely to be true. Young Al misbehaved so frequently at the home that he was placed in solitary confinement in a monk's cell, where he stayed until Cantor Yoelson came to pick him up. That was probably just long enough for word to reach Washington that Harry had been caught and for the cantor to realize that his younger son was the one in custody.

In later years, Al teased Harry by telling him, "Remember, I did time for you once, son."

In 1948, Al took his wife to see St. Mary's. "The gate's open," he told her. "It was always shut when I was here. I remember bars all around. Once I hit a boy on the stairs, coming down from chapel. They put me in solitary. That's bad enough. But to look out the window—and watch the others playing—well, honey, I screamed and hollered until I ran a temperature. So they had to let me out."

Harry joined Al back in Washington for a while. They sold watermelons in the streets of the capital and kept on singing in the streets. This time they sang outside the burlesque theatres, places with names like Kernan's and the Raleigh, which their father hated so much. To him they were dens of evil and sin.

At the age of seventeen, Harry left Washington again, vowing never to return. Al stayed at home for a while, but he felt that even if he wanted to remain, it was not the life he needed. Hessi was kind to him, all the more so because she felt Moses Yoelson was doubly strict with his son. But her hands were now full with children of her own. She and Al's father were well on the way to having a complete new family—three sons and a daughter.

Not even bouts of coughing—early stages of tuberculosis were diagnosed when Al was at St. Mary's, but he recovered as soon as he left the institution—could persuade Al to stay at home. Singing made him feel better, he'd tell his father. But not the magic of the Hebrew prayers.

Hearing a band play "Good-bye, Dollie, I Must Leave You" really set the future entertainer on the trail of show business success. It also gave him his first chance to sing to men in uniform.

It was 1898—Al was probably thirteen or fourteen—and the fife-and-drum bands marched, one after the other, down Washington's Pennsylvania Avenue on their way to Cuba. The battleship *Maine* had been sunk in the dispute over whether America or Spain had territorial rights in Cuba, and the two countries were at war.

Al was spellbound as he heard the bands playing and, like many other small boys, eagerly joined the marching ranks. The bandmaster took a liking to the small curly-haired youngster with the big eyes, and when he heard him singing to the rhythm of the marches, made Al his first theatrical proposition: "Why not become our mascot? You'll be able to sing."

To actually be asked to sing—such joy had never come his way before.

Al went all the way to Florida with the Fifteenth Pennsylvania Volunteers. But at the camp, the commanding officer decided the boy was much too young to be taken to a battle zone and ordered Al home before his men sailed for Havana and the charge of San Juan Hill.

So for a brief moment, Al was home again. But his feet itched once more and for the first and only time in his life the smell of sawdust was in his nostrils.

He saw a poster advertising the arrival in Washington of "The Greatest Show on Earth—Walter L. Main's Travelling Circus." Never much of an animal lover, for him the magic of the circus was in the word "show": the color of the bandsmen's uniforms and the sound of the ringmaster shouting act after glorious act under the big top.

Al talked his way into a job in the circus as an usher. But his fascination did not last long. The uniforms were tacky, the animals were mangy, and the people didn't pay the price of admission. The circus folded—and Al went home once more.

Then one day he sneaked into the gallery at Washington's Bijou Theatre, just as Eddie Leonard, one of America's great vaudevillians, was singing his specialty, "Ida, Sweet as Apple Cider."

"Come on, everybody," shouted Leonard from the gaslit stage. "Join in." The audience did—but not too enthusiastically, except for one young boy soprano up there in "the gods." For the first time, the voice of Al Yoelson was heard *inside* a real theater.

Leonard was so impressed that he made young Asa sing the song as a solo. He also insisted that the boy meet him backstage. The next day, Al was at the Bijou again, singing with Eddie Leonard just as spontaneously and just as well. The act was repeated day after day.

33

The old trouper asked the young beginner to join him permanently and make it an act. But Al Yoelson had no ambitions to sing from a mere balcony. He wanted to be down there on the stage with the spotlight shining on *him*.

Harry, meanwhile, had got himself a job as an usher at the Bijou and tried to persuade his brother to take up Leonard's offer. But it wasn't easy. Besides, Cantor Yoelson had heard about it all—and gave Al a few more cuffs about the ear. Regretfully Al said farewell to Eddie Leonard, but the memory of singing inside a real theatre, a theatre full of that warm, stale but inviting smell, lingered on.

Not long afterward, he ran away from home again and ended up with a troupe called Rich and Hoppe's Big Company of Fun Makers. This didn't last long either. The company was so prosperous that it gave Al Yoelson, as he was now being billed, a tablecloth for a cummerbund. In fact, he lasted only a week with Rich and Hoppe. But by the end of that week Al Yoelson had become Al Joelson; it sounded more American that way.

When he came back to Washington, Al spent most of his time walking the streets, wondering where the next break would come. It came unexpectedly soon.

Harry had risen in the world by now. He was selling peanuts and popcorn at the Bijou instead of merely showing the customers to their seats. He managed to sneak Al into the balcony once more, in time for him to watch one of the most daring acts that the Naughty Nineties had yet developed, the bump and grind of Miss Aggie Beeler, burlesque queen.

Taking an ample leaf from the book of Lily Langtry, she billed herself as Jersey Lil. In feathers and rouge, the busty Miss Beeler held Washington men in the palm of her well-manicured hand. She, too, called for help from the audience and, once more, the only real sound from the customers was Al Joelson's soprano voice, crooning for all he was worth, "You Are My Jersey Lily."

Aggie Beeler succeeded where minstrel man Eddie Leonard had failed. Al decided to defy his father once more and agreed to "sign" with Aggie and join the act. He was to sing along with her from the balcony whenever her own voice needed a rest. As a member of the Villanova Touring Burlesque Company, Al was really in show business now.

34

He was a great attraction, Aggie realized. Fourteen-year-old Al was being talked about. When Cantor Yoelson heard about it, he was so angry that he forcibly prevented Harry from leaving the apartment to go to work at the burlesque theatre.

But to some people being forbidden to do a thing is all the encouragement they need to do it. Harry left home for good and went to New York, where he got a job as a singing waiter. Al, on the other hand, was in no position to argue with his father. There had been a row with Aggie because she would not give him the billing he felt he was entitled to expect. Nor would she let him join her on the stage.

So the businessman in Al emerged for the first time: he resigned. He decided to join Harry. Walking the streets once again, he hummed the songs he could not get out of his mind. Trudging through New York's Orchard Street market, where the Jewish peddlers sold everything from oranges to prayer shawls, Al had the break that finally launched him into show business once and for all.

He was spotted by a talent scout looking for youngsters to play in a crowd scene—on a real stage.

3

IS IT TRUE WHAT THEY SAY ABOUT DIXIE?

IT WAS probably the luckiest thing that had ever happened to him. The scout was looking for a youngster with noticeably Jewish features—and Asa Yoelson had those, all right. His hair was curly and jet black, his eyes were big. He was just the sort of healthy specimen the man from the Herald Square Theatre had in mind for the American premiere of the play that had drawn the crowds from the East End of London for years: Israel Zangwill's *Children of the Ghetto.*

To the scout, Al had the right background and the right appearance. But to Al Joelson, it was something more—a special feeling about appearing before hundreds of people. It was nice to have a dollar or two at the end of the week with which to buy food and pay for a room on the top floor of a tenement building. But the money was only a part of it.

He could feel a magnet drawing him closer to the audience every time he glanced over the footlights. When the extras in the crowd scene were supposed to disperse to allow the leading performers to stand in the spotlight, he lingered behind. The stage was as magical as his expectations had led him to believe it would be.

Children of the Ghetto opened on October 16, 1899, and ran for a mere three performances. But it was enough to infect Al with the show business bug.

For three months, Al was out of work. He jogged along with Harry, but for him being a singing waiter didn't offer much in the way of compensation. He was now a man of the theatre and nothing was going to drag him away from his ultimate ambition: to find his public.

A man named Fred E. Moore helped him find it. Moore had been a stage electrician in the Dewey Theatre on New York's Fourteenth

Street when Al had played there with Aggie Beeler. Fred had always wanted to be a performer, but the money came in more regularly on the wrong side of the lights.

Al was walking aimlessly down the Bowery early in 1900 when he bumped into Fred. Al was little more than a child, but Fred, having heard his story, knew that he could help the boy break into show business.

"Why not join me in an act?" he asked Al. "We'll be the best song illustrators in the business."

The idea appealed to Al.

Fred didn't think the name Al Joelson did anything for the lad. "Call yourself Harry," he suggested.

And so, as "Fred E. Moore and Harry Joelson, Introducers and Promoters of High Class Ballads and Popular Songs," they caught a train out of Grand Central Station and made for the big time. Fred's buxom wife went along and cooked the stew; Fred and "Harry" grabbed what work they could find. Once they were seen in Baltimore, the offers came in thick and fast. The fine Irish tenor of Mr. Moore and the light Jewish choirboy soprano of Master Joelson made a popular pair. They were never billed very well, but there was always work.

Al thought this was real success. And it was, until the day his voice started to change. Suddenly no sound emerged when he tried to sing high notes. And when he tried to go down for a more comfortable sound, all he got was a croak. Al Joelson's voice would never sound the same again.

His soprano voice was gone—and so, he feared, was the Al Joelson career. When those notes seemed as impossible to reach as a real fortune, he fell into one of the deep depressions that in later years were to haunt him constantly.

How was he going to live now? Certainly not by singing. At night, he slept on park benches. By day, he trudged around the New York theatre district, hoping that when he next opened his mouth, there would be a voice.

But his voice had gone—forever, it seemed. While walking along the Brooklyn freight yards in despair, he decided to jump a Washington-bound train. The tears in his eyes came both from utter remorse and from the cinders flying up from the track.

When the train arrived in Washington, he managed to jump clear just

37

before it reached the station. Head hanging, he crept up the stairs over the feed store and knocked on the door of what had once been his home.

Hessi was there with her own young children. She gave her Asa a warm hug and made him a glass of tea. When his father walked in from the synagogue a little later, his words were sharp, but the boy noticed a twinkle in his eyes.

"No more with the loafers?" asked the cantor. "Now your place is in shul with me."

But Cantor Yoelson knew that this was not to be. And his son knew it, too. When Harry arrived at the apartment shortly after this—his own attempt at finding jobs singing in saloons had fallen as flat as his younger brother's voice—it was the end of the happy family reunion.

The boys' father couldn't stand their blasphemous talk about the theatre, and they couldn't tolerate the old life. The boys decided to run away again. But not before they planned what they were going to do. They decided to form an act. With an eye for faces, and an ear for the language those faces spoke, they now had an idea that seemed to contrast the two worlds in which they were living.

They called themselves "The Hebrew and the Cadet." Harry was the "Hebrew"—a cross between Fagin and a Hassidic gentleman just off the boat from Poland—and Al was the cadet—smart in West Point uniform, his hair brushed neatly back, his face sparklingly clean, representing all that was wholesome about America.

The problem of Al's singing voice didn't arise. Harry did all the singing the act needed and Al whistled. That in itself was the beginning of a staple of the Jolson theatrical diet.

The two were billed as the Joelson Brothers. They stole most of the dialogue they "wrote" for the act.

"You're a monkey," said Al.

"Vot—you call me a monkey?"

"Sure. You know what a monkey is? A monkey is a very fine person."

And Harry the Hebrew replied:

"I know dat. Mine father, mine mother, and mine brothers and sisters are all monkeys, too."

Apparently, it went down well enough. The act was booked for the theatres just off Union Square, then the center of the vaudeville business. They went on tour, too.

But in September 1901, the people who paid for admission to vaudeville theatres weren't spending their money. President William McKinley had been shot.

This was one time when the show did not go on. And the people who went off first and came back last were newcomers like the Joelson Brothers.

It was back to the park bench and Tin Pan Alley in the hope that someone, somewhere, would hear them. And someone did. Al's voice was coming back.

The boy soprano was gradually turning into a mature but high tenor. In a country that went crazy over Count John McCormack, that was no great hardship.

An agent booking a new burlesque show called *The Mayflowers* heard the boys and gave them a chance. They were undoubtedly the best part of the bill, playing the Hebrew and the Cadet routine one minute and Harry blacking his face as a minstrel another. Al had decided not to play around with burnt cork; it didn't seem to go with his cadet routine. (Years later Harry was to be accused of imitating Al as a blackface artist.)

The Mayflowers lasted several weeks. Next came *The Little Egypt Burlesque Show,* in which Harry and Al were only as good as their jokes were dirty. The two boys had been around a bit now, but Al was still probably only sixteen and the two of them were little more than novices in that kind of territory. The sort of jokes they knew hardly turned a hair—but they were strong enough to upset the Gerry Society, which did what it could to make the management reluctant to hire the boys.

But when the panic lifted, the boys were asked back and given a contract: $17.50 a week between them. Between acts they sold song books containing naughty pictures of women wearing Eastern costume. Anyone who struck a match behind the semitransparent paper could see the ladies wearing rather less.

When *Little Egypt* folded, it wasn't as difficult for the two Joelsons to get work as it had been before. People were beginning to notice them. A line had even appeared in the show biz papers.

For Al, at least, it was to be the first of thousands of entries.

In the world of burlesque, a gentleman called Billy B. Van had a reputation for providing a few hours' good entertainment—and for being shrewd enough to pick up the best acts for the smallest financial outlay on his part. He heard about the Joelsons and booked them for his *Patsy Bolivar Revue*. They were to get forty dollars a week each.

But they weren't due to start for a few weeks. They filled their spare time by crossing the border into Canada and getting on the bill at the Royale Theatre in Montreal.

But they never got further than the wings of that theatre. Harry fell in love with a chorus girl, much to the dismay of one of the stagehands, who had taken her out before the "American big shot" appeared on the scene. He pounced on Harry and seemed likely to break his neck, so Al joined in the melee.

The Joelsons were immediately struck off the bill. But this incident created a brotherly love between them that somehow had never been there before.

They didn't mind that they had lost the Montreal job. They had the big *Patsy Bolivar* contract to fulfill. But that was not to be, either. Soon after arriving at Van's theatre, the boys had an argument with him. He ordered them to stay behind with the chorus after rehearsals while the stars went home. They told him that as the real stars of his show they were insulted. He replied by firing the pair and demanding the return of the twenty-dollar advance they had been given. Van didn't get his twenty dollars and they returned to the park benches.

Dixon and Bernstein's Turkey Burlesque Show booked them next, in spite of a succession of rows in which Harry demanded advances on salary and Bernstein refused. Before long the boys bought a typewriter on the installment plan, sold it for twenty dollars, and disappeared. They felt dishonest, it is true. But they were also hungry.

Their next job, with a man called Dan Casey, was to play a couple of Irishmen in a show called *The Brigadiers*. Neither had ever played anything but Jews before. The accents, particularly Harry's, were none too successful. When Casey chided him for this, Harry replied, "What's the matter, haven't you been to Ireland?" Casey had to admit that he had not.

"Well, I have," said Harry. "And they have Jews in Ireland, too. I'm an Irish Jew."

That was enough to sustain the pair for another few weeks, this time at fifty dollars a week, already a reasonably big advance on what they had earned before.

When they got an offer to open at the modern Odeon Theatre in

Baltimore, they really thought they had made it big. In the world of burlesque the Odeon had a reputation as a nursery for Broadway. As far as the Joelson brothers were concerned, it remained a mere reputation. The Odeon burned down the day before they arrived.

Baltimore was near Washington, so once more they pocketed their pride and went home to fill their stomachs. They had the usual kisses from Hessi, the same sarcastic comments from Rose and Etta, who had now married but had returned home, too, for a visit, and more chastisement from Cantor Yoelson—although he now did not bother to talk about their following him in the religious life.

His son Hirsch had always seemed a downright no-good and now he was even worse than that, for he had led Asa astray. What Moses never seemed to realize was that when things were going badly for the boys, it was usually Al who had persuaded Harry not to give up.   Certainly Al was the one who found it harder to leave the theatre atmosphere and who got depressed at any prospect of having to do so.

Being home was the same old story. Father and sons couldn't live under the same roof. As soon as the two youngsters had saved enough money from the jobs they picked up singing in Washington cafes and saloons, they were off again. Their destination was New York once more.

When they arrived, they had enough between them for a room on Fourteenth Street across the road from Lew Scharf's Restaurant, which Al in later years was to describe as the "Stork Club of the nineties."

It wasn't much of a room, he observed. "More like a broom closet. But I was able to see the fancy people going into the restaurant—people like Diamond Jim Brady and Lillian Russell. And I could smell the fancy food.

"Most important, though, I could hear the music. I'll never forget the thrill one rainy night when I first heard Jim Thornton play 'Sweet Sixteen.' All the years in between haven't dimmed the thrill of that moment, because whenever I sing that song, I'm a young kid again staring out there on Fourteenth Street in the rain."

But the thrills were few and far between. When there was no more money to pay the rent, the boys were back on the park benches and knocking on the doors of agents' offices.

Then came the break they had been looking for. On a summer afternoon in 1903, they bumped into a man named Ren Shields.

Shields was none too successfully trying to write vaudeville acts. One of the people he had been trying to write for was Joe Palmer, a man who in his day had headlined a reasonably prosperous act. But he had been struck down with multiple sclerosis, and in those days there was little but sympathy for an actor in a wheelchair.

Shields needed a break as badly as Palmer. He had had his moments—notably when he had written the lyrics of "In the Good Old Summertime"—but the royalty checks were small and didn't come in very often.

The Joelson boys seemed to be the answer to his problem. He would team them up with Palmer in a new musical comedy act. What's more, he would build the act around the old trouper's wheelchair. Palmer would play the patient in a nursing home, Harry would be the doctor, and Al the bellboy.

For once Al would have all the punch lines in the comedy skits and Harry would be the straight man. Palmer was the "feed" for them both.

The first thing any new vaudeville act had to do was to advertise, if they could afford it, in the theatrical press. In any case, they had to have cards printed. But they couldn't find a printer who would prepare the sort of cards they had in mind: their names engraved over little oval pictures of each partner, and above the portraits the names "Joelson Palmer and Joelson."

"The names are too long for the card," said one printer. "How about shortening them?" Palmer's name wouldn't make much difference, he said, but the boys were different. They both had the same name—and a foreign-sounding name it was at that. "Take the e out," he said.

The boys decided to give it a try. Their act was to be called "Jolson Palmer and Jolson." For the first time an audience saw a performer called Al Jolson. The audiences loved the act. It made them laugh until they were dry—which pleased the vaudeville houses; they sold more beer.

Playing in Brooklyn, Al Jolson's career was really launched.

Only eight years later, Al described the scene: "I had a Negro dresser who told me, 'You'd be much, much funnier, boss, if you blacked your face like mine. People always laugh at the black man.'" In 1912 no one thought that was in the least offensive and, when Al told it, he had the audiences in fits.

It was a good, colorful story of those times. Much more likely, however, was the other legend about a decision that made Al Jolson the most successful minstrel man of all time.

On the bill with him was a blackface comedian and monologue man called James Francis Dooley. "Why don't you try some of the burnt cork yourself?" he asked the youngster. "It'd go perfectly with that Southern accent of yours, and you'd make a much better bellboy."

The resulting act was better than it had been before. Al's confidence had been sagging, but from the moment he blacked up, he felt he owned the whole of show business. Before very long show business owned him.

In later years, Jolson's blackface routine was to be condemned as an insult to the Negro. It is fair to say that he never considered it to be that. At the turn of the century blacking up was just another vaudeville routine. No one believed that minstrels with burnt cork on their faces were really Negroes. In a way, they were a race of their own: they were rarely as insulting as non-Jewish actors playing characters like Fagin or Shylock.

To Al Jolson, it was the passport to a completely new world. When that makeup was on his face he never seemed to worry. It was like a mask behind which he could hide his problems. It also seemed to make him twice the personality he had been before.

The act toured the country, billed as *A Little of Everything*. As far as the Jolsons were concerned, "everything" meant a salary check and a reference from the management to go with it.

In April 1905 came what they thought to be the biggest big break they had a right to expect. They were offered a contract by the famous Tony Pastor to play at his Music Hall. Second only to the Palace on Broadway, Tony Pastor's has gone down in history as the top spot in vaudeville. It was there that Irving Berlin worked as a singing waiter when he wrote "Sadie Salome Go Home," his first hit.

The offer included a fee of forty dollars a week each, the kind of money no one sneered at in those days. The Jolson brothers took turns carrying the contract, it was so precious a document.

By the time they got to New York to cash in on the contract, the paper was ragged and dog-eared. As it turned out, it was never to be more than just a piece of paper. Just before the act was due to go on at Tony Pastor's, Harry and Al had their first really big row—one that was big enough to drive their careers apart for good.

The two quarreled over who was to look after Joe Palmer, whose illness was becoming more and more debilitating every day. In the end they had to take turns washing and dressing their crippled partner. Finally, they came near to blows when both decided they wanted the evening off at the same time.

The row ended with Harry walking out and Al and Joe going it as a twosome at another theatre. But it didn't work out. Al, increasingly restless, thought he could do better on his own. Joe found another partner who shortly afterward managed to stop the crippled performer from driving his wheelchair over a window ledge.

Al desperately needed to make a success of his career. On his own now, he placed an advertisement in *Variety:* "Watch me—I'm a wow."

Harry temporarily discarded his blackface makeup and worked up a routine as a Jewish juvenile. In a brown derby and striped frock coat and trousers, he billed himself as "The Ghetto Sport." He got bookings, but nothing like those that were suddenly coming Al's way as fast as he wanted them.

Al had left Joe in California, and from the moment he pranced around the boards for his first solo audition, he got the work he wanted—on the West Coast.

He arrived in San Francisco in 1906, a week after the earthquake. Within days of the quake and its fires, temporary theatres—some tents, some huts—went up in the city. The local administration decided that entertainment was vital for morale.

Al Jolson was paid seventy-five dollars a week to play in one of those makeshift theatres. Within weeks, his fee was doubled. Harry Jolson wrote many years later that San Francisco was the town that loved Al the best.

Al Jolson made an enormous impact on San Francisco in 1906. It was as though another earthquake had hit the city. No one had ever seen a single performer who was so dynamic. He had only to open his mouth and it seemed the crowds flooded into the box office. The only competition seemed to be revival meetings—and in many ways that's just what Jolson's shows were. Al Jolson was responsible now for a completely new kind of adoration and worship.

By the time he left San Francisco at the end of 1906 he was earning two hundred dollars a week. He had also begun to perfect the act that was soon to make him famous. As for his personality, it was there already.

Standing on a makeshift stage in one of those temporary San Francisco theatres, he first made the statement that has gone down as his own epitaph.

One didn't have to be in show business to see what the crowd was doing to the young man of about twenty-one that night. They were shouting at him, demanding one new song after the other. Hard-bitten laborers with grimy hands and faces sitting next to men in evening dress and women in fashionable long gowns were as brothers and sisters in the near-religious frenzy.

Al, his collar loosened to allow the sweat to escape below his chocolate makeup, saw what was happening, and felt an elation he had never felt before. He stood up, stretched his hands out over the footlights, and called back, "All right, all right, folks—you ain't heard nothing yet."

For the next forty-four years, there was never to be a Jolson performance where that phrase was not uttered, and when it did not evoke just the same sort of response that greeted it that night. The audience screamed and shouted for more.

Enrico Caruso was in town at the same time. Al liked to joke that the Italian tenor didn't receive the same sort of response as he was getting.

None liked the handsome young singer more than the girls of the city. Whether they knew it or not, they were bolstering the Jolson ego, which was always to play such an important part in his story—and few had better opportunities to show just how much they admired him than the girls who were working on the same bill as Al. They flattered him and even asked him for dates.

And they got them, too. All, that is, except one of the chorus girls, who held back while the others pushed. And because of her apparent disinterest, she was the one he wanted most. Her name was Henrietta Keller, a tall, blond, breathtakingly pretty girl, whose stern Norwegian father had ruled her with a rod of iron before she left home in Oakland, California.

Mr. Keller did not like the idea of show business. But he became reconciled to his daughter's going on the stage on one condition—that she did not develop too close an attachment with show people. As a dutiful daughter, who accepted that she must never fall in love with a man in the business, she didn't allow herself to be tempted. She turned down all the offers of dates that came her way, including those from Al Jolson.

It hurt his pride deeply. He even told her it was harming his image. But she said that her own happiness was what she had to be concerned about most. Nevertheless, there were signs that Henrietta was weakening.

There were shy smiles when he rolled his eyes on stage in her direction. When he sang directly at her, she responded in spite of herself. Soon she had not only agreed to go out with the young star; she had also accepted his proposal of marriage.

The ceremony, before a justice of the peace in New Jersey, was the climax of the first romance Al had ever had. The only person he had confided in about the marriage was his old friend and mentor, Fred Moore.

He only hinted at it in letters to Harry, who himself was doing well now with the leading Keith Circuit under the billing "The Operatic Blackface Comedian." He had given up his Jewish act and was following his younger brother's lead, although he insisted he was merely continuing where he had left off in the *Turkey Burlesque Show* four years before.

Harry found out about Al's plans to marry through Fred Moore and tried to stop Al before it was too late. Marrying a Gentile girl, Harry pointed out, was just about the worst thing a Jewish man could do. Wouldn't Al reconsider? If his younger brother had any such thought, Harry's request was all he needed to fire his determination to go through with the marriage.

When the news filtered through to Washington, D.C., Cantor Yoelson went through the ritual he had last performed after burying his first wife, Naomi. He sat on a low chair and recited the Kaddish, the prayer for the dead.

Al, meanwhile, had a recurrence of his old tubercular trouble and with Henrietta went into the hills of Washington state to recuperate. As soon as he showed signs of improvement, he and his bride went south again, back to work.

The idle months in the hills had made Al restless, far more than he had ever been before. He wasn't just relaxing with a new wife. Henrietta felt she was just along for the trip, while his real love was thousands of miles away.

In those first weeks he showed her that she was no substitute for the raucous crowds who had filled his life for the past year. When an offer came from the Sullivan and Considine Circuit to join them in tours of the Middle West and West, he jumped at the chance. They paid him $250 a week, and he placed more advertisements in the trade papers. Billing himself as "The Blackface with the Grand Opera Voice," he announced: "Perhaps you've never heard of me—but you will."

When Harry saw the title under which Al was billing himself, he threatened to report his brother to the theatrical profession's disciplinary body, the White Rats. Al made a few choice comments about Harry and carried on just the same. He played in the West, Harry in the East, and deliberately, the two never met.

Between bookings, however, Al suffered the indignity of being asked by agents if he and Harry Jolson were related. One after the other they told him, "He does a routine similar to yours." One critic wrote, "It's going to be a toss-up as to who has the better act of the two, Harry Jolson or his brother Al. Harry accomplished something at the American last week at nearly every performance which I have often read about and heard talked about, and that was to stop the performance."

And he went on, "If it had been a prearranged affair it might have been understood, but the applause was so insistent, and so enthusiastic were the demands, that he returned and began all over again and it was absolutely useless for the act following him even to start.

"Jolson was some hit and already the Broadway managers are squabbling for him."

Alas for Harry, the managers squabbled over him on very few occasions, although for a while he was riding high.

He was playing the William Morris Circuit when it went bankrupt, leaving Harry and a thousand other artists completely stranded. He couldn't get work anywhere. When Eddie Leonard, the man who had first realized the potential of Harry's brother Al, heard about this, he offered Harry a place in the new minstrel troupe he was planning.

But Leonard had a row with his "angels," the show folded, and Harry went off to England to find work in the music halls there.

He now had a bride of his own to take with him. The man who had scolded his brother for marrying a Gentile had done the same thing—and eloped. He later told his father that the cantor's brother, Rabbi Julius Hess, had given him his blessing. But in England, he said, what he needed most of all was luck.

Al, meanwhile, was being noticed, drawing rave reviews from the press wherever he went. What was even more important at the time, people in the profession were noticing him.

In 1907 a dapper young agent named Arthur Klein saw Al at work in one of the country's earliest cinemas in El Paso, Texas. Later he recalled, "Black face, white socks, straw hat—the man electrified me. I followed him through Texas and Mexico, traveling by train to catch his act." He tried to persuade Al to let him sign him up as his agent and make him a big name. But Jolson was convinced he could do it on his own.

He was playing at the Pantage Vaudeville House at Little Rock, Arkansas, the same week as another blackface outfit—Lew Dockstader's Minstrels, the biggest name in minstreldom since the days of E. P. Christie and Stephen Foster.

An impresario named Will Oakland had advised Dockstader to go and see Jolson. He watched young Jolson from the wings and then convinced him that he could do better as part of his firm than by trying to make it on his own. He could play as a single within the framework of the minstrel show.

No longer would he have to hope to play in towns where his name would mean something. As part of the Dockstader show, he knew there would be standing room only wherever he went. Jolson needed to hear no more. Besides, he was shrewd enough to gamble on the future.

Dockstader promised him big billing, and the people who saw him at the end of the minstrel line would never be allowed to forget. He had the promise, too, that he could choose not only the songs he wanted to sing but the way the orchestra played the accompaniment, too.

In America at the turn of the century, the minstrel show was reaching the apex of its success. It had been a nationwide institution for fifty years, with a never-changing pattern. Like the minstrels in Tudor England who went from house to house with a song and a tale, troupes like Dockstader's went from town to town creating their own kind of folk art.

Like the circus they were, they marched from the railway station to the theatre, dressed in top hats and tailcoats, at that stage without their blackface makeup. At city hall, surrounded by swarms of people, they would stop, while the leader of the minstrel company recited platitudes about the fair town they were visiting.

48

There were always precise rules on how the minstrels dressed—striped trousers, big floppy bowties, tall hats—and particularly on how they wore their burnt cork. The big circles around their eyes and the oval border to their lips might have been considered a caricature of the Negro—but it would have been difficult to mistake one of Dockstader's men for the genuine article.

Their routine on the platform—whether in a tin hut or in an ornate theatre—never varied. In the center was the one man in the company with a white face—Mister Interlocutor, who was to the minstrel company what the conductor is to the symphony orchestra. When he took his place, a rattle of tambourines greeted his instruction, "Gentlemen, be-ee-ee seated."

The leading performers were the end men in the front row of the company. They traded insults with each other and were the butt of the interlocutor's jokes.

By the time Jolson joined Dockstader, the first signs that the day of the big minstrel show might be ending had appeared. Vaudeville was drawing youngsters away from the old traditions and had progressed into theatres, leaving the beer parlor and saloon far behind.

The motion picture had proved that it was plainly here to stay. Short comedy reels, dramas, and early science fiction had come to the nickelodeon. Movies were no longer just peep shows. The first cinemas were being built.

And in the home, the parlor piano was now struggling to hold its own against the phonograph, from which resounded the first sounds of what was soon to be called ragtime.

Dockstader gave Jolson his head because he thought this powerful young performer would help him prolong the success of the minstrel show in the face of such competition.

When, forty years later, *The Jolson Story* recreated the young Al's constant battle with the frustrations of the minstrel show—a set routine with little opportunity to branch out on his own—it was only telling half the story. What Dockstader did was to give Jolson the opportunity to develop a style that he never totally abandoned.

If he was able to hide the constant battle with his nerves behind his blackface, he was able, too, to prove to himself that when he was alone on the stage he could hold the audience in the palms of his outstretched

49

hands. He exaggerated a Southern accent because it helped him cover up what vestiges still remained of the Lithuanian-Yiddish sounds he had brought over from Srednik.

Al was not content merely to sing. For him singing meant using every movement of his body. He discovered that a small on-the-spot dance while he sang helped him to attract that part of the audience whose attention seemed to be wandering. By stretching out his arms at the same time, he could include the audience. By shaking his head, he showed that he was firmly in control.

. The days with Dockstader also proved that success on stage was a two-way affair. Sometimes he played in halls where the house lights couldn't be dimmed. But he reveled in that situation, for he could see the faces of the people out front. If they were smiling at him, he smiled underneath his makeup and responded even more engagingly.

By 1909, after only one year with Dockstader, it was evident that he had eclipsed Dockstader himself and his other star, Neil O'Brien.

Dockstader led his men in old minstrel numbers like "And he played to her his fiddle-e-dee." Jolson sang the current hit songs like "Sweet Sixteen" and his very first Mammy number, "It's a Long Way Back to Dear Old Mammy's Knee." Before very long, Dockstader had to face the fact that the customers were coming to see Al Jolson, and not simply his minstrel show.

But Dockstader was happy as long as the cash flowed in. Amid a crescendo of bones and tambourines he would proclaim the entry of "Our premeer end man—Mistah Al Jolson." Al received the same salary Dockstader claimed to be paying himself, seventy-five dollars a week.

In 1909 the troupe came to New York and played at the famous Fifth Avenue Theatre. For the first time, *Variety* opened a Jolson file. Their columnist Sime noted: "Haven't seen a demonstration for a single act, or any act for that matter, as was given Al Jolson."

Al left Dockstader for a brief time, fed up with the routine in which he had to join forces with Dockstader and O'Neil for what was called the "Possum Club Picnic." The big star no longer felt happy in the bellboy's uniform the act demanded. He felt he had left that life behind when he said goodbye to Harry and Joe Palmer.

In 1912, he told *Variety*, "I have never regretted becoming an end man and was very happily situated when we reached the Grand Opera House, New York."

Just how "happily situated" can be appreciated; at the Grand Opera House he was spotted by a pack of vaudeville talent scouts.

It was just part of the job. The agents and talent scouts haunted theatres like the Opera House, hoping to spot new artists. When they saw Jolson, there was an immediate rush to the stage door.

For the young singer, it was an opportune moment. Dockstader wanted to rest, and closed the show in midseason, so Al was open to offers. He accepted one to open at Oscar Hammerstein's new theatre, the Victoria.

On his first night there, he introduced a new Jolson ritual. He walked straight to the front of the stage and shouted to the electricians, "Bring on the house lights. Ya know, folks—this is the happiest night of my life. Yes, siree. I'm so happy. Ya wanna listen . . . " And he then went into all the most cheerful songs in his repertoire.

Jolson was successful, but not as successful as he had hoped. He went on circuit around the Orpheum chain in the East. What gave him the most satisfaction was that he was becoming so well known that he could call the stagedoor keepers by their nicknames. That was real fame.

What he described as "this delightful tour" folded in Louisville, Kentucky, when he became ill with a recurring throat infection. For the first time in his life, Al Jolson made a claim on an insurance policy. "I shall never forget the agile intern who was sent by the accident insurance company to examine me," he told the *Variety* reporter in a 1912 interview. "He was to make sure that I actually was sick enough so as to get the $12.50 a week they were good enough to allow. From the way the young doctor-to-be went about his work, I felt that he was afraid that I was shamming illness for the $12.50."

In December 1909, he was back in New York at the Colonial Theatre, singing "Hello, My Baby," one of the first big ragtime hits. When one of the billed stars refused to work during the Christmas holidays, Jolson stepped in as a replacement. This time, he was the hit he wished he had been on opening night at the Victoria.

The audience cheered and tears rolled down Al's cheeks as he stood on the stage. The building resounded with the audience's applause.

A party was thrown for him after the show and he rushed back to the hotel where he and Henrietta were living to tell her about his success. Instead of being ecstatic the way he thought she should be, she managed a faint smile and turned to the bedroom. Somehow, the excitement on her husband's face seemed to confirm her worst fears; the more successful he became, the harder they would find it to live a normal married life.

Because Al was working in the heart of New York, that was where they had to live. And because the heart of New York meant one of two things—a luxury apartment or a tenement—the only sensible place for a home was a hotel suite. That, at least, was how Al worked it out.

Henrietta had other ideas. She told Al to go to the party without her. She had a headache, she said.

Early in 1910, he went back to Dockstader, again singing the current hits, but never having the chance to introduce a new song. Nevertheless, Tin Pan Alley was already courting him. A young man in a music publisher's office persuaded him to try a number that he predicted would be very big.

Jolson sang it in the show's olio that night. It was called "Alexander's Ragtime Band." At one end of New York, Al Jolson and the minstrels were singing the number to the sort of syncopated beat Dockstader himself detested. At the other end of the city, the song's composer, Irving Berlin, was making a fortune, playing the same tune on his own one-key piano.

The publisher's fifteen-year-old song plugger, meanwhile, was busy searching out more potential hits for Jolson. It was a job he did with loving care for the next forty years. His name was Harry Akst.

Dockstader didn't like the ragtime tunes, but he had to admit that they drew the customers. And he watched what was drawing them in at other theatres, too. When he found out what other headliners like Nora Bayes and Jack Norworth were singing, he made sure Al sang them, too. "Come Along, My Mandy," which Bayes and Norworth had written for their show "The Jolly Bachelors," became an established hit of the *Dockstader Minstrels.*

Jolson sang the Bert Williams specialty "Why Adam Sinned." He also perfected a new routine, whistling some of the passages. What had previously been a substitute for his broken voice was now becoming a trademark.

Then Art Klein appeared on the scene again. He decided that Jolson was underselling himself. And that, Klein said, he could not allow.

"I'd like to sign as your manager," Klein told him. "I think you ought to go back to vaudeville. I know a lot of people have got their eyes on you. But I think you're such a great artist that there should be really great things in store. And now for the first time, you're really going to get a chance."

In a cafe on Columbus Circle, Jolson and Klein signed a ten-year contract.

Klein, as always dressed immaculately in trousers with razor-sharp creases, smoothly pressed jacket, white shirt, and black necktie, booked his new protégé for $250 a week into two theatres simultaneously. Jolson had enough energy in him to commute from one theatre to the other in the course of an evening.

Al continued successfully for a year—so successfully, in fact, that he was able to snub the great Florenz Ziegfeld. Ziegfeld asked Klein to bring Al down for an audition. In what the showman regarded as the supreme folly of youth, Klein told him, "Jolie doesn't audition for anyone." It was a gamble, but he confessed to his shattered client that he did not want Al to be lost in the midst of the big Ziegfeld production extravaganzas. He said he had bigger plans for him. But it was a chancy decision. "I was determined to get Al on Broadway," Klein said years later.

When he saw demolition teams move into the old Horse Exchange in the midst of what was already the street of dreams and disasters, he saw his opportunity.

The place had been taken over by the Shubert brothers, experts in staging the sort of magic Klein knew Al could weave for them. Jake and Lee Shubert were on site every day, watching the last remnants of the straw and the smells of the Horse Exchange being consigned to oblivion.

When Klein approached them to use Jolson in their first show they weren't interested. "He's from vaudeville, Art," they told him. "We're legit. This is going to be the classiest musical theatre on Broadway."

Neither he nor Jolson ever argued with that. The theatre was going to be called the Winter Garden.

4

GIVE MY REGARDS TO BROADWAY

IN 1911, some of the lights of Broadway were still fed by gas. The roadway echoed to the sound of clattering horses' hooves and streetcars trundling their way to and from the Bowery.

There was straw on the pavements everywhere and when theatregoers in their finery crossed the road, they had to be wary of what their feet might pick up. But there were signs that the old order was changing. The automobile had arrived—although even on Broadway people still turned their heads to look when they heard the sound of a horn.

The Shubert brothers, who had by now established themselves as the biggest names in the musical theatre business, had built a tasteful gold-encrusted palace. The Winter Garden symbolized the new age into which that business was now entering. It was located just where the streetcars turned around.

A young song writer named Jerome Kern had been asked to produce a complete score for the theatre's first production, *La Belle Paree.*

It would be nice to think the Shuberts had the foresight to decide that a theatre of such magnificence with such a brilliant composer providing the music also needed a bright new star called Al Jolson. They didn't. He was part of a package the Shuberts bought when they took over *Dockstader's Minstrels.* Klein simply persuaded them to change his role.

Even so, they didn't think Jolson was right for a Broadway musical. He was allowed on only in the very last scene. When they saw Jolson perform, the Shuberts believed their worst fears had been justified.

No one seemed to be taking any notice of him. *The Cook's Tour Through Vaudeville with a Parisian Landscape,* as the show was subtitled, seemed to take second place to the landscape of the theatre itself.

Eyes were wandering throughout the long evening and the newspaper writers seemed as impressed with the decor as the audience was. After all, they had heard that one man had paid $19 for a $2.50 seat, just to be there on what he was sure was a historic occasion.

One columnist wrote: "Crowds began to arrive at the Winter Garden long before eight o'clock until the sidewalk was almost blocked and the lobby filled to overflowing. The line of carriages and automobiles extended for two blocks when the first nighters were coming more plentifully. . . .

"Once inside the theatre, the people seemed disinclined to go at once to their seats, but filled all of the wide promenade space back of the orchestra seats until the overture began.

"Large baskets of flowers, bouquets, and elaborate floral designs were banked in the rear until the walls were hidden. Garlands of flowers were draped around the box fronts and the side of the proscenium arch. Not the least attractive part of the Winter Garden is the simplicity and harmony of the decorations of the auditorium. The walls and balcony front are in old ivory and gold and the ceiling marked off in latticed squares in old ivory behind which is an artificial sky of blue. . . .

"The audience last night found the seats wide and comfortably spaced, with a receptacle for cigar ashes attached to the back of each chair."

The writer did not record that they were equally enthusiastic about Al Jolson.

The show had been running more than three and a half hours when the little blackfaced figure walked on stage and announced he was Erastus Sparkler, "an aristocrat of San Juan Hill cutting a wide swath in Paris."

"Paris Is a Paradise for Coons," he sang, but few took much note. The audience was noisy after listening to what had proved to be a pretty nondescript score. Many had already gone home; they had not only suffered the earlier scenes of *La Belle Paree,* but had endured, too, a Spanish ballet performed by "Sixteen Moorish Dancing Girls" and "Bow Sing" which was described as a "one-act Chinese fantasy opera."

Al was nervous by the time his music struck up and he had forced himself to dance out onto the stage apron. The people out front were a kind but largely indifferent audience. Blackface had never been featured in a "legitimate" show before and the men and women who had paid to come along to the Winter Garden on March 20 were clearly not in a mood to be impressed.

Most of the critics had already left to make sure their reviews were in the next morning's papers. But there was one who did stay—Adolph Klauber. Writing in the *New York Times,* he said: "Among the very best features were those provided by the two unctuous ragtime comedians, Miss Stella Mayhew and Mr. Al Jolson, both of whom had good songs and the dialects and the acting ability to deliver every bit of good that was in them."

The number that took Mr. Klauber's fancy was the one in which Al, still in blackface, joined Miss Mayhew, to play a clown.

Klauber saved Jolson for Broadway. Art Klein recalled: "Jolson was very, very sad about this. He told me I had no right to sign him for such a big place. He was happy in vaudeville—and making more money there, too.

"That night, he was an absolute failure—because he really didn't have faith in his work." Jolson himself wrote: "I felt so nervous that night that I walked to Ninety-fifth Street instead of Fifty-third, where I was living, before I realized what I was doing. You can understand how I felt."

After reading Klauber's review, the Shuberts gave Al a new position on the bill for the second performance, the Thursday-afternoon matinee. They thought his reputation as a showman meant he was big enough to cope with the sort of traumatic experience that opening had been. And he proved them right.

He came onstage and poked his head through the still-closed curtain. With that one gesture, he began not merely to entertain the people out front, but to spellbind them. And he used a number that symbolized this new age in which people were buying automobiles to impress their neighbors and particularly their sweethearts.

In the middle of the song "He Had to Get Out and Get Under" Jolson pulled a trick out of the air that once more gave him the audience's full attention. The huge, ornate Broadway stage bounced with the sound of his whistling between choruses. The audience opened up to him in the sort of frenzy that he was later to demand as his right.

As Art Klein said: "In those days there were no microphones. But this man had the most resonant voice of any human being I ever knew. I stood at the back of the theatre with my hands on the wall—and I could feel the bricks vibrate."

Variety saw the way the tickets were being bought and billed *La Belle Paree* "Double Sockeroo." In the show business Bible's language that meant "standing room only" on all fronts. Jake and Lee Shubert finally appreciated what they had bought when they signed for Dockstader's troupe of minstrels.

Jolson's fame grew. The critics came to see what they had missed the first night and wrote about this magnetic new singer, Al Jolson. The Social Register people, who had been reluctant to be seen anywhere less than in the Metropolitan Opera House's Diamond Horseshoe, realized that it was now the fashion to go to the Winter Garden.

They came from Park Avenue and from Brooklyn and the Bronx. And they came from out of town, too. Some people even came by train from Chicago to catch this new marvel in blackface.

They came to catch the ever-changing Jolson personality and routine. From the word go, he showed he wasn't going to be like the other characters in a Broadway show, the ones who simply read their lines or sang the songs the composer had written for them. From the moment Jolson introduced "Get Out and Get Under," he showed he was going to sing his own songs, despite what poor Mr. Kern had hoped. So he sang "That Lovin' Traumerei," which had been adapted from the original by Robert Schumann, and another, called "That Develin' Rag," by Billee Taylor.

The people who came to hear him once came again and again. Not only was there the novelty of seeing what he would sing next; there was also the anticipation of discovering *how* he was going to sing his songs. Even when he repeated songs in subsequent performances, he changed the way he delivered them. The Winter Garden regulars played games with each other, spotting the changed lyric, the different treatment of a chorus, the substituted phrase.

Oscar Radin, conductor of the Winter Garden orchestra (he was an uncle of Oscar Levant, the pianist who a couple of generations later became Jolson's foil on his post-World War II radio shows), was completely thrown from one performance to the next.

Al reveled in the games he played with the musicians and, because it made people talk and the talking made more people buy tickets, the Shuberts reveled along with him. They let him decide which numbers to use for the show. His own part in *La Belle Paree* got bigger and bigger while the other, more experienced, performers found their lines declining in significance, and their songs suddenly disappearing from the orchestra's repertoire.

For a time, Jolson joined the cast of *Bow Sing* as well as *La Belle Paree* itself. But largely through his pressure, the second feature was removed from the bill—and the other artists from the payroll—after a mere thirty-two performances. *La Belle Paree* went on for another seventy-two.

When the show came to an end for the traditional summer break, the sound of the audience's applause was too strong for Al to want to take a rest. Henrietta thought differently. To her this was the perfect opportunity to start the family she had planned, although nothing had yet happened to indicate that this would be accomplished easily. Her doctors had said that Al was probably too tired.

Henrietta was becoming increasingly aware that her husband was happier going to the racetracks than staying with her. He certainly found it more convivial to spend the after-show hours at one of those floating crap games Damon Runyon later immortalized in his Broadway stories. Henrietta begged Al to spend some time with her, but all he could really think about, even when playing the dice, was his own career.

He gave Jake Shubert the idea straight: "Why not take the show on the road?" he asked. "We'll take the same scenery and cast and use all the same songs. It won't cost very much."

Lee and Jake Shubert had intended to concentrate on the new show they were planning for the Winter Garden next fall. But the thought that Jolson could be onto something big was irresistible.

So the people who had read about Jolson in their newspapers now had a chance to see and hear what all the fuss had been about. More important in the history of the theatre, they were for the first time being given the chance to see a complete Broadway show, right in their own backyard.

A former haberdasher from Missouri confessed to Al nearly forty years later that a ticket for *La Belle Paree* somewhere in the sticks had

58

been his first opportunity to see a Broadway import. His name: Harry Truman.

By October, the cast was back on Broadway. Gaby Deslys, the sensation of the Paris music halls, had been booked by the Shuberts for their next Winter Garden performance and Al Jolson was there, too, to take second billing.

On Novebmer 20, 1911—five days later than originally planned, because the Shuberts didn't think Mlle. Deslys knew her lines and songs well enough—the curtain went up on *Vera Violetta*. Al Jolson played Claude—once again a blackface role in a European setting.

Also in the cast was the darling of London's Gaiety Theatre, Josie Collins, who sang her famous Cockney number, "Tar-Rar-Rar-Boomdiay." Jolson had a number with a similar title, "Rum-Tum-Tiddle."

Meanwhile Jolson began to acquire the first trappings of stardom. As a big Broadway star, he felt he needed status symbols. So Klein bought him his first second-hand car and a fur coat. It was mid-August when they negotiated the salary terms for *Vera Violetta*. The weather was oppressively hot, but nothing would stop Jolson from wearing the fur coat for this meeting with the Shuberts.

"I don't want any of your summer salaries here," he told them, and pulled the collar of the fur coat tighter around his neck.

The Shuberts need not have worried about the money they paid Jolson. He was a fantastic hit in the new show on its first night. And in that microphoneless age, he developed yet another gimmick: he danced, marched, and hopped up and down the Winter Garden aisles from the front of the stage right up to the back of the theatre. He would launch himself into a number behind the footlights and then prance to the street doors singing and whistling as he went.

The *New York Times* was not slow to catch on to Jolson's effect. They wrote: "There was Al Jolson in the role of a colored waiter who succeeded in rousing the audience into its first enthusiasm in the early part of the evening and kept them enthusiastic much of the time afterwards."

Gaby Deslys played the sweetheart of a professor and, the *Times* said, she performed "remarkably well." Much more happily, in fact, than she performed offstage. Never before had she acted in English, and

59

now she felt that the rest of the cast were making fun of her. Even worse, she sensed that though Jolson's name was billed below hers, it was he the audience wanted to see, and it was he the rest of the cast were interested in talking to.

One buxom eighteen-year-old chorus girl in the show made a constant play for his attentions, and more than once succeeded in having him walk her home. Her name was Mae West.

Miss West got no notices for *Vera Violetta.* Indeed, every time the show was mentioned in the press, Jolson's name seemed to appear more often than anyone else's. "Stella Mayhew and Al Jolson made the two hits of the night," said *Variety.* "Gaby Deslys went big also with Al Jolson singing with her in a song 'I Want Something New.' Jolson just kidded while she sang. Al Jolson opened with 'That Haunting Melody,' and after he got through with that, the audience called for 'Rum, Tum, Tiddle,' and he certainly can sing that song."

On November 23, he placed another ad in *Variety.* "Everybody likes me," he wrote. "Those who don't are jealous. Anyhow, here's wishing those that do and those that don't, a Merry Christmas and a Happy New Year—Al Jolson."

During Christmas week, he went to the Victor studios to stand for the first time before the big acoustic horn which served as a microphone. He sang "Rum, Tum, Tiddle" and "That Haunting Melody." He also performed the two songs just as he had on stage, dancing from one end of the room to the other. The recording engineers went berserk at his antics. If they were to get their record, they insisted, the artist had to stand still in front of the horn.

Al promised to cooperate, but when he got to a particular part of "That Haunting Melody," he began to dance a few steps again. In the end they placed a coat around him, buttoning it at the back like a straitjacket, sat him on the chair, and told him to sing without moving. Surviving copies of that first recording show that he performed none the worse.

In fact, the record drew even more people to the Winter Garden and ensured *Vera Violetta* a run of 136 consecutive performances. Jolson told *Variety:* "When I look back and see how things have been made easy for me, I feel more than grateful to the Shuberts."

On March 5, 1912, that gratitude was returned when Jolson starred in his own right at the Winter Garden in *The Whirl of Society,* in which

Jolson appeared for the first time as Gus, a stock character he was to re-create in further Winter Garden extravaganzas and in films. Again, he was teamed with Josie Collins and Stella Mayhew.

For *The Whirl of Society*, the second item in a three-part bill, Jolson sang early hits like "My Sumurun Girl" and "On the Mississippi." He also introduced an early Irving Berlin piece called "Ragtime Sextette." Berlin was being billed as "The Ragtime King"; people thought he was the only one writing that kind of music. When Jolson sang it, some couldn't believe that any other performer had the right to sing it.

On March 15, 1912, he was back in the Victor studios again to record "Brass Band Ephraim Jones" and "Snap Your Fingers." Every time a new Jolson disc hit the streets—with another artist on the reverse side—it meant more tickets for the Winter Garden. Who was on the bill with him or what the story was about didn't seem to matter any more. The audiences wanted to see Jolson.

Many years later, in 1947, Charles Hastings wrote in the magazine *Motion Picture*, "Because of his tremendous vitality, Jolie never had a flop on Broadway and some of his shows were pretty bad. Some of them had little else but Jolson in them. But that was enough, because Al sang in a way that rattled your backbone and made you want to jump up and dance."

Jolson loved every aspect of his new-found success. But there was something more he wanted, even craved. He wanted his peers to know how good he was. And for him, this was even more important than the views of Henrietta, who was being shifted more and more into the background of his life. He desperately wanted the applause of the people who had thumbed their noses at him a few years before. To hear them acknowledge his success and, more important, his talent, was what he really needed.

Jolson talked it over with the Shuberts. "Why not Sunday performances—just for show folk?" he asked them. The two brothers, seeing more dollar signs before their eyes, realized that Jolson could be leading them to a new fortune. They jumped at the idea. And so did the show people.

They sat on both sides of the footlights, in the promenade section at the back of the house, to watch, openmouthed, as this comparative newcomer kept things throbbing in a one-man show for two hours at a time.

Al was twenty-seven, but he was already holding court for people double and treble his age. When they stood to cheer him at the end of that first Sunday concert, it was obvious that a new Jolson institution had been born. Another show was booked for the following Sunday, and another for the next week, and so it went.

On March 23, 1912, Sime, *Variety's* columnist, wrote: "The Shuberts may run the Winter Garden, but Al Jolson owns it. That dandy performer does as he will with the audience, whether Sunday or on weekdays. He had to sing three songs with his ad lib stuff, thrown in for good measure, then close with the melodrama."

And on a Sunday in November that year, Sime noted: "Al Jolson arrived before that time [11 P.M.] and kicked up the usual riot in the theatre that always follows his appearances. It's marvelous what Jolson can do or say at the Garden and get away with. He thinks nothing of removing his coat, collar, and tie after having been dragged to the stage. Sunday night he demonstrated his popularity in New York."

The following March, Wynn, another *Variety* writer, noted: "Jolson was the loud noise of the evening. He sang many songs, one or two new, and had Melville Ellis as accompanist for a couple. Jolson kidded so much, he broke himself up in 'The Spaniard Who Blighted My Life' and had to make a fresh start with it. When it comes to ad-libbing on the stage, Jolson makes some of the others look foolish." And the writer noted something else, "He appeared in whiteface."

Blackface or any other theatrical rig was strictly banned on Sunday nights, but Jolson could dominate a theatre without the aid of props. He could do it, too, without the help of the stories then being written for Broadway shows.

In *The Whirl of Society,* he developed another technique of getting into the audience. The aisles were not big enough to contain him and all that he had to offer, so he went to the Shuberts with another idea. Instead of simply running down the aisles, why not, he suggested, perform on a runway right through the middle of the house leading from the stage to the promenade section? That way, he told them, he could get close to his audience while remaining on stage. The whole theatre would become the one stage.

At first, the Shuberts dismissed the suggestion: it would cost them money. The runway would take up valuable seat space and if there were fewer seats to sell there would only be less money coming in. Jolson's answer was that the show would last that much longer.

The Shuberts were convinced.

As far as Jolson was concerned, the runway was yet another path on the road to success. It brought him closer to the audience he adored, and with the house lights all turned up as he instructed the theatre electricians to do each night, closer to their faces, too. When they smiled, he sang twice as confidently. Again the Winter Garden rocked.

When Jolson heard the response, he felt he had to top it. "You ain't heard nothin' yet" became a signal for more songs and more patter, none of it related to anything in the script.

They thronged to the Winter Garden in spite of below-freezing temperatures and the blizzard that had swept New York for days.

When *The Whirl of Society* went on tour, Al made sure that his old hometown, Washington, D.C., was on the schedule. He had not seen his father for several years and, with Harry trying his luck in England—not too successfully—Al's ties to his family were getting weaker as his success increased.

He kept two reserved seats for Cantor Yoelson and his wife on the opening Friday night in Washington. But they didn't come. Al had forgotten that nothing could persuade his Orthodox Jewish father to venture outside his home or synagogue on the eve of the Sabbath.

When he went to the old flat above the animal food shop after the show, there was more chastisement from the man who had never been in a theatre. "A father doesn't call on a son, Asa," said the cantor. It was something Al never forgot.

On future visits to Washington, Al made a point of bringing tickets to the Yoelsons' flat before appearing on stage. Usually the cantor would use the seats, although the old man would never agree to meet Henrietta.

While he could reluctantly accept his son's unholy path, he could never reconcile himself to a Yoelson's marrying someone who was not Jewish.

At first he never mentioned his *shiksa* daughter-in-law. It seemed better to pretend that she never existed. Then later through curiosity he ventured to ask why a man should be away from home so frequently without his wife. He couldn't resist asking whether she was pregnant.

When he heard she was not, he shrugged his shoulders, not knowing whether to be pleased that there was no member of his family being born into a strange faith, or sorry that there was not a new generation on the way.

Infrequently, the gray-haired cantor visited New York.

On one occasion, newspapermen recognized him in a store and pointed out the rabbinical figure to the assistant. "That's Al Jolson's father," he said. "Nonsense," said the man behind the counter. "Everyone knows Al Jolson is Italian."

It was the nearest the old man ever came to exchanging blows with a stranger. Despite his bitter disappointment with the way his Asa's life had gone, there was still pride when he heard his son's name mentioned in public. But to call him an Italian! It seemed as bad as hearing that his daughter-in-law's parents were Norwegian.

Sometimes Henrietta went on tour with Al. But more often than not, she stayed in their New York apartment. Al was more concerned with his own show business friends and the people who could further his career than with her, it seemed.

By September 1912, he had his first press agent, an attractive girl named Nellie. When he opened at the Lyric Theatre, Chicago, in *The Whirl of Society*, Nellie was constantly at his side.

One evening, when she was acting in a purely professional capacity, the *Sunday Recorder-Herald* of Chicago reported a performance as amusing as anything on stage. A writer noticed Al's determination never to let the facts spoil a good story.

"Nellie is the greatest of the new tribe of women publicity artists," Katherine Synon wrote in that paper. "But she was operating the spotlight and dodging it whenever a stray beam caught a glint of her evening gown. 'It's Al's show,' she declared, 'and I wouldn't necessarily be in it at all if he weren't so shy.' But because he was shy she coached from the sidelines until the Jolson monologue finally was launched.

"The dressing room was the scene of the informal production. Nellie had made a way from the stage door through ranks of chorus girls who greeted her with acclaim and flung after petitions to be exploited in airships.

" 'I'll put you all together in a hydro and sink you off the pier,' she had threatened over her shoulder as she knocked at the door of the Jolson dressing room. The 'come in' was not cordial, especially as it was followed by a sotto-voiced remark, 'If there's room to get a mosquito in here, I'd like to find it.'

"But we went. Al Jolson. Blackface comedian. Atlas of the song revue whose weight falls from his slender shoulders, will never look any funnier on the stage than he did then. His close-fitting wig, pushed high from his head to give him air, left a Caucasian streak that endowed him with a zebra effect. He stopped his frantic search for a clean white tie, to roll startled eyes at Nellie as she explained the design of the rest of her party of two. 'She wants you to talk, Al,' she said soothingly.

" 'Oh, Nellie, you won't leave me, will you?' he cried in panic—and Nellie stayed . . .

" 'Al started his stage career in Chicago,' said Nellie. Jolson rolled surprised eyes at her. 'It was Chicago, wasn't it, Al?'

" 'Oh, yes . . . it was Chicago.'

" 'And you were only six years old?'

" 'Only six.'

" 'Where was it, Al?'

" 'It was at a vaudeville theatre. It must have been the—'

" 'The old Olympic, Al?'

" 'Yes, the old Olympic.' "

And so, the paper reported, the interview went on. Nellie made up the lines, Jolson approved.

On February 6, 1913, the hoardings outside the Winter Garden announced a new production. But this time "Gus" was the star beyond all doubt.

Gaby Deslys was still the female lead, but now the name Al Jolson was billed above hers. *The Honeymoon Express* was a two-act "spectacular farce," and Jolson made a great hit with one particular tune. "My Yellow Jacket Girl" had been written for the show by the men who provided the score for the production, Jean Schwartz and Harold Atteridge. Jolson made an even greater hit with a song he had introduced at a Sunday concert, "The Spaniard That Blighted My Life," written by Billy Merson, an English music hall star. That number became the subject of a legal wrangle.

When he reached Hollywood stardom a decade and a half later, Jolson recalled the days of *Honeymoon Express* and his Broadway triumphs. In an interview with *Theatre* magazine, he reminisced, "The big kick on the legitimate stage is the first night, the nearness of that audience, and the realization that you can play on their moods."

The truth of the matter is that Jolson was never at his best on opening nights, certainly not until the last hour or so. His stomach was so knotted that he could neither think straight nor remember his lines. But he mastered the situation that opening night in 1913 by a device he later used to master Broadway itself.

Two thirds of the way through the evening, it was obvious that the final curtain was going to be hours late. So he called to his audience, "Do you want to hear the rest of the story—or do you want me?"

Once he was sure he was the one the people in the orchestra seats and in the gallery really wanted, Jolson let rip. He sang not only the songs from the new show, but the numbers from his previous attraction, too. And he sang the song he had just recorded for his new label, Columbia Records, "You Made Me Love You." When a Winter Garden audience heard him sing that, they wouldn't let him sing anything else. He gave them one chorus after the other. And when he turned to another tune, they made him return to "You Made Me Love You."

If there was a comedy number in *Honeymoon Express* to rival "The Spaniard That Blighted My Life," it was the one in which he was to play around with a whole succession of dialects, "Who Paid the Rent for Mrs. Rip Van Winkle?"

It soon became obvious, though, that whatever Al sang, the audience wanted him to go on singing. Gaby Deslys sat and sulked between performances. Once, Jolson even dismissed the cast while she was still on stage. She walked out in a crashing crescendo of high heels. But the people out front didn't mind.

Nor did the Shuberts. When Jolson first got involved in a lawsuit in December 1913, they happily paid up. A writer named Junie McCree sued for $250 because she claimed an act of hers called "Razor Jim" had been rewritten for Jolson without her consent. But Al Jolson was plainly worth the $250 to the Shuberts.

In fact, they had just signed him for a new seven-year contract—at two thousand dollars a week, thirty-five weeks of the year. The Jolson troupe was full of young talent. But Jolson outshone them all, including a Latin youngster named Rudolph Valentino.

Fanny Brice, the original "Funny Girl," played one of her first roles in *Honeymoon Express*. So did a songwriter named Harry Fox, who later married one of the Dolly sisters after making a fortune with "I'm Always Chasing Rainbows," based on a melody Chopin had called "Fantasy Impromptu."

Fox was one of the earliest Jolson imitators. They tried—and generally failed completely—to sound like him. To look like him, they blacked their faces and wore his kind of slim jacket and short trousers. They threw their arms out as he did. They got down on one knee as he did. But few of them ever knew how Jolson devised the technique that he turned into yet another trademark. It happened during the run of *Honeymoon Express,* when Al was plagued by an ingrown toenail.

He tried hopping from one side of the stage to another, but couldn't relieve the pressure that way. In those days he couldn't sit on a stool either—audiences demanded to see their entertainers work. So when "Down Where the Tennessee Flows" came to a poignant moment— when he was expected to beseech his Mammy to allow him to go home—he got down on one knee. It not only took the pressure off his toe; it also gave to posterity another Jolson mannerism.

Performers all over America heard about it and adopted the idea. So did Harry Jolson. Harry had been having a tough time ever since he first left for England in 1910. He had arrived in Britain to begin a theatrical tour just at the time when the country was in no mood to go to the music hall; King Edward VII had died.

Harry went back to England a year later and did moderately well. But he decided to go home again, convinced he was underpaid. But he couldn't get top bookings anywhere in America. While Al Jolson was playing Broadway, Harry Jolson was playing Brooklyn.

Furthermore, he was being billed as "AL JOLSON's brother— Harry." When he said it hurt him to be featured that way, he was told that either he accepted that billing or there would be no billing at all.

Al, galloping from one success to another, was not particularly concerned about his brother's plight. Harry said Al ought to help him as he had done once before by talking things over with the Shuberts. A few weeks before Al signed his new contract with them, the Shubert Brothers also handed Harry a contract to look over. He was to star in a new production to be called the *Review of Revues.*

Al objected. His brother's routines in the new show dwindled as the day for signing his contract approached. Before long Harry realized why the Shuberts were using the elder brother as the carrot to get the younger one. They knew that Al wouldn't tolerate having another Jolson under the prestigious Shubert banner, and the less they offered Harry the more they were likely to get Al to agree to terms.

Finally, when they agreed to cut Harry's routine down to one number at the end of the show, Al signed—and Harry walked out in disgust. He pleaded with other managements to give him a chance on his own, but they insisted that he either agree to capitalize on Al's name or forget about it.

His act was too similar to Al's, they pointed out. His high tenor voice might have been all right for England, but Broadway could do without it. Harry went on tour.

Al stayed on Broadway, relishing the notices the New York press gave him. When he appeared as Gus in yet another Winter Garden hit called *Dancing Around* in 1914, the New York *Sun* wrote: "Al Jolson had been too long absent from his public as its particular star. He was welcomed back with enthusiasm born of the hunger to see and hear him again.

"He was never more amusing, never acted with more evident enjoyment of the task for its own sake, never sang with more artless delight in the occupation. Nothing ever checks the wave of contagious magnetism that spreads through the theatre whenever he appears, and makes him and his audience the best of friends.

"He is the spirit of rough gaiety and his admirers sit in happy captivity under his irresistible ministrations." The paper noted that Al could do "about the most refreshing characterization in the world of stage humor. Almost any actor would give anything to be able to reproduce such a characterization. But only one man can, and he happens to be Al Jolson—so he need not trouble about any other role."

But Al did trouble. And the papers noted that, too. They remarked on the way he had "mastered eccentric dancing." They'd never said that about him before. But he knew he was great. When the Shuberts wanted him to play in one of their other theatres between the runs of *Honeymoon Express* and *Dancing Around,* they paid him $2500 for the six-day run.

The only real loser was Henrietta. She went out for walks alone. She met friends for coffee. And she sat in her apartment. When Al came home, it was usually to sleep. If he stayed at home in the afternoon, barely a word passed between them. He was indifferent toward her, while she had grown used to simply accepting her portion of his paycheck. She had the clothes she wanted and all the jewelry she could wear. But Al was married to the sound of people lining up at the box office, and hearing them mention his name.

And that was also the only thing keeping Harry Jolson in business. When he stood on a stage once and begged the audience to listen to him for his own sake, they just laughed. In his autobiography, *Mistah Jolson,* Harry wrote, "There were two Jolson brothers appearing on stage—and Al was both of them."

It was a difficult situation; while Al was quickly establishing a reputation as the most outstanding artist on Broadway, Harry was no more than a mediocre also-ran.

At one point, when Art Klein and Al were having negotiating problems, Al suggested that his brother join him as manager. Harry turned him down, his pride deeply hurt.

For a third time, he want back to England and happily sent Al press clippings of his sensational success in Leeds, singing "Put Your Arms Around Me, Honey." Three thousand miles away, Al was pleased that Harry was doing well. If it had been nearer home it would have been another matter entirely.

Dancing Around, aided by a score from Sigmund Romberg, ran for 145 consecutive Broadway performances. Again, the hits of the show were the ones that the composer didn't write. The big Jolson hit was "When the Grown-up Ladies Act Like Babies" by Joe Young, Edgar Leslie, and Maurice Abrahams. There was also the first number Al sang by a husband-and-wife team he was to use time and time again, Gus Kahn and Grace Le Boy—"Everybody Rag with Me." He sang "It's a Long, Long Way to Tipperary," imported from England and the trenches of France, and "I'm Glad My Wife's in Europe." Friends in the know were not far off in believing he wished she was there.

When the run of *Dancing Around* finished, Jolson took it on tour. One of the first ports of call was Washington, D.C. But it was to be a very different visit from his last.

Two messages awaited him at the stage door. One he had been expecting from his father, wondering when he would be coming home. The other, on White House stationery, was an invitation from President Wilson to breakfast the next day.

The President greeted the young star and told him how much a

Jolson fan he was. "I've heard some of your records," said Wilson, "and I've read all about your great success on Broadway, but I haven't been able to see you perform."

It was the perfect cue. "Wait a minute," he said with a twinkle. "Wait a minute—you ain't heard nothin' yet." And he sang "You Made Me Love You" as Woodrow Wilson ate breakfast.

When he left the White House, Jolson's chauffeur drove him directly to the feed store, where Moses and Ida Yoelson were waiting to greet him. They still did not approve of show business, but if it meant their Asa being received at the White House, then who were they to object? Perhaps he was not quite the loafer they had imagined. Al spent the day with his father, stepmother, and three half brothers, and their sister.

At the parlor piano, he sang "I Didn't Raise My Boy to Be a Soldier." Jolson was very much impressed by Wilson, the man who won the following year's election on a "No War" ticket.

The city's papers were full of "local boy makes good" stories and when he pranced through his *Dancing Around* routines, Washington audiences showed themselves even more enthusiastic than those who paid to sit in front of the stage at the Winter Garden. When the local Methodist church asked him to sing at their charity show during his Washington run, he quickly agreed to help.

Moses and Ida gladly accepted Al's invitation to the next performance of *Dancing Around.* But they didn't go to his dressing room after the show, as he had expected. Al had to go to them as they sat in the empty orchestra. "I told you, Asa," said the old man. "A father doesn't call on a son." But he and his wife had plainly enjoyed this new taste of show business. What was good enough for Woodrow Wilson was all right by Moses Yoelson, too.

On June 29, 1915, Jolson and the show's company played at the Panama Pacific International Exhibition at San Francisco, which gave them a worldwide reputation. But Henrietta was no more impressed by this than she had been by his Broadway triumphs. She told friends that a wife did not enjoy being insulted by a husband who was a star any more than she did by one who was a failure. Rumors spread of his shouting at her and calling her names on the few occasions when they were seen together.

Not only did she not like his being away from her on the evenings and afternoons that he was on stage; she also resented his constant restlessness when he was with her. He had taken his car on the train to San Francisco with him so that his chauffeur could drive them on a leisurely trip back East when the exhibition was over. But once he had arrived in San Francisco, he couldn't get back to Broadway quickly enough. He told the chauffeur to drive the car back to New York, and caught the train, while Henrietta stayed behind in Oakland.

He had important business to discuss with the Shuberts; nothing should be allowed to interrupt the strategy he intended to use when talking with them. For his next show he did not want to be merely co-starred. He was determined to be the only star.

His wish was the Shuberts' command. For the opening of *Robinson Crusoe Junior,* Jolson was for the first time described as "America's Greatest Entertainer." (A decade later, he was to be called "The World's Greatest Entertainer.")

Robinson Crusoe was the nearest Jolson had yet come to a show with a real plot, although from opening night on, it was quite plain that the story was not going to interfere with his domination on stage.

He was the little native boy on the desert island who helped Robinson Crusoe find his destiny. In fact, he was Good Friday. But in some scenes, he changed back to the old familiar Gus and even in one act to Fatima.

Three songs in the show became very much part of his personal repertoire: "Where the Black-eyed Susans Grow," always to be one of his own favorites; "Yaka Hula Hickey Dula," a Jolsonesque version of the Hawaiian Love Song; and the inevitable "Where Did Robinson Crusoe Go with Friday on Saturday Night?" a ridiculous piece of nonsense which Jolson somehow managed to turn into a reasonable ballad. The rest of the show was simply Jolson.

One evening he told the Shuberts: "This show's a lot of bunk. Let's get a Negro chorus to sing in the background and I'll do a couple of spirituals. I'd like that."

Who were the Shuberts to contradict their star? If Jolson said he'd like it, they'd have to like it. The Winter Garden audience, which liked anything Jolson did, would like it, too.

So for no apparent reason, the desert island scene suddenly became a backdrop for a Negro choir. Al sang "The Old Folks at Home" by

Stephen Foster and traditional tunes like "Swing Low, Sweet Chariot." Both Sigmund Romberg and Harold Atteridge could be seen pulling their hair.

But the Shuberts stood in the wings, arms folded, wide smiles on their faces. For 139 performances the customers lined up to get into the Winter Garden.

In 1916 Jolson was invited to go into a new medium—films. He did a short picture for the Vitagraph Co., but he didn't like the result. "I'm no good if I can't sing," he said. But since it was to be shown as a benefit for the Traffic Police's Benefit Fund, he decided not to worry too much about it. When word came that the picture was getting a wider release, Al was furious, and promptly ordered all the showings to cease and copies of the film to be confiscated.

Harry Jolson's career was hitting one of its frequent rough periods at this time. For him the Jolson name was by now more a handicap than an advantage. He was being compared more and more with his younger brother, always unfavorably. It became increasingly clear that Harry had little or no talent.

Al was advised by Klein that his brother's lack of any ability to hold an audience could ricochet on himself. "It's no good, Al, to have this guy held up as your brother. He's doing you a hell of a lot of harm."

Al took Art's advice and went to see Harry at his run-down apartment. "I'll give you twenty-five dollars a week to get off the stage," he told him. Since Harry had no work at all at that time, he accepted the offer.

But it was difficult, even in those days, to manage every week on twenty-five dollars. Harry's wife Lillian eventually got up enough courage to go and see her brother-in-law. "Al," she told him, "we just can't manage. Do you think you could make it thirty dollars?"

Al's reaction was immediate: "Why, you ungrateful . . ." he shouted at her. "You won't even get your twenty-five dollars." So Harry was forced to go back looking for work. Sometimes he got jobs that paid good money. Frequently, he did not.

Still, when there was money for him to make, his brother was often responsible for Harry's getting a job. Georgie Price, the man Al once said could impersonate him better than anyone else, suggested that Al was somehow ashamed of letting anyone know he could do a good deed, or give money to charity.

Al once went to the United Booking Office and asked them to book Harry. "I'll give you all my arrangements and all my orchestrations—and whatever you pay him I'll pay half his salary. You can give him my songs and my jokes—but don't tell him I had anything to do with it."

When Al was in California he heard a young ukulele player in a six-piece Hawaiian band and liked what he heard. They were not the sort of tunes being played in Tin Pan Alley. Jolson, always on the lookout for other people whose talents would help his own, was very impressed.

He introduced himself at the end of the show. The young musician told him his name was Buddy DeSylva. The tunes were his own, he said, and he wanted a chance to play them in the big time. Until then, he had had to be content with writing music for college shows and band concerts.

Jolson told DeSylva to come to New York and call at his Park Avenue apartment—and to bring along some of his music. DeSylva took him up on the offer. One of the songs he brought was called "'N' Everything." Within six months it had earned the young songwriter twenty thousand dollars. It was his first royalty check and it had come to him because Jolson had interpolated the tune in his new Winter Garden show, *Sinbad*.

On February 14, 1918, the night *Sinbad* opened, the Winter Garden public was looking for something to help them take their minds off the war. The Yanks were coming all right, but the war in France was going badly.

Jolson had volunteered for war service, but was told that his country needed him most to boost morale at home. So he sang for the troops before they left for France and at war bond rallies. And of course he still sang at the Winter Garden.

In the two-act extravaganza Al sang roles as Sinbad the Sailor, the old familiar Gus, and even as the front half of Emil, the Talking Mule. With his new collection of songs, the Jolson ego took new shape. He fancied himself a songwriter. For each tune in which he found slight alterations necessary to the lyric or to the phrasing, the name Al

Jolson appeared among the credits for the songwriters. It was there, together with those of Buddy DeSylva and Gus Kahn in "'N' Everything." And it was featured for their song "I'll Say She Does," and again in "Chloe." Altogether Jolson's name appeared in the *Sinbad* song credits seventeen times.

But his name was not on three other numbers Jolson introduced in this show, songs that were to be among his greatest. On opening night, the audience was enthralled as Jolson started to sing a tune obviously made to measure for him. When Al had finished, the audience started leaping over their seats in a mad rush for the stage and the runway.

The song began conventionally enough for a Jolson tune: "Mammy mine, your little rolling stone that rolled away, strolled away. . . ." But it ended, "Rockabye your rockabye baby with a Dixie melody." Al always said that it was his favorite song. He certainly put more punch and more enthusiasm into that number than he had put into anything else.

The second song that became the sensation of *Sinbad* was one written for another show with an altogether different kind of performance in mind. A nineteen-year-old song plugger had scribbled it on the back of a menu card over dinner—in about twenty minutes.

The song plugger and a young lyricist called Irving Cesar believed they had the answer to the current Tin Pan Alley sensation, *Hindustan.* The producer of the Capitol Theatre's *Demitasse Revue* thought so, too—and bought the tune.

He gave fifty chorus girls the opportunity to dance to it, each one with an electric light bulb glowing on her satin slipper. Everyone on stage sang it, backed by the powerful theatre orchestra. But barely a copy of the song on view in the theatre lobby was sold. And it certainly wasn't being bought outside the theatre.

The song was "Swanee." The young songwriter was George Gershwin. And through Al Jolson—and Buddy DeSylva—it became Gershwin's biggest hit.

It was DeSylva who suggested to Cesar that he bring Gershwin along to a Jolson party. Like all of Al's parties, it was to be an evening of his singing. Guests brought other guests and those people brought more strangers. There were so many unknown faces that it was impossible to tell who had been invited and who was gate-crashing.

When Al sang, it was only after a piercing series of shouts for

"Jolie," a nickname reserved for his intimates in the business. The shouts were always as loud and persistent as those from the Winter Garden.

The night Gershwin went to a Jolson party for the first time, he was determined to get to the piano in time to demonstrate what he had come for. He sat down and played while Cesar sang the words: "Swanee, how I love you, how I love you, my dear old Swanee. . . ."

It had exactly the desired effect. Four days later, Al Goodman, who led the Winter Garden orchestra, had dusted the number up, and within two weeks Jolson was dancing up and down the runway to it, singing and whistling while the audience stamped their feet. Al Jolson had found a hit that seemed to be the end of all hits.

Sinbad opened and closed twice—when Al decided he wanted to take things easy. When it reopened in 1921, Jolson produced a new show stopper. Today, it is the song every mention of Jolson recalls. To some people, it is the only song he sang, "My Mammy."

As was true with "Swanee," Jolson was not the first to sing "Mammy." But like "Swanee," he turned it into a hit that made money not only for him but for its writers, Sam Lewis, Joe Young, and Walter Donaldson. Al Jolson made it his theme song.

By the time *Sinbad* opened at the Winter Garden, Al Jolson could have turned Humpty Dumpty into a record breaker.

The supreme accolade for a man who wanted the admiration of his peers more than he needed to eat a meal came on April 1, 1918. The Friars honored him at a dinner at the Hotel Astor. They produced a special written program for the occasion which showed cartoon figures lining up for a Jolson performance. One said to another: "I've got a chance to see this show—if I don't die of old age." The *New York Times* recorded that the dinner turned into a patriotic rally. The guest speaker was Colonel J. S. Dennis of the Canadian Expeditionary Force, the man who had organized the British-American recruitment drives.

Jolson was notably chagrined at having been upstaged by a colonel. But seeing the colonel inspired him to go with his chauffeur to the nearest recruitment office, where he insisted on being called up. The chauffeur was rejected. Al was accepted and told he would be called that December. Then, on November 11, 1918, the Armistice was signed.

The end of the war meant raising money for the war veterans, who were going to need homes and work on their return. A mammoth concert was organized at the Metropolitan Opera House and Jolson was invited to take part. It was the sort of bill he had never been on before. He was just one among a whole group of stars. His turn to go on stage came immediately after the hall had rocked with applause for another singer of a very different sort.

Enrico Caruso had just finished "Vesti la Giubba" when Al Jolson ran onto the stage. Before the applause for the tenor had died down, Jolson, dressed in an immaculate blue suit with a rose in his buttonhole, threw out his arms and called, "Folks, you ain't heard nothin' yet."

He really didn't have to do much else. The sheer bravado, the chutzpah of it, brought the house down. The audience, stiff in stuffed shirts and tight corsets, was in the palm of his hand, just as if it were the Winter Garden.

George Burns was in the audience that night. "Imagine it," he said, "this cute little Jew saying, 'You ain't heard nothin' yet'—after Caruso—in Caruso's own house." The opera critics were confounded and wrote columns to condemn the Jolson "insult" to Caruso.

The tenor himself was delighted. He sent word to the Winter Garden, inviting Al to join him in his hotel suite, where he gave Caruso an impromptu private performance of "Swanee" and "Rockabye."

"Come, Al, and sing with me at the Met," said Caruso.

"No, 'Rico," Jolson answered. "They couldn't have two of us on the same bill again. The critics would go daffy."

But the box office appeal of Jolson on a concert stage was not lost on the promoters. On May 18, 1919, Jolson gave a song recital at the Boston Opera House. It was the first time in history that an entertainer from Broadway—and certainly one who had grown to fame and fortune from the Russian ghetto via minstrel shows and vaudeville—gave his own soiree at an opera house.

Jolson sang seventeen of his favorite songs including "Rockabye," "Where the Black-eyed Susans Grow," and "Night Boat to Albany," accompanied by the Boston Symphony Orchestra. More than $4100 was taken in that night; the most expensive seats were two dollars. More than two thousand people were turned away.

Art Klein arranged the Boston concert with the help of a newcomer on the Jolson scene, Louis Epstein. To Epstein, the sun shone out of Jolson's face and the stars gleamed in his eyes.

It was the beginning of a devoted friendship that lasted until Jolson's death. When Art Klein's contract with Jolson expired, Epstein stepped in as the star's manager. But he was more than that. "Eppy," as Jolson called him, was his friend, his father confessor. And the way his private life was now going, he needed that.

On June 26, 1919, Henrietta Keller divorced Jolson after thirteen years of marriage. To be married to someone like Al required a superhuman effort, and she wasn't willing to make it.

She alleged that Al "cannot stand success—because with that success his tastes ran far stronger—to wine, racehorses, and other women." She also alleged that he deliberately arranged for her to go to California the previous March while he stayed on in New York. "He said he loved me best when I was 3400 miles away, because I'm only a small-town hick, anyway."

Henrietta demanded and received two thousand dollars a month alimony. "Why not?" she asked the judge. "He's earning more than $3400 a week."

Al said he was dumbstruck by Henrietta's charges. "Outside of my liking for wine, women, and racehorses," he said, "I'm a regular husband."

He tried for a reconciliation, and sent his secretary, Frank Holmes, to Oakland to try to get Henrietta to change her mind and cancel the decree. When Holmes brought her a note from Al—"Come back to me and I'll give you all the money and clothes and motors you want"— Henrietta told him, "I don't want Mr. Jolson's money and motors now. What I want is my freedom."

Soon after the divorce, Henrietta went to stay with her former brother-in-law Harry and his wife, Lillian. She told them the familiar story of Al's days and nights away from her, of how he only wanted to be out with his gang and to be worshiped by his public.

They sensed that she desperately wanted to feel loved, and when Al called at their old apartment to meet her, Harry and his wife felt there might be a reconciliation. But it was not to be. Henrietta met someone else and was soon married again.

In private, Al joked with his friends about the girls he was going to take out now. After he had taken them out, he regaled his friends with the details of the previous night's experience. The tabloids loved the stories secondhand, and Jolson loved to tell them.

Henrietta faded away. But Al couldn't completely forget her. He gave her a house and when they occasionally met there, he seemed to be more tender toward her than he had been during all their years of marriage.

Meanwhile, Harry placed himself under Al's personal management. As for Al, he took on the rest of the profession.

Actors Equity called a strike and almost all Broadway's theatres were closed.

Two men held out against the strike more vociferously than anyone else: Al and George M. Cohan, the Yankee Doodle Dandy who loved to go on stage trailing the Stars and Stripes behind him. He was the man who was once asked, "Can't you write a show without a flag?" Cohan replied, "I can write without anything but a pencil."

But the strike was too much for George M. He said he would rather never get out pencil and write again than help the unions to change the face of Broadway. Jolson sided with him, and for months it appeared that Al's career was in as much jeopardy as Cohan's. George M. retired to the country. But Al Jolson couldn't foresee that sort of fate for himself. Show business meant too much to him; his principles didn't stretch far enough to include the thought of never putting on burnt cork again.

He was also concerned about the way he behaved on stage. He told one writer, "If I don't get laughs and I don't get applause, the mirror will show me who is to blame."

But he agreed that the audiences had something to do with the way he behaved on some occasions and was none too kind about them, either.

"I know of nothing worse than the audience in New York," he said. "I often do not come on stage until half an hour after the curtain rises. While the play is actually going on, I sometimes stand in the rear of the orchestra seats to watch the people coming in.

"I just can't describe the noise and confusion. People stop to shout hello to friends. They block the aisles in making engagements with friends for a month distant. They argue about their seats and their programs and do everything except recognize the fact that the curtain has gone up."

Jolson was being unusually modest. He might have been expected to state the obvious: that until he came on stage, there was nothing worth watching or listening to.

He told *Green Book* magazine in 1915, "I've never given the same performance twice for three reasons. I'm always trying something new. I'm a believer in spontaneous humor, and I'd go insane if I had to do the same thing every night."

Offstage he was the same kind of performer. When he went to pay $7600 in back income taxes in 1918, he climbed six floors, patted the collector, Big Bill Edwards, on the back, and sang for thirty minutes while the tax office staff gathered round. There was so much bustle in the crowd that the pickpockets did almost as well as the tax man—one man was relieved of a wallet containing seventy-five dollars but said it had still been a good show.

Al still had his problems. For one thing, there was another lawsuit to worry about. The Puccini estate had sued Al for plagiarism—stealing the melody of Puccini's "E Lucevan le Stella" and quickening the tempo to turn it into "Avalon."

Jolson and Vincent Rose had to find twenty-five thousand dollars. The singer learned the hard way what being a songwriter meant. But it was a good investment. He continued to sing "Avalon" for the rest of his career and every time someone bought a copy of his record, there were double royalties for Jolson, as singer and writer of the melody.

Not that money seemed to mean all that much to Jolson now. He was a free man; he had girls around him wherever he went; and the people who bought the tickets on Broadway thought he was king.

If he could hear people talking about Al Jolson in the street—and he always could—it was worth more to him than money. At the age of about thirty-five, the world's riches were at his command—and the world seemed to want it that way.

5

I'M SITTING ON TOP OF THE WORLD

NOTHING made Al Jolson happier than standing on the terrace of a skyscraper overlooking New York's theatre district, watching the lights flickering below. He would smile and say to whoever was with him, "Broadway—that's my street."

When people first started talking about the Jazz Age, Broadway *was* Jolson's street. He belonged to it from the top of his shiny black hair to the soles of his shiny black shoes. If he had been born in a trunk in a theatre dressing room instead of in a poor Russian town, and if his ancestors had been acrobats instead of cantors, he couldn't have been more a part of the scene.

But if he belonged to Broadway, even more assuredly, Broadway belonged to him. In these days before mass communication, important men in all walks of life could strut through the streets unrecognized— but not Jolson. He was mobbed wherever he went: when he left his dressing room, when he went to his own table at Lindy's, and when he bought his newspaper from the boy near the Times Square subway. As far as he was concerned, it was merely the audience's way of returning the love which he gave them across the footlights, seven nights a week.

The shouts of "Al, Al, Al," every time he entered or left a theatre made it all seem very real. For the first time ever, New Yorkers were reacting to an entertainer the same way they acclaimed a President or visiting royalty. And for Jolson, their acclaim was vital.

When attendance began to drop off for performances of *Sinbad*, the Winter Garden manager would worry to distraction. He knew what Jolson's reaction would be at the sight of empty seats in the house.

As always, it was Eppy, the resourceful friend, who solved the problem. He would run out into the street and accost the nearest passerby. "My wife's been taken ill," he'd say. "Would you like two tickets for the Winter Garden? It's Jolson—and he's great."

Before the amazed pedestrian could say anything Eppy would disappear into the crowd, knowing the two empty seats would be filled.

Sometimes, Jolson got wind of his manager's game. If he was the least bit suspicious of genuine ticket sales, he would sit in the box office himself. Bowler hat firmly placed at the back of his head, he would find out for himself exactly how well tickets were selling.

One night when it became obvious to Jolson that *Sinbad* had little more to offer, Jolson told Jake Shubert, "Gotta terrible sore throat. Can't sing a note," and slunk out of the theater. His chauffeur drove him to Grand Central Station and he was on the next train to Florida. Shubert reacted by offering Jolson a new two-thousand-dollar contract for two Sunday concerts.

This was an election year: 1920. The man who had sung for President Wilson sensed that postwar voters were going to call for a change. "I like to be with the winner," Jolson told reporters, and promptly signed up to work for the Republicans' Warren G. Harding.

Jolson became president of the Harding-Coolidge Theatrical League and wrote both the words and music of the party's campaign song, "Harding, You're the Man for Us," which he launched at a ceremony at the candidate's home at Marion, Ohio.

Newsreels showed him wearing a straw hat, playing golf with the candidate, silently mouthing the lyrics of his tune,

> We think the country's ready for a man like Teddy.
> We need another Lincoln to do the nation's thinkin'
> And Mr. Harding, we've selected you.

This turned out to be one of Jolson's less enlightened judgments. But when he appeared at the Harding inauguration the following January, there was no hint of the scandal in the President's life which many say was responsible for his death two years later. On the contrary, everybody was cheering, Jolson along with them. He wrote special lyrics to his old song "Down by the O-hio." He also sang "Take away the gun from every mother's son."

81

Jolson had something else to be happy about: a new love. He met dancer Ethel Delmar at a party, when she was being slapped around by an inebriated gangster.

"Leave her alone," said Al, throwing the drunk into a chair. When he took the girl home, he asked her about herself and found out that she was dancing in the chorus of the George White *Scandals* and her real name was Alma Osborne.

He proposed and offered her a part in his next show, but she turned him down on both counts.

Jolson went back to work and to the racetrack, and dated other girls, but the memory of the tall brunette dancer haunted him. He saw her a few times walking her dogs on Broadway, but he couldn't get up the courage to talk to her. The extrovert Jolson was uncharacteristically shy with girls he wanted to take him seriously.

Then one night, he went up to the chorus dressing room at the theatre where the *Scandals* was playing and waited. The next day, Al and Ethel were sailing to Paris on their honeymoon. A local judge had performed a hurried ceremony and there was a new Mrs. Jolson to compete with the Broadway audiences.

But it was tough competition, too tough for a twenty-two-year-old girl who had never wanted anything more than to marry, settle down, and have a family.

It became increasingly obvious that she was as unlikely to have children by Al as her predecessor had been. It was also obvious that nothing a wife could do could possibly satisfy Jolson as much as the roar of applause from a crowd of people sitting in a theatre. He yearned to get back to work—with good reason.

The Shuberts had a new theatre for him, just off Seventh Avenue; this one was going to be named after him—Jolson's Fifty-ninth Street Theatre. For the opening, there was the most spectacular show in which he had yet appeared—*Bombo.*

On opening night in October 1921, every one of the theatre's 1645 seats was filled. *Bombo* had the same loose plot that all of the previous Jolson shows had. But the crowds roared and shouted for more, just the same.

Jolson again played a character called Gus, this time a slave brought over by Christopher Columbus who until that time seemed to have escaped mention in the history books.

The new score for the show had been written by Sigmund Romberg. But once again it was the tunes Romberg had not written and Jolson's ad libbing that earned thirty-six curtain calls on the first night.

Bombo had the greatest tunes Al was ever to sing: the fabulously successful "Mammy" from *Sinbad* and another twenty or thirty new songs. No one was ever sure how many. It depended entirely on the mood Jolson was in, and as before, he always changed the numbers he sang from one performance to the next.

In this show Jolson introduced a song that he later described as his second favorite. It was also the last he ever sang in public: "April Showers."

The audiences cheered ecstatically. When he jumped onto the runway, pointed his right arm to the gallery and proclaimed, "Look, look, they're not clouds, no, no—they're crowds—crowds of daffodils," the packed auditorium was near frenzy.

Bombo not only won Jolson bigger audiences; it also helped Buddy DeSylva. He wrote "April Showers" with the Jolson Theatre's orchestra leader, Lou Silvers. And with Jolson chiming in a chorus or two, he produced another *Bombo* showstopper, "California, Here I Come."

Gus Kahn benefited from *Bombo,* too. He provided Jolson with a number that for the next twenty-five years was always introduced with simulated train noises: "Toot Toot, Tootsie."

George Jean Nathan saw Al at work around this time. "The power of Jolson over an audience," he wrote several years later in the *American Mercury,* "I have seldom seen equaled. There are actors who, backed by great dramatists, can clutch an audience in their hands and squeeze out its emotion as they choose.

"There are singers who, backed by great composers, can do the same. And there are performers who, aided by external means of one kind or another can do the same.

"But I know of none like this Jolson—or at best very few—who, with lines of prewar vintage and melodies of the cheapest tin piano variety, can lay hold of an audience the moment he comes on the stage and never let go for a second thereafter.

"Possessed of an immensely electric personality, a rare sense of comedy, considerable histrionic ability, a most unusual music show versatility in the way of song and dance, and, above all, a gift for delivering lines for the full of their effect, he so far outdistances his rivals that they seem like the wrong ends of so many opera glasses."

Sigmund Romberg, who wrote many of the tunes for *Bombo,* described Jolson less charitably. "Simon Legree in blackface," he called him. For Jolson was relentless in demanding perfection from the people who were writing his songs.

"Work, children," he called to Romberg, Buddy DeSylva, and Harold Atteridge, who would rather have gone drinking than sit by the piano on the empty rehearsal stage.

They planned to drive to Montreal one night to escape Prohibition. "Sorry, children," said Al. "I've got some friends coming from Washington tonight and I promised to let them hear your songs." So the songsmiths stayed and Jolson had some new tunes. Among these friends who came to visit was Lillian Harris, who was later to become Mrs. Sigmund Romberg.

While he was appearing in *Bombo,* Al received the greatest plaudits that had come to any performer for his work in the First World War.

Al stopped a matinee to read a telegram that had just arrived from the hero of the British navy, Admiral Lord Beatty. "All good wishes to you and the American theatre," it said. "The theatre and its people contributed a mighty part in winning the war. It helped to maintain the morale both at home and on the front."

Throughout the run of *Bombo,* war veterans came to thank him for what he had done for them. One of Al's jokes in particular had sped along the front line in France: "I'm looking for barbed wire to knit a sweater for the Kaiser."

The American Red Cross thanked him, too. After a big benefit show for the Red Cross, one journalist wrote, "It was the most sensational performance ever given in the history of New York's theatrical benefits. Al Jolson outdid himself. During the performance, he asked all the soldiers and sailors in the audience to step onto the stage, and then he auctioned them off. The evening finished with Jolson conducting the orchestra in a rousing chorus of 'The Star Spangled Banner.' "

After more than two hundred consecutive performances, *Bombo* closed, and Jolson turned his attentions to a different kind of show in a very different medium.

For years, David Wark Griffith, the acclaimed director of *Birth of a Nation* and *Intolerance,* had been trying to persuade Al to try his luck on the screen. Jolson turned him down time and again. He remembered his experience with the Vitagraph film company in 1916 and didn't like it. "I'm no actor," he protested each time Griffith asked him.

But the director was persistent. Eventually, over dinner one night, Jolson succumbed. He agreed to make a film in blackface. It was to be called either *Mammy's Boy* or *Black and White*. But Al insisted on one thing: there was to be no contract.

"I tell you, I'm no actor," he repeated every time a lawyer suggested putting the deal in writing.

Meanwhile, the Griffith publicity machine got working. *Movie Weekly* devoted a full-page spread to "Famous Black Face Comedian becomes Griffith Star."

Al was quoted as saying, "Sure I'm going into pictures. They won't let Valentino act, so I have to step into the breach." Which wasn't exactly what he'd been telling Griffith. But he played along to the *Movie Weekly*'s writer, Charles E. Dexter.

He told him that he never worked hard on Broadway, despite what other people thought. "Going out on the stage and letting myself go—that isn't work. I'd rather crack jokes and sing songs than breathe or eat. It's all fun. . . .

"You know, they say that picture making will be a vacation for me—a rest in the out-of-doors and all that. But no jumping off the cliffs for me."

Dexter was quite astute, however. "It's pretty hard to say how Jolson will get along without his tongue in pictures. The Jolson tongue wags faster than any other tongue in show business. Belonging to his company is like being with an animated joke book. But it is safe to say that D. W. Griffith will make Jolson forget that he can't tell jokes in pictures. In the first place, Jolson is a talented actor."

As the days of shooting the picture in New York's Mamaroneck studios went by, Jolson became more and more disillusioned with the whole operation. He was right about acting, he felt. Griffith and *Movie Weekly* were wrong.

He couldn't respond to a camera lens and, worse still, the lens couldn't respond to him—not like the audiences at the Winter Garden. And if there were no songs to sing and no jokes to tell, what was the point in continuing? He demanded to see the rushes and his worst fears were confirmed. As soon as the lights in the small studio theatre went up, he told Griffith he was not going to finish the picture and walked out.

Meanwhile Griffith had inserted an advertisement in the newspapers: "Mr. Jolson's wonderful personality registers on the screen as dynamically and delightfully as it does on stage."

When reporters asked him whether the film would be finished, he told them, "Certainly. It'll be ready for release this fall."

Six reels of the film had been run off when Al decided he had had enough. He had already made that decision when an advertisement signed in Jolson's name appeared in *Exhibition Trade Review*. "I'm in a new business now," it said. "I'm in good hands—and whatever I've got, I'm going to give it all to you."

Jolson drove with Ethel to one of the New York piers and sailed for Europe. He was photographed giving his wife a big au revoir kiss.

On the outward voyage, he telegraphed Griffith: CIRCUMSTANCES OVER WHICH I HAVE NO CONTROL SUCH AS ILL HEALTH MADE ME LEAVE STOP FEEL BETTER ALREADY AND WILL RETURN NO LATER THAN AUGUST STOP ON MY RETURN WILL SIGN CONTRACT WITH PROPER CONDITIONS AND START WORK IF AGREEABLE STOP.

Griffith, who earlier had said he was so "delighted" with Jolson's work, now stated he was not agreeable. "I've invested seventy-one thousand dollars in this project and I'll sue," he said. And he did.

Al was in Europe with Jake Shubert, patching up a quarrel almost as bitter as the one with Griffith. Jolson had complained that he was being made to pay "extraordinary" sums toward the cost of his shows.

The Shubert brothers, who hated each other in almost every regard, had one thing in common—a desire to make as much money out of each other as possible. When that wasn't possible, they joined together to make as much money out of the public and their artists as they could.

On one occasion Eddie Cantor received a bill for $1900 for glue. He was told it was needed for the elaborate sets the Shuberts were providing. Al was billed four hundred dollars—for costumes for his supporting cast.

Moreover, the Shuberts were grooming Georgie Price to take over Jolson's place at their Sunday concerts. It was, they reckoned, the one thing that would keep Jolson within their fold. They made a new deal with him, presented unacceptable conditions to Georgie Price—making

86

him report to the train in the freight yard eight hours before departure, and insisting that he stand around for four hours on stage without uttering a sound—and finally canceled his contract for twenty-five thousand dollars. Price went into Wall Street; Jolson went to Paris with the Shuberts.

Al was photographed next to the gargoyles of Notre Dame, wearing a monocle, and was reported complaining about the English weather. "I'll never go abroad again," he told *Billboard*. "Unless, that is, with Mrs. Jolson—and then I'll just go for the sea voyage."

And Griffith? The New York *Tribune* reported, "Jolson's olive branches for Griffith wilt." They quoted Al: "Now Mr. Griffith will have nothing to do with me. Neither will any other film director, because I cut and bolted. Yes, it's true. I bolted.

"My doctor said, 'For goodness' sake, Al, go away—or you'll go crazy.'"

The *Tribune* said Al was "disgusted and disappointed" at the way the picture had gone, especially since he was not expecting Griffith to change camera crews halfway through production as he had.

Without knowing too much of the true story, they added, "One of the ambitions of Mr. Jolson's life has been to re-create his musical-comedy success on the screen. 'That was why I wanted Mr. Griffith to direct me. I was afraid of being a failure. When they brought round a contract for me to sign and this provided for a second director to interfere I cut and bolted.'"

When the Griffith affair came to court, the jury could not agree. In 1926, judgment was finally made against Jolson. He was ordered to pay $2627. Griffith's demands by then escalated to five hundred thousand dollars.

Ethel was as stunned as anyone by Al's sudden decision to break with Griffith and go to Europe. "He was on the verge of a nervous breakdown," she told the press. And she denied that he had intended to stop work on the picture completely. However, already it was obvious to her friends that she was anything but happy with the situation; she had begun to drink heavily.

When Al returned from Europe, he announced that he was going back to work in *Bombo*. And once more, he triumphed—singing the same old songs as well as many new ones.

He was frequently tired, however—which meant that he spent the nights in hotels, instead of going home to Ethel. To try to relieve the strain on their marriage, Jolson took Ethel with him to Chicago when *Bombo* went on tour. The audiences who greeted every Jolson visit with enthusiastic adoration welcomed his wife, too. But she found that she was no more a match for the Midwest public than she had been for the Broadway crowds.

Chicago was sensational. Understandably—with *Bombo,* Al refused to tour with anything but the best the Shuberts could offer. Other performers might be content to take inferior companies on tour and rest comfortably on their own laurels, but Jolson insisted that the Chicago public see a show every bit as good as the one the Broadway audiences had seen.

This did, however, have an effect on business. The takes for the second house were always less, even though the theatre remained full, because Jolson never sang the same songs twice the same way, and audiences bought tickets for the first house and stayed in their seats for the next performance.

They lingered even after the performance. On one occasion Jolson kept the theatre filled until the early hours of the morning while he rehearsed with full orchestra the first performance of Gershwin's song "Who Cares?"

There were Chicago fans outside the theatre as well. But not the sort he was used to. Early one afternoon, he opened the door of his hotel suite to two men dressed in black. They asked him to follow them. Jolson wouldn't normally have accepted such an invitation but there was something about these visitors that convinced him to go with them. He followed them into the elevator, out of the hotel, into the street to their car. They didn't talk much on the ride—the gun inside the car seemed to make conversation somewhat superfluous.

When they reached their destination, Jolson was politely told to go with his companions into a big house, where he was shown into a palatial room and asked to sit down. Before long, the big ornate doors opened and two of the men who had driven him to the house walked in, followed by a small, chunky third man with a scar on his face.

"You sing to me," he said to Al.

"What de yer want?" Al asked, understandably confused.

"April Showers," came the reply. "My name's Al, too."

Jolson didn't need to be told that. The face of Al Capone was in the newspapers every day of the week. For the next two hours an audience of Chicago hoods sitting in the big house at Cicero heard Jolson sing. It was the only recorded meeting of the two Als; but it was some time before Al Jolson had any further trouble from gangsters.

Bombo finished its run in Chicago in the midst of one of the strongest continuing feuds in show business history.

Jolson and Eddie Cantor were always close friends—and professional rivals. The rivalry was never more intense than it had been in December 1923, when Al fled to Florida with what he claimed to be an attack of laryngitis.

Jake Shubert knew exactly where to find him. As he thought, Jolson was lying in the Miami sun, by a swimming pool, a white silk scarf around his throat in case anyone got any wrong ideas.

"How are you feeling, Al?" asked Shubert.

Jolson reached for a pad. "Terrible," he scribbled. "How's Broadway?"

It was the right question for the tactics the cunning Shubert had in mind. "Not too exciting," he answered. "But Cantor's not doing badly. In fact, he's had his biggest week ever in *Kid Boots.* They took forty-five thousand."

It was a flag to a bull. "It's a damned lie!" Jolson thundered, forgetting his sore throat. "We must get the next train back to New York. No, find out the first plane."

After that he didn't miss a single Broadway performance of his show.

But this time in Chicago, there could be no doubt that Jolson's throat really was bad. Cantor, despite an attack of pleurisy, was playing to packed houses in a neighboring theatre. The doctors had strapped his back in a corset and ordered him to rest. But he refused. Years later, Cantor confessed that he couldn't bear to see the newspaper headlines reading "Jolson drives Cantor out of Chicago." When he finally collapsed, Cantor's doctors put their patient on the train to New York.

Jolson came to see him off at the station. "No show *has* to go on, Eddie," Al told him. "You're being wise."

On arrival in New York, Cantor was greeted with the news of a second closure in Chicago. Jolson's show had folded too. In fact, Jolson was much more ill than Cantor had been. But nothing could have persuaded him to close his show while Cantor was still packing them in.

Once his rival was out of the way, though, he could bring down the curtain on *Bombo*.

To Ethel, the show's closing offered another chance to settle down. There were times when it seemed that married life was now agreeing with both of them. News leaked out that they were considering adopting a baby. They applied to the New York State Charities Board and went through a rigorous investigation procedure. Jolson told the officials, "My wife and I have a splendid country home at Scarsdale. We have horses, dogs, cats, canaries. But there's always been something missing."

But the void was not filled. The Jolsons never went ahead with their family plans. They did put on a brave front for outsiders, however. When they entertained Harry and his wife Lillian at the Scarsdale house, Al and Ethel were the picture of domestic bliss. Not only was the couple getting on fine, but the two brothers appeared to be hitting it off well, too.

Harry heard that Al was to play a jockey in his next show, *Big Boy*. "And if you're a jockey, Al," he suggested over drinks, "what about the horse? You must have a horse to ride—so make it a big real one."

When *Big Boy* opened at the Winter Garden on Thanksgiving, 1925, the scene that stopped the show was Al's appearing—on horseback.

Harry was delighted. He phoned Al to congratulate him on the show's reception. The hit number was "Keep Smiling at Trouble." Harry told him that youngsters were already humming and singing it wherever they went. And wasn't the horse a good idea. "I thought it would be," said Harry.

"*You* thought so," Al gasped. "*You* thought so. It was *my* idea." Another row between the brothers had broken out—and this one was not any easier to patch up than the previous ones.

The horse turned out to be one of the great sensations of the show. It brought together two of Al's greatest loves—the theatre and the racetrack.

He had been known to cancel a matinee in order to back a horse he considered to be a certain winner—and treat the cast of the show to free bets at the same time.

In 1921, Al had established his own stable with a six-year-old called Snapdragon the Second. But he rarely had more than one or two horses at a time. He preferred to bet on other people's animals. Horses and racing were a vital part of his life.

"A horse is a very good tonic," he'd say. "Mind you, I've had a few relapses in my time. There was once a horse in which I had every confidence. It betrayed me! For reasons of its own, it tried to pretend that it didn't know the right way round the course. It seemed to think that running backward would win races."

This was one of the rare occasions when Jolson admitted he'd lost a race.

Jolson always bet big money at the races. According to one legend, he and a member of the celebrated Vanderbilt family went to the track together and bet on the same horse. Vanderbilt, the American aristocrat, put seven dollars on the nose. Jolson bet four thousand dollars—and the horse romped home at forty to one.

Racing was Jolson's way of letting off steam—but more important, it gave him a chance to prove that he was everybody's top guy.

But no matter how seriously Jolson took other things, it was still his work on the stage that caused the real excitement.

Writing in *Life,* a pocket magazine of the period, Robert Benchley said that to sit in on a Jolson performance in *Big Boy* was "to know what the coiners of the word 'personality' meant."

He explained, "The word 'personality' isn't quite strong enough for the thing that Jolson has. Unimpressive as the comparison may be to Mr. Jolson, we should say that John the Baptist was the last man to have such a power. There is something supernatural at the back of it, or we miss our guess.

"When Jolson enters, it is as if an electric current has been run along the wires under the seats where the hats are stuck. The house comes to a tumultuous attention. He speaks, rolls his eyes, compresses his lips, and it is all over. You are a member of the Al Jolson Association.

"He trembles his underlip, and your heart breaks with a loud snap. He sings a banal song and you totter out to send a night letter to your mother. Such a giving-off of vitality, personality, charm, and whatever all those words are, results from a Jolson performance."

Big Boy was by any definition a sensation. Audiences were eating out of his hand, just as they had always done. And Al was feeling generous—as he always did when things were going well.

There was one song in the show that he never really liked—so he gave it to Eddie Cantor. It was called "If You Knew Susie"—and it became Cantor's biggest hit. Some twenty-four years later, the two stars sang it as a duet on the radio—just to show that there were no hard feelings. But he told Cantor after the show, "Eddie, if I knew it was that good, you dog, I'd never have given it to you."

Of course, a song is a valuable show biz prop. But there is something that is worth even more to a young performer—encouragement. Jolson gave just that to a young actor from London during the run of *Big Boy*.

Ralph Reader had come from England to try his luck on the American stage and was given a small part in the new Jolson show. The star took an instant liking to the youngster he always called "English." In his autobiography, Reader says Jolson made him feel at ease as soon as he went out on the big Winter Garden stage and stood alone with him.

"Don't worry about me," Jolson told him. "Just look at me. No matter who might be watching, if you keep your eyes on me, they're bound to look at you. If you watch a searchlight, they'll nine times out of ten look back to where the light's coming from.

"Remember that your eyes are searchlights and if you keep them fixed on me, the audience will look back and see where those eyes are coming from." Reader described this as the soundest advice he had ever received. To him, Jolson was "electricity—entertainment in lights and yard-high capital letters."

But although he was "electricity" to everyone else in the twenties, too, the old insecurity intermittently raised its head. There was nothing like a few empty seats to make him think he was finished. When he saw there were seats unfilled and before his dresser had time to get out his makeup, Al was speeding to the station and on the way to Atlantic City.

The Shuberts offered the crowd their money back, but the people who had paid to see the world's greatest entertainer were not going to be so easily put off.

Lee Shubert rang the hotel in Atlantic City and stayed on the line until Jolson arrived there. "Al, you can't let us down," he pleaded. "There may be a few empty seats—but that's because it's so cold and there are people with coughs and flu. It doesn't mean they don't want you. I've got a thousand people out here who won't go away until you return."

Jolson got the message. The people stayed in their seats for four hours—until Al returned to sing to them.

By now, Jolson was not only established as an extraordinary entertainer; to many people, he was superhuman. The sophisticated *New York Times,* not usually overcome with ecstasy when discussing "light comedians," shared those sentiments. "According to common report," they wrote on September 6, 1925, "Al Jolson has been discovered walking with a purely human tread the public pavements of Broadway and entering a purely vulgarian dining room where common folk seek their sustenance.

"Those who have seen him as Gus, the joyous blackface jockey in *Big Boy,* know how false these reports must be. At best it is only the shade, the apparition of the astral body of the energetic Al. For the blackface Al himself never passes out of the theatre. His being is circumscribed by the stage. The gods cannot breathe the air of fleshly mortals. Al Jolson cannot leave the stage."

And then the writer pondered, "It would be interesting to know what his astral body seen walking in the streets would say about the way Al behaves on the stage."

The truth was that Al Jolson behaved in any public place the way he behaved on the stage. If he was in a crowd, the people with him were his audience. He could even turn a courtroom into a theatre. Only a couple of months after the *Times* gushed about Jolson the god, his "astral" body came before Judge Isaac N. Mills, who was hearing an application from wealthy Leonard Rhinelander for his marriage to be annulled.

Rhinelander had married a former housemaid, Alice Jones. In court, he produced letters from his wife that showed "she was one of the most sought-after girls in the world. . . . Al Jolson had noticed her and so had Irving Berlin."

She tried to get Rhinelander to marry her by telling him how many other men of substance wanted to take her out. In one letter she wrote, "I was talking with Al Jolson today. He was swimming—but he's sure some flirt with the girls."

The meeting, she alleged, had been at Paul Smith's resort in the Adirondack mountains. But the judge seemed unimpressed. "Who is Al Jolson?" he asked. The court dissolved into fits of laughter.

The judge ordered Jolson to appear before him. And, when the singer arrived in court, he gave the sort of performance his public expected of him.

"The comedian," noted the *New York Times,* "smiling a broad smile, got into the box. After dusting down the chair on which Rhinelander had been seated, he carefully sat down."

"No, I've never seen Alice Jones or talked with her," he told the judge. "I have enough trouble with *my* wife. *She* won't talk with me or even have breakfast with me."

Big Boy closed in the middle of what seemed destined to become a record run. He had never been better on any stage before and no audience had ever warmed to him—or anyone else—the way it was reacting to him now.

But Al's throat was troubling him again and his doctors advised a complete rest for two weeks. Jolson spent the period on one of his favorite pastimes—trying out medical remedies, although he claimed it was the racetrack that really cured him.

During the two weeks off stage, he sent away as many doctors as he called to see him. One doctor insisted on wrapping him in an electric blanket all night. He lost weight, but not his cold. Another insisted on sticking electric needles into his neck. "I was straddling a chair when he put the needle inside me," said Al. "It was supposed to wander around and locate the pain. After it had wandered around for ten minutes, I arranged to have the doctor thrown out—machine and all."

"Then there was the army doctor who cured two divisions in three weeks. He shoved a spoon down my throat and before I knew it, he had me black in the face. The scheme, I guess, was to cure the patient of his cold by diverting his attention to a broken neck."

The bout with the doctors didn't cure Jolson of his acute hypochondria, either. He went on building up his fear of sore throats, thinking this might rob him of his voice for the rest of his life.

During the run of *Big Boy,* Al repeated the trick he had used during *The Honeymoon Express.* He stopped cold right in the middle of the show, walked down to the footlights, and shouted, "Do you want me—or do you want the show?"

From all over the packed Winter Garden came the cry, "We want Al. We want *you.*" The entire cast was dismissed. Al undid his collar and sang until he had breath for no more, then ordered all the house lights up and asked the people out front to sing to him.

On another occasion, Orville Harold, then a famous tenor at the

Metropolitan Opera, came around to the wings while the show was still in progress. It was Saturday night and he wanted to take his daughter Patti home before midnight.

"Sure," said Al, completely unconcerned that Patti, the show's leading lady, was on stage at that moment. Jolson went right onto the stage, gently held Patti's hand, and told the audience, "Listen, folks, Orville is in the wings waiting for his little girl. You wouldn't like to keep an opera star waiting, would you? Would you mind if I send her home now and put her understudy on? I'll sing to you while she gets changed." And for thirty minutes he did.

Jolson's conceit, it seemed, knew no bounds. But Larry Adler, the harmonica player, who says that Jolson influenced his show business career, completely disagrees. "You're conceited," he asserts, "when you *think* you are better than anyone else. Jolson *knew* that he was the best. It was, as far as he was concerned, an established fact." It was certainly an established fact that when he dismissed his casts they'd stay on to see Jolson perform for the rest of the evening.

He had the same sort of effect on audiences away from the theatre, too. After a late performance Jolson and a crowd of his associates, including Eppy and his new piano player, Harry Akst, would usually go on to a nightclub. Late one Saturday night, while Ethel stayed at home with the gin bottle, Jolson and the gang wound up at a smart hotel where the country's top bandleader, Ben Bernie, held court. Bernie was famous for his catch phrase, "So help me." On this occasion, he announced to an audience sozzled with illegal Prohibition booze, "So help me—we have Al Jolson with us." From the tables went up one continuous shout: "Song. Al. Song."

To the virtually uncontrollable crowd, Jolson called, "Folks, this used to be my mother's birthday." Suddenly the place was hushed. "Because this was my mother's day, I'm going to sing a song she loved."

He told them that since the song was about a little village in Russia and he was going to sing it in Yiddish, he would explain the words to them first. It was, he said, about the small Jewish congregation who sent three men to audition a new cantor—a tailor, a coach driver and a shoemaker. The tailor describes the man's singing as like a perfect stitch. The coachman said it was as elegant as a royal carriage and as strong as a horse. The shoemaker said it was like the best pair of boots he had ever made.

Recalling that evening, George Murray wrote in the Chicago *Ameri-*

can, "Jolson made his audience live with him, momentarily, in that faraway ghetto in a tiny Russian village. Having told them what the song was, he sang it. Bernie, who knew the song, accompanied him on a fiddle. Did I say Jolson sang it? It was more than singing. He wept it. He laughed it. It played in his heart and the hearts of all responded to it.

"For fifteen minutes or a half hour, Jolson sang the song of his mother's childhood. And in that Saturday-night audience, not an eye was wholly dry. There was Jolson, no bigger than five foot six inches, slender, puckish, singing in a foreign tongue of a foreign place."

And as he sang, he must have been aware of his own father, still living the old life in Washington. Al decided he had to go to see the old man. It had been a long time.

Jolson in 1913. The fur coat meant he had really arrived.

Top: La Belle Paree and Jolson's first night on Broadway in 1911. He was still only one in the line-up (sixth from the right). *Bottom left:* By the second night Jolson was stealing the limelight from more established performers whose names have long been forgotten. *Bottom right:* Leaflets like this were distributed all over New York. In 1916 Al Jolson's name was the biggest at the Winter Garden—and the biggest on Broadway.

Francis, Day & Hunter

Francis, Day & Hunter

Jolson the minstrel. His own tunes became the popular songs of the day.

A typical minstrel line-up, with Jolson in the center, of course.

Warner Brothers

Al Jolson on honeymoon with Ruby Keeler . . .

. . . and in 1945 with Erle.

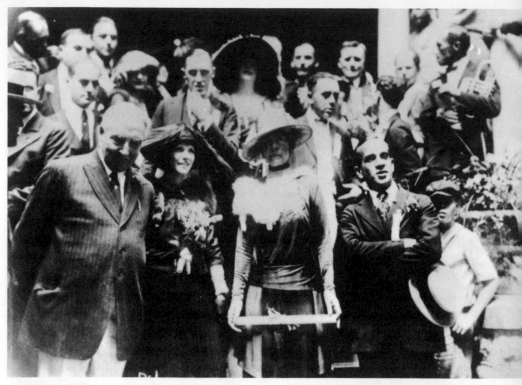

Ve
Øje
Ve
Øje
J
ha:
De
va
tilf
m
„Den
gende N
og at De
saa vil sy
om „Jazz
geren", naar den kommer frem.

Med venlig Hilsen
Deres

„Jazzsangeren" udkommer ogsaa som Tale- og Sangfilms-Roma

Top: Jolson in politics. In Marion, Ohio, with Warren G. Harding (left).
Bottom left: Jolson the racegoer. Next to audiences, he loved the thrill of the
racetrack best. *Bottom right: The Jazz Singer* and Jolson were hits everywhere, including Scandinavia.

6

APRIL SHOWERS

CALVIN COOLIDGE invited Al Jolson to help him launch his 1924 election campaign at a White House breakfast. When Jolson accepted and agreed to pose on the lawn outside the presidential mansion, Coolidge and his staff breathed a sigh of relief.

The idea of press cameras clicking as Jolson sang "Keep Cool with Coolidge" was enough to win millions of votes.

> The race is now begun,
> And Coolidge is the one
> The one to fill the presidential chair
> Without a lot of fuss.
> He did a lot for us.

It was probably the worst set of lyrics Jolson ever sang, but Coolidge was delighted. When Al and Mrs. Coolidge joked over the breakfast, the President laughed loudest.

Coolidge wrote Al a letter thanking him for his efforts for the Republican ticket, "With a very definite recollection of the service which the [Harding] League did in 1920, I want to thank you for your offer of help."

Al was once more president of the Republican Theatrical League. Once more, he saw his candidate win. Al was offered the post of Scarsdale constable as a measure of Republican gratitude. He turned it down; he said he was more concerned about his own business. But he left no one with any doubts about how much he enjoyed the extra fame his political involvements brought him.

And the Coolidges' near neighbors, the Yoelsons, and the congregation of the synagogue at East Street West, reveled in it all. Moses and Ida walked proudly in the streets of the capital. Al's half-brothers George, Myer, and Emil, and their sister Gertrude, took it all for granted. Asa was their celebrity brother and as far as they were concerned, he had never been anything else.

In *Big Boy,* Jolson had only a horse for competition—and a pretty mangy one at that. Eddie Cantor had all the trappings of the big Ziegfeld productions, the most magnificent sets, the most gorgeous girls, and a hundred and one lesser lights who could have topped a vaudeville bill on their own account. Cantor took thirty thousand dollars a performance. So did Jolson.

It was uncanny. Cantor and Ziegfeld tried to work out the secret. Cantor thought a visit to a Jolson Winter Garden matinee might suggest the key. So he bought his ticket for an orchestra seat and waited. He took five weeks to get over the experience. "Something happened that afternoon," he confessed privately to friends. "For five weeks I just couldn't work properly again. I couldn't compete with Jolson."

Looking back now one wonders why he even tried. Jolson could take many things—the occasional thumbs down from a girl he tried to date, the jealous comments from other performers—but he couldn't accept competition.

When he entered his star dressing room at the Winter Garden, he walked through the narrow whitewashed corridor backstage like a Roman emperor in procession. When he reached the top of the stairs, Louis Shreiber, his dresser, would be there to give the royal welcome.

Wherever Jolson went, Shreiber went too—until he became an agent for the William Morris Organization. And then he represented Jolson. At the Winter Garden his job was to brush the king's clothes and to turn on the water taps: if it ever seemed likely that another artist in the show was about to get a generous round of applause, Shreiber turned on the water taps to drown out the noise of the clapping hands.

On one occasion, Jolson had a team of performing elephants fired because he felt the audience liked them too much. He wanted the audience literally to starve for his entry. He wouldn't allow anything that even partly satisfied them to appear before him. In any case, he had little to fear. He could walk onto the stage an hour after he was due to appear and prance along the runway with his overcoat over his arm and his hat still on his head and be met by thunderous applause.

"Sorry I'm late, folks," he'd tell them. "But it was cold and I stopped by for dinner at the little restaurant next door. It was such a good dinner that I just couldn't leave it. But now that I'm here, do you mind if I make up on the stage?"

The audience, of course, roared "No." So Schreiber and Eppy were instructed to bring his blackface kit on stage. The house lights would go up, and while Al joked and chatted, they made the preliminary black ring around his mouth and painted on the burnt cork.

When he finished, he sang his first song. "Don't bring the horse on yet," he shouted to the nearly frantic stage manager. "I'm going to sing to the folks by myself tonight."

Comedian George Burns remembers that sort of evening as one of the milestones in the history of show business. "He'd tell the ushers to buy half a dozen five-pound boxes of candy, and while he was singing, he'd pass the candy around to everyone in the audience.

"When it was all over, Al would say, 'I'm feeling hungry so I'm going back to that restaurant now. But there's a swell piano in there, and if any of you feel like it, why don't you wait till I've had something to eat and join me, then I'll sing a couple more songs for you.' The entire Winter Garden seemed to empty and pour into that little restaurant. Jolson sang to them till three o'clock in the morning."

Jolson's Sunday concerts were normally death to anyone else on the bill.

After one Jolson concert, he retired to the back of the theatre for a drink and a smoke while another act, the Ponselle sisters, filled in. Rosa Ponselle sang "My Buddy" at the top of her voice; it was the most powerful voice Al had heard and he didn't like it.

Without going back ostage, Al ordered the Shuberts to fire the Ponselles. They ended up at the Metropolitan Opera. But months afterward the theatre's talent scout was still looking for a new job.

About this time Jolson took one of his increasingly frequent vacations in Florida. To keep the money pouring in, the Shuberts hired comedian Jack Osterman to head the Sunday bill. Osterman did moderately well the first week and Jolson turned over in the sun and puffed his cigar. The second week, *Variety* reported, Osterman received the cheers of the Winter Garden audience. Jolson was back on the next train into Grand Central Station.

He took *Big Boy* on the road and it was a smash hit, like all Jolson shows. Since Jolson always had a piece of the show now, he was the first star since the days of the great actor-managers ever to have a financial interest in one of his productions—the money coming into the box office was now almost as important as the faces before him.

The take was so good in Buffalo that Jolson insisted on an extra performance. One Friday evening the *Big Boy* company were told there would be a special Saturday matinee at ten o'clock the next morning.

The following week, the Saturday matinee had to be canceled—and Al took everyone in the show to the racetrack.

Early in 1926, Al Jolson was billed to take over the star spot in the Winter Garden's revue *Artists and Models,* the Shuberts' answer to Ziegfeld and his Follies. When Al took over, he never got on stage much before ten o'clock. He'd take a look at the mountains of white flesh—the "models"—around him, make an appropriate comment, and allow them to exit.

Did anyone mind? His audience was as enthusiastic as it had ever been before—probably the only time in theatrical history that nude girls have been overshadowed by a balding man in his late thirties.

Jolson's return was a perfect way to celebrate the fifteenth anniversary of the Shubert Theatre's opening. The *New York Times* reported, "Mr. Jolson gave of his utmost, as is his custom, for nearly an hour. He sang and talked and talked and sang." Some evenings, he talked and sang for three hours.

The *Times* commented, "How does he do it, year after year? How does he manage to alchemize these base metals of sentimentality and vulgarity into pure gold of entertainment? The pundits offer no satisfactory analysis. He destroys the usual barriers [that] stand between audience and entertainer."

Jolson and *Artists and Models* ran for four weeks. He couldn't commit himself to more. Later, he took the show to Chicago, where it grossed more in one week than any other show in the history of the stage—$60,400.

Those who had never seen a Jolson show on Broadway or on the road could always hear him on their phonographs. Columbia Records had signed him to an exclusive contract until the end of December 1923. By May of that year, there was still a chunk of that bargain unfulfilled. So Jolson cut seven new discs at seven thousand dollars a side, a phenomenal fee for that time.

The Brunswick recording people were willing to pay even more. Jolson signed a new contract with them for ten thousand dollars a side. The Columbia executives were bitterly angry with their star. They decided to release the Jolson pressings they had just made one by one at the same time as Brunswick released theirs.

Meanwhile the new label elected Jolson to their board of directors. "We feel that anyone who can enjoy such widespread popularity as a singer can bring real ideas and help to our company," said Brunswick's vice-president, R. F. Besinger.

Columbia regarded Al's Brunswick deal as disloyalty and defection. For years they had nurtured his recording career, they told him, but Jolson remained unimpressed.

He hadn't been any more cooperative all the years that they had supplied him with a road manager, a man everyone knew as J.P.J. Kelly. He followed all the Jolson shows on tour and plugged Al's latest discs at the same time. On one occasion at Dayton, Ohio, Kelly was approached by a gentleman who called himself Bonesetter Reece. Reece was an osteopath who had been giving exhibitions of his skills, attracting a nearly revivalist following. He asked Kelly if he could get him a couple of tickets for the next Jolson show.

"Sure," said Kelly.

"No," said Jolson. "I've got a piece of that show and if you think I'm going to give away tickets to some quack, you're mistaken."

Kelly paid for the tickets himself. But he wasn't worried. He had several sons of his own, one of whom looked as though he was going to do very well in show business—a youngster named Gene Kelly.

But although Al was hard to some people, he was remarkably generous to others. He passed the front door of the Winter Garden one day to hear an usher telling a boy of about eight to go away and not come back to Broadway until he had enough money to pay for a ticket.

"What's your name, son?" Al asked him. "Al Cooper," said the boy. "Well—we Als should stick together." He ordered the usher to find young Master Cooper a seat in the front of the theatre and to show him around to the dressing room at the end of the show.

Jolson probably soon forgot the incident. But twenty-five years later, Al Cooper was among the mourners at his funeral.

Al's visits to his father in Washington were more frequent now than they had been for many years. The older man's antagonism to show business and his son's participation in it was gone. When Al offered to buy the Yoelsons a new house, the cantor accepted graciously.

He found he was able to talk to his Asa now. Over a glass of steaming tea, they could discuss the world's problems. Al enjoyed the sessions. They gave him a chance to slip into the old Yiddish vernacular, to hear some of the old stories, which he embroidered into jokes for his act.

The Winter Garden audiences—which always included a large Jewish element—liked the way Jolson inserted the odd Yiddish word into his monologues. He'd tell them about his father, for example: "I bought my dad a coat last week. It cost two hundred dollars. A lovely coat. But I knew what my dad would say about that, so I persuaded the clerk to change the label for one that had a twelve-dollar price tag. Yesterday, I asked him how he liked the coat. 'Fine,' he said. 'It was a wonderful coat for twelve dollars. So wonderful that I sold it to Uncle Moshe for twenty. You didn't know your father was a businessman, did you?' " To his dying day, Al swore that was a true story.

To Jolson being Jewish was something he took in his stride. Big-time show business was very much a Jewish affair in the twenties. Jolson and Jessel, Eddie Cantor, and Georgie Price, the Shuberts, Gershwin, Irving Berlin, Fanny Brice—all were Jewish.

And so was Harry Richman. In May 1926, Al invited Richman to join him at the Westchester Biltmore Country Club for a round of golf. The club trustees refused.

"Sorry," one of them told Jolson, "but you see—he's Jewish."

"So am I," said Jolson. "And you know what you can do with your club and its membership lists." Later, when he finalized his resignation, he quipped, "I shoulda told 'em Richman was only half Jewish—and please let him play nine holes."

But Jolson had enough friends and enough places to go to without bothering about the Westchester Biltmore. He didn't have much time for golf, anyway. It was much more fun to go out with girls—girls who wouldn't demand his constant attention, and particularly girls who didn't drink.

He and Ethel rarely even talked to each other now. She would arrange to be out walking the dogs when he was at home, which wasn't very often.

Al didn't like having to go out to get his own girls. As far as he was concerned, he could safely leave that job to Eppy. The papers showed Al in restaurants with brunettes, at the racetracks with blondes, and getting into cars with redheads. To be seen with a pretty girl was almost as important to him now as being applauded by an audience.

There are still a few aging matrons about today bearing the scars of their encounters with Jolson. Few of them talk about it. One did venture the comment, "He certainly knew how to use his hands."

One of his dates was reported extensively at the time. While he was on tour in Billings, Montana, he decided to take a member of the chorus out for dinner. After the meal, Jolson started paying the usual compliments and whispering the usual suggestions. He put his hand on his companion's knee—and had it sharply brushed away.

"Don't give me any of that business about loving me like a sister," Al said angrily. "No," he was told. "But I'll love you like a brother." At that point, his date pulled off a blond wig to reveal what was very obviously a man's head underneath. Jolson got up immediately and ran out of the restaurant.

At the end of July 1926, he and Ethel tried to patch things up by sailing to Europe. They said they were going to Paris "for a second honeymoon." They sailed on the *Leviathan,* occupying the Grand Suite—three bedrooms, three bathrooms, and a sitting room.

But the trip was not successful. Ethel secretly consulted a firm of French lawyers, and went to court and obtained a divorce. She returned to America the next day. Al stayed in Paris for another week and returned alone in the same suite he had shared with Ethel on the outward trip on the *Leviathan.*

Whether or not the pair were divorced was a matter for speculation. Ethel denied it when she arrived in New York. When reporters questioned him in Paris, Al shouted, "It ain't true."

But the Shuberts said they believed there had been a divorce. "It's common gossip," said an official working for the brothers. "Everyone knew they went to Paris just to get divorced."

Al continued to deny the rumors until the divorce was made final, later that year.

For days after his return from France, Al seemed morose, not because he did not have Ethel around him any more—they hadn't been close to each other for years—but it was obvious that the Jolson ego had taken a battering. He sought her out and telephoned her day after day.

But she would have no more of him. He consoled himself with more days at the races, more orders to Eppy to find more girls. But most important, he wanted the one thing he couldn't live without—hard work and plenty of it.

Jolson required perfection now even more than before. If he couldn't keep his wife, he had to prove to himself as much as to anyone in the show that he could keep his audience.

In Syracuse, New York, he did an unheard-of thing: At the end of the performance, he refused to give an encore. "My throat's not up to it," he told the startled manager backstage. "Why didn't you tell that to the customers?" he was asked. Jolson's answer: "I didn't want their sympathy."

What he really wanted was a girl—and Eppy knew it. He regarded it as his principal function now—but he wasn't always able to deliver.

When Al wanted a "special" girl, Eppy thought of Ruby Stephens, a pretty blond dancer Al had met in Atlantic City.

He was in the New Jersey resort to judge a Charleston contest. When young Ruby came on the scene, he was immediately enamored of her. At the end of the evening, he sidled up to the winning dancer and said, "You know, I've got thirty million in the bank. Why not help me spend it?"

It was a temptation the young girl found hard to resist. Al believed he had persuaded Ruby to go away for a weekend with him. A day or so before the planned rendezvous a telegram was sent to Jolson's suite at New York's Ritz Hotel, where he had been living since his breakup with Ethel.

Two doors away from Jolson's suite was another occupied by Jimmy Walker. Between them was a smaller room, rented by George Jessel. By mistake, the telegram intended for Jolson went to Jessel. He opened it and saw it was from Ruby, calling off the affair. Jessel resealed the cable and gave it to Al.

That weekend, Jolson left for his destination as planned. He did not want anyone to know that he had been sent a "Dear John" note. It was a long time before Jolson got over his infatuation for Ruby Stephens.

She decided to stick to her career and become an actress. She also decided to change her name—to Barbara Stanwyck.

Jessel, who was now starring in a Broadway play called *The Jazz Singer,* said nothing about the telegram. At that time, he and Jolson were close friends, and he did not want anything to come between them.

On April 30, 1927, a new dimension was added to Jolson's career. He sang "What Does It Matter?" by Irving Berlin on the radio. His debut for NBC—as part of a benefit program for victims of the recent Mississippi flood disaster, was hailed by the entertainment industry.

Almost everyone else in show business had been rushing to get to the microphone, but Jolson was deliberately holding back. "Why take the risks?" he asked. "Besides, I like to see the people I'm singing to."

The first radio critics noticed that Jolson seemed nervous when he sang over the air; but they welcomed his entry into the field. Not long afterward, a picture of Al singing into the horn mike was featured on the cover of a radio enthusiasts' magazine. "Just think," it said, "you can hear Al Jolson just by turning a little knob."

Another kind of microphone beckoned, however, and no one knew what was going to happen with that one. On October 7, 1926, an audience in the Colony Theatre in New York heard Al Jolson singing "April Showers"—not on the stage but from the screen.

Sitting in a hut in the midst of a Deep South cotton plantation, he also sang "Rockabye Your Baby with a Dixie Melody" and "When the Red, Red Robin Comes Bob, Bob, Bobbin' Along." The audience saw the flickering on the screen and heard the voice almost synchronized with it.

Warner Brothers' Vitaphone Company was experimenting with a one-reel short. People came out of the theatre, chuckling at what they had seen. It was a good gag that no one was taking very seriously.

George Jessel made a similar short and no one bothered with that, either. The other film studios took note of the films and quietly suggested to Harry and Jack Warner that it might be a good idea to show the pictures in fairgrounds.

The Warners were in financial trouble. They needed something to put them on their feet. A new young executive with the Vitaphone Company, Darryl F. Zanuck, suggested a full-length sound film.

113

They couldn't afford a new story, so they would have to choose one they already had. The one most likely to succeed was one that had already shown its worth on Broadway: George Jessel's *The Jazz Singer.*

The story had an interesting pedigree. Before the war, Samson Raphaelson, a student from Champagne, Illinois, showed Al Jolson a story he had written called *Day of Atonement,* about a Jewish cantor who couldn't persuade his child to give up the theatre. It was very much like Jolson's own life story, but Jolson thought it was so much out of his field that he politely declined.

A young actress named Vera Gordon heard about the story years later when she was starring in the Broadway show *Humoresque.* Raphaelson changed his story to allow a girl to play the main part and changed the title to *The Jazz Singer.*

But before it went on the road, Jessel heard about the play. He persuaded Raphaelson that it would be much better to return the story to the lines of the old Jewish folktale, the story of the cantor's son who wanted to sing in grand opera.

The play ran to packed audiences for three years and it looked as though it would never end its run on Broadway. What killed the play was Warner Brothers' Vitaphone—and Al Jolson.

When the studio finally decided to film *The Jazz Singer,* Jessel was the obvious choice to star in the picture. But with the uncertainties of a talkie and the effect it might have on his career, Jessel wanted insurance to the tune of one hundred thousand dollars.

Warners said no, and approached Eddie Cantor. He, too, said he was too worried about the effects of talking pictures on his career to contemplate the idea.

Darryl Zanuck suggested they try to get Jolson.

They knew Jolson loved a gamble. "What about asking Al Jolson to put money into the picture and draw stock from its takings?" Zanuck asked.

Jolson insisted on complete secrecy about the whole matter while he thought it over. He was staying at the Biltmore Hotel in New York at the same time as Jessel. The two had arranged to go out one Sunday for a game of golf. Al knocked at his friend's door and told him to go back to sleep. "I'm going out for a walk."

Jessel turned over and went back to sleep. The next day he read in the papers that Jolson had signed with Warner Brothers to make *The Jazz Singer.*

"Is it any wonder I always felt bitter?" Jessel asks. "I felt sick. It was my part and partly my story. Jolson got the role because he put money into it. But he *was* better at it than I would have been."

7

CALIFORNIA, HERE I COME

WHETHER Jolson could have imagined what *The Jazz Singer* would mean to show business, no one knows. He certainly had an uncanny knack for breaking new ground, setting precedents for everyone who came after him.

No secret was made of his trip or of its purpose. But when he arrived in Hollywood for the first time on that day in 1927, the movie capital had no idea what was going to hit it.

Jolson was met at the railway station by Jack, Harry, and Sam Warner, with Darryl Zanuck hovering behind. And he hadn't been in California very long before the other stars of the city—among them Charlie Chaplin and Douglas Fairbanks—came to pay homage.

The King of Broadway was being feted now as the King of Hollywood—but with a grain of salt. Hollywood was flattered that the great Jolson had come to join them, but they couldn't believe that he would really have any impact on their world.

Fan magazines were writing about the new movie star-to-be and Jolson posed with the Warner brothers for more pictures, among them a celebrated one in which the Warners held the mouthpiece of a giant telephone while Jolson held the earpiece. There was something symbolic in the shot: without Jolson, Warners and the whole Vitaphone invention were useless.

Originally, *The Jazz Singer* was to be a completely silent picture with just a sound track of Jolson's songs and occasional background music. The Warner-Vitaphone film *Don Juan* the year before had proved that synchronized background music could be made to work.

If anyone but Jolson had starred in *The Jazz Singer,* that probably is what would have happened. But with Jolson in charge—and that was precisely the way he saw things from the moment he first walked onto the set—nothing could possibly turn out the way it had been planned.

There were subtitles for the picture—just as there always had been. So no one was terribly concerned when Jolson started ad-libbing in front of the cameras, disregarding the screenplay, just as he had always abandoned the book on stage.

The orchestra tuned up, the cameras with their crews in a stiflingly hot soundproof box were whirring, and the microphones were all switched on. All was ready for Jolson to go into his first big featured number, "Toot, Toot, Tootsie, Goodbye."

But Alan Crosland, the director, had never worked with Jolson before. Just as he gave the signal for everything to roll, Al got into the spirit of the thing. "Wait a minute, wait a minute," he cried. "You ain't heard nothin' yet. Wait a minute, I tell yer. You wanna hear 'Toot, Toot, Tootsie.' All right, hold on." And then he called to orchestra leader Lou Silvers: "Lou, listen. You play 'Toot, Toot, Tootsie.' Three choruses, you understand, and in the third chorus I whistle. Now give it to 'em hard and heavy. Go right ahead . . . "

No screen playwright could ever have put those words in a script and gotten away with it. But the mikes were switched on, the film and Jolson were in motion and those sentences were preserved for posterity. The film industry would never be the same again.

Later, when the rushes were run, the Warners were shrewd enough to realize what they had on their hands. So an additional scene was written for the stars—in sound. Young Jakie Robin (Jolson) comes back to his aged mother (Eugenie Besserer) and fools around on the piano, chirping "Blue Skies." The scene, a happy incident in the film, comes to an abrupt end as Warner Oland, playing Jolson's father, storms into the room and shouts, "Stop!"

The novelty of sound made *The Jazz Singer* a success. But there was something more to it, something that went beyond the maudlin sentimentality. For one thing, great efforts were made to ensure accuracy—greater efforts, in fact, than were usual for Hollywood, the town of make-believe.

To make sure that Cantor Rabinowitz really looked the stern father, Warner Oland—later famous as Charlie Chan—studied how the patriarchal Jews of the New York ghetto mastered their children. When he was ready to play the part himself, the camera crews moved from

Hollywood to Orchard Street in the heart of the Lower East Side of Manhattan.

Oland sat by the window of a restaurant and, when Alan Crosland gave the word, walked into the street to get lost in the crowd. His beard was long—much longer than the one to be worn twenty years later by Ludwig Donath playing Papa Yoelson in *The Jolson Story*—and his skullcap was much taller. He fit in perfectly with the Orchard Street throng. When he caught a young boy by the sideburns and pulled him into one of the street's shabby little houses, no one took any notice. It happened there all the time.

For days, too, camera teams studied the services at the old Orchard Street synagogue. Studio artists noted every detail of the architecture and created an exact replica weeks later on the Burbank stages.

The same attention to detail was given to the Winter Garden scenes. The interior of the theatre was photographed and then rebuilt in the studios. For some shots, only the real Winter Garden would do—and the filmgoers saw Jolson on the runway of his own theatre.

While the camera crews worked on Broadway, a giant tarpaulin covered the usual flickering sign. The temporary fascia proclaimed "Warner Brothers Pictures, Inc., will shoot scenes today of the New York Winter Garden for their forthcoming production, Al Jolson in *The Jazz Singer*." It pointed out that there would be no interruption of the current Shubert success, *The Circus Princess*.

At night, the temporary sign was removed to reveal the electric letters spelling out the legend "Winter Garden—JACK ROBIN—The Jazz Singer."

For the next twenty years, Al Jolson would have to be content with the pseudonym. But with *The Jazz Singer* he already had his memorial. The world's first talking picture was really very much Jolson's own story.

Not that he particularly enjoyed the filming. "I thought the picture would be a terrible flop," he said soon after it was finished, "because everything was new and strange to me. I would do a scene five times with tears in my eyes and then Alan Crosland would say, 'Do it again—and put some feeling into it!' "

"I wanted to go away and hide," said Jolson. "But the Warner brothers got me by the collar, threw me on a train, and packed me off to New York for the opening, which went over with a bang and made me very happy."

118

It won a special award from the Motion Picture Academy, largely for its novelty value. But it was a novelty that rocked the old Hollywood to its foundations.

People stood for hours on the night of its premiere to catch a glimpse of the stars. Those who managed to get into the Warner Theatre for the film had no idea of what was in store for them once the projectors started to roll. What they did see and hear sent them reeling.

Rival film producers in the audience shook in their seats. The next day the wires between New York and California burned with instructions from movie moguls to wire their studios for sound.

Careers crumbled as studios realized that faces that had previously sent millions of women into swoons belonged to voices that would now transport them into hysterical laughter.

For Al Jolson it was the greatest moment in his stupendously successful life. He loved to see the crowds gather nightly outside the Warner. Every evening for weeks, he and Lee Shubert would go into the theatre just before the film's end to hear Jolson singing the Kol Nidre in the synagogue as his father lay dying.

The talking picture took its toll on show business much faster than anyone could have guessed. It killed not only the silent picture, but also vaudeville.

The Keith-Orpheum circuit, which controlled a vaudeville empire that stretched from one end of the United States to the other, wrapped up its theatre interests and joined with the Radio Corporation to form a new film studio, RKO.

Jolson and Warner Brothers knew they had a hit on their hands and that was the way they liked it.

The story of *The Jazz Singer* differed from the one in the Jessel stage play. Instead of the erring boy returning to become a cantor, there was a different happy ending. Jack Robin sang the Kol Nidre to make his dying father happy, but he went on to see his mother cheering proudly from her seat as he sang "Mammy" on the stage of the Winter Garden.

It had to be like that. No audience could really be expected to see Al Jolson give up show business—even in a film.

The film was shown all over the world; if there were European cities without sound equipment in their cinemas, it did not matter. *The Jazz Singer* was shown from the Danube to the Dnieper as a silent picture.

The film went on to make three and a half million net profit. Before

119

long Jolson's own stock in Warner Brothers was worth four million. His stock as a film property was priceless.

Publicly other studios and other stars dismissed "this novelty—talking pictures." Chaplin—of whom Jolson had written glowingly in *Variety* the year before, praising his picture *The Circus* as "the greatest thing I've seen. Dem's my sentiments"—vowed in the press never to make a talkie.

Privately, everyone who counted in Hollywood was having nightmares. The local electricians had never had so much work in their lives. Studios changed overnight. Half-finished silent films were scrapped completely or had sound sequences added.

And, of course, Warner Brothers wanted Jolson for another picture.

There were only two Warner brothers now. Sam had died of a heart attack on October 7, 1927, the day after *The Jazz Singer*'s triumphant premiere. Harry and Jack were convinced that they had a hot new story for their hot new property.

The Jazz Singer had made Jolson, above all, a sentimental actor—a mistake Al himself was to regret a few years later. The new film script cast him in the role of the father of a dying child. All the emotions he had used as a son escaping from the fringes of his father's prayer shawl he was now displaying again, running after his little boy's pram. The picture was to be called *The Singing Fool*.

Again, it was a silent film with snatches of dialogue and a few songs which Jolson sang both with and without his blackface makeup. Looking back on the film now, it is easy to see where he was happier. He was stilted singing to an empty camera lens. He needed live voices to shout back at him when he sang. But even without audience participation he could escape from reality easier in burnt cork. The mask helped him as it had on Broadway, although only a fraction of his magnetism showed through. But for those people who had never seen Jolson live, it was enough.

The Singing Fool was racked with problems. For one thing, there had to be a little boy to appear with Al as his son. For weeks, mothers managed to break the Warner Brothers' security net and get onto the lot just in time for Al's entrance or just as director Lloyd Bacon moved in. Cleaners mysteriously produced little boys from behind their aprons. Waitresses managed to find them hiding on their coffee trolleys.

In the end, the part went to a youngster called Davy Lee—who years later said his principal recollection of the film was "Uncle Al's bony knees."

Finding a suitable new song for the film was another problem. One by one, songwriters submitted melodies and lyrics, and one by one Jolson threw them in the wastepaper basket.

In the end, he tracked down his old sparring partners, DeSylva, Brown, and Henderson, who among them had supplied so many of the old Jolson hits—including three that were to be included in *The Singing Fool* already, "It All Depends on You," "I'm Sitting on Top of the World," and "Keep Smiling at Trouble."

The songwriters were at a party in Atlantic City when the long-distance operator announced that Al Jolson was on the line from California.

"Listen, fellers, I've gotta have a song, ya hear?" he told them. "It's a song to a little boy—a little guy who's dyin' and his dad's near heartbroken about it. Do Jolie a favor and yer won't regret it."

At the suggestion that King Jolson, the man who had taken the Winter Garden by storm, who had thundered through the Metropolitan Opera House singing "Swanee," wanted a silly song like that, the trio dissolved into hysterics.

"We've got to do it as a gag," said Buddy DeSylva. "Who could take a thing like that seriously?"

They threw every ounce of schmaltz they could into the song. By the time the song was finished, they were so ashamed of what they had written that they got a bellboy to mail it to Jolson for them. None of them could bring himself to actually deposit the number in the box.

Jolson laughed, too—all the way to the bank.

The new song was called "Sonny Boy." When audiences heard Jolson weep over the gray skies in the picture, they wept. When Jolson smiled before the song reached its climax, they smiled. When he broke down over the boy's death, the people out front broke down with him.

The recording became the first disc in the world ever to sell a million copies. It went on to sell two and then three million.

Warner Brothers decided to stage the opening of *The Singing Fool* on Jolson's own stamping ground, the Winter Garden. Once more, he was the king of his own theatre. When he wanted to go out, the latest Rolls-Royce import was provided for him. When he wanted to go to a ball game, De Pinna's, New York's smartest men's-wear store, provided

121

him with a vicuña coat—which he promptly returned after the game. "I only took it on approval," he insisted.

For ten years, *The Singing Fool* remained the most successful movie of all time. Only in 1939 did *Gone with the Wind* overtake it.

The picture made five and a half million dollars. By the end of 1929, Warner Brothers—near bankruptcy when they made *The Jazz Singer*—had made a net profit of $7,271,805. Someone calculated that it was a 745 percent profit. The once tiny studio was now the giant of Hollywood and their prize asset was Al Jolson.

Eleven months later, a new Jolson picture opened at Broadway's Warner Theatre—*Say It with Songs.* Songs that Jolson again sang to Davy Lee.

DeSylva, Brown, and Henderson were brought in again to repeat their "Sonny Boy" success. This time they didn't laugh, and this time not as many people cried. But "Little Pal" was a reasonable enough follow-up to "Sonny Boy." Jolson and Warner Brothers continued to make money at the box office.

It had not yet dawned on the Warner moguls that they were hardly doing justice to their hottest property. Nor did Jolson yet realize what was slowly happening to his career.

He was making five hundred thousand dollars a film—a phenomenal sum at that time—and the audiences were pouring into the cinemas to see him. Or were they?

There were already rumors that each Jolson picture was turning out to be just a carbon copy of the one before. Not enough people in high places, however, had realized it. No one began to wonder whether, as the novelty of the invention wore off, the public might not be more demanding.

When films were advertised as "All talking—all singing—all dancing," Jolson's were not among them. The monster he had created had begun to bite. Even before *The Singing Fool* was released, Al was saying unpleasant things about the films he was making.

"It ain't so bad," he said about one picture. "But *The Jazz Singer*—a monkey could have played it—and did."

Jolson was made to measure for the big Hollywood spectacular musical. But he didn't get one. Perhaps the studio bosses realized he would have ordered all the other singers and dancers off the set and taken the cameras over for himself.

Given the right director, Jolson the actor might have emerged, just as Jolson the dynamic personality had on Broadway. But it didn't happen.

He didn't get the directors he needed—probably because the best were frightened of him—and his talent did not get the chance it deserved. Jolson on the screen was in more ways than one just a moving shadow of the real Jolson.

But other things were happening to him. The Shuberts had managed to get him away from Hollywood for four weeks to play in the Chicago production of *A Night in Spain.* He got ten thousand dollars a week for the stint and so broke all records for show business fees. Eddie Cantor reputedly had earned five thousand a week from Ziegfeld, and Marilyn Miller, the darling of the age, who had won the hearts of Broadway audiences singing "Look for a Silver Lining," had taken a weekly check for six thousand.

Lee Shubert got Jolson to agree to the Chicago deal only after a fee-chasing battle between them. Shubert said Jolson could have five thousand for the show. Al refused. "Six thousand?" Again Jolson shook his head, lit a cigar, and walked to the door.

"All right—ten thousand," Lee agreed. "You realize this makes you the highest-paid actor in the world?" he said with obvious pain. "Sure," said Jolson, "but you're the richest producer, ain't you?"

"I won't be," said Shubert, "if I have to pay actors like you."

The conversation might have had some poignancy ten years before. But Jolson was used to the sort of superlatives Shubert put to him. He had always been the greatest—and as far as he was concerned he always would be.

As he told *Motion Picture Classic* magazine, "Not that I don't have a lot of fun in life, understand me. I'm always kidding. If I break a leg I enjoy that experience. If I make a million I enjoy that one. I like all sorts of things, too. I like to eat in a hash house with a bunch of galoots and I like to doll up in an open-face suit and have the headwaiter in a swell hotel call me by name."

He also enjoyed going to Texas Guinan's night spot in Manhattan. Tex, like Jolson, had been a Shubert star. And like Jolson, she frequently appeared on stage with a horse. But at her own nightclub, Tex was queen just as much as Al had been king of the Winter Garden. She announced her own acts, introduced the girls of the chorus, and welcomed her celebrated guests publicly.

123

One night at Tex Guinan's place profoundly affected Jolson's life. He walked into the club in full evening dress—as always, looking immaculate—and acknowledged the welcome the assembled company gave him.

He sat down with Eppy and Harry Akst, trying to keep his mind on the show in front of him. Just sitting in an audience was always hard. But then a girl in the chorus caught his eye.

"What's the name of that cute little dark one?" he asked Tex.

"Her name's Ruby," the club owner replied. "Ruby Keeler. But keep away. She's Johnny's girl."

"Johnny?"

"Yeah—Johnny Irish."

Al was shocked. Johnny Irish Costello was taking over the New York crime rackets in much the same way that Capone had taken Chicago. One did not cross razors with Costello or his gang too lightly.

For Al it was a ticklish predicament. He was attracted to the girl. But he certainly did not want trouble from Johnny Irish, nor did he want to admit defeat to Tex. And in situations like that, Jolson, always a gambler, had to be brave.

He went up to Ruby after the show. They talked and liked each other. But at that stage neither was taking the other very seriously. To Al she was just a pretty face and what appeared to be a nice trim body. It seemed just another case of the big star using his charm to approach a chorus girl. Her mother had warned her about such things before she left home and there wasn't much a chorus girl didn't know. She was prepared for any likely advance.

They said good night to each other and that was the end of it—or so it seemed.

Months later, Al was at a Los Angeles railway station to meet Fanny Brice on one of those show business welcomes that delighted the publicity agents. She got off the train accompanied by two young girls. Fanny introduced them to Al, "Mary Lucas—" Al smiled like a gentleman—"and Ruby Keeler." The young brunette blushed as she was introduced to Jolson. Of course she remembered him. How could she possibly have forgotten? But did he know who she was?

"I know," said Al. "Tex Guinan's place. You were that cute tap dancer."

124

Because this was a show biz gathering, the agents were there in force, too—including Al's own man, William Morris. Looking at Ruby, Al told Morris, "Get that girl a job dancing for $350 a week. Say Jolie says she's the best little hoofer he's ever seen."

Morris, whose New York office was already managing Ruby, thought it a wonderful idea. Whether Ruby was worth $350 a week was irrelevant—he was on ten percent.

The next day Morris made the calls. "Jolson says she's great," he said to the owner of one of Hollywood's smartest clubs. "I'll think about it," replied the man—and then did what both Jolson and Morris knew he would do.

He called Al at his apartment. "This kid Ruby Keeler?" he asked. "Is she really that swell?"

"Really is," said Al.

Ruby opened the next week at the club for $350 a week. Every night after the show there was a bouquet waiting for her from Al.

When she returned to New York, Johnny Irish sent for her. Irish was as soft as far as women were concerned as Jolson was, and when he saw that Ruby was quite clearly more interested in Jolson that she was in him, he had the word passed through the gang grapevine that it might be a good idea for Jolson to come and see him.

Like a prospective bridegroom calling on his father-in-law, Al went to see the gangster.

"Ruby loves yer," said Johnny Irish without any formalities. "So you'd better marry her—or there won't be a certain singer on Broadway no more. Get me?"

Jolson got the idea. "See, I got this picture opening next week," he said, adopting the vernacular of his would-be executioner. "As soon as it opens, I'll marry her. I love the dame, I tell yer."

Al and Ruby were married at Port Chester, New York, on September 21, 1928. He was forty-three. She was nineteen. Ruby's parents objected to the marriage right up to the time the ceremony was performed by a justice of the peace. Cantor Yoelson and Hessi shrugged their shoulders at a new shikse daughter-in-law. They had resigned themselves to the fact that their Asa was following the traditional show business pattern, marriage-divorce-remarriage-divorce-marriage again. They did not like it, but they accepted it because they had no choice.

The papers, meanwhile, splashed the story "Abie's Irish Rose Come True." *Abie,* the big Broadway stage success, was now being made into a film. Jewish Al and Catholic Ruby seemed to have realized the dream. The gossip columnists loved every detail of the story. Wherever Al and Ruby went, the newspaper men and women went, too.

When word leaked out that the pair were going to Europe for their honeymoon, every pier in New York was blocked with press photographers and reporters trying to seek them out.

"This is for keeps," Al told them on the deck of the S. S. *Olympic,* and gave Ruby a fond squeeze. "How about you, honey?"

"For keeps," she said.

In London and in Paris, they were feted as the stars they were. They made a surprise visit to London's Piccadilly Theatre, where *The Jazz Singer* had just opened. When Ruby saw the crowds gathering around her new husband, she wondered whether she had married a man or a cult.

On October 14, 1928, the London *Daily Sketch* reported, "Al Jolson, America's highly paid revue star—he gets £3000 a week—has at last overcome his fear of appearing before a British audience.

"Until last week, Jolson was so nervous that English audiences might not like his work that he refused offers to appear here for fifteen years.

"Now he has made a personal appearance at a London theatre. He made an instantaneous hit.

"Jolson came on the stage of the Piccadilly Theatre on Friday night following the showing of his talking picture *The Jazz Singer* to say a few commonplace words of appreciation at being in London. He stayed twenty minutes, keeping audiences in roars of laughter with funny stories. Even then they would hardly let him go.

"Jolson was thrilled with the reception. 'It's better than New York,' he said again and again. 'After this I simply must appear on the London stage. I would like to appear in revue. Anyway, I promise I'll be here sometime soon."

In America, the public was looking forward to Jolson's fourth picture, *Mammy.*

Jolson never did play live in a London theatre, but his pictures were eventually to be even better received there than they were at home. In Hollywood, the studio heads were beginning to worry about Jolson's screen image; but he was still universally known—and mimicked.

Theatre owners organized Jolson contests, one of which Al entered himself under a false name. He came in third.

By the time *Say It with Songs* came out—in this film Al was sent to jail on trumped-up charges, to be deprived of his baby girl—more than one critic noticed the sameness of the offering.

Al, however, was happy to collect his half-million-dollar salary check, and the Warners were more than happy to add their signatures to the paper. They talked about the future but didn't worry about it. If it didn't last—well, what did?

Even Al thought it wise to tell one newspaperman, "As for 'Mammies' and 'Sonny Boys,' of course they aren't real. In real life Sonny Boy would generally rather sock you on the jaw than climb upon your knee. Most of the Mammies, instead of having hands all toil-worn and that sort of thing, are stepping out with their boyfriends and having a good time. But that's just the very reason why the public loves 'em."

To Al, the public was still everything.

When he and Ruby returned from their European honeymoon, a new home was awaiting them at Encino, near Hollywood. Al carried Ruby over the threshold for the cameramen. The couple had a meal together and just as the bride was settling in, Al decided to go for a short walk—"to help the food go down, honey," he explained.

He was away the rest of the evening and a few hours into the morning besides. "The guys at the fire station saw me as I passed by," he told Ruby, "and I gave them a song or two."

Ruby didn't argue. After all, she wasn't married to a man. She had teamed up with a legend and she knew she would have to share him.

Hollywood was responding to Jolson as it had never responded to anyone before. Jolson film premieres in those days weren't just a matter of searchlights, screaming sirens, and microphones. For Jolson films, special Jolson tickets were produced, made of real silver foil on which a black-and-white Jolson silhouette was superimposed.

Early in 1929, while Al was still in California, Ruby took the long train journey to Pittsburgh. Flo Ziegfeld had signed her for a tap-dancing role in the new Eddie Cantor show *Whoopee.* Al regarded it as a whim. And he knew that Ziegfeld was only trying to capitalize on her marriage.

When Al joined her in Pittsburgh soon after the show opened, he saw red. Billed as Ruby Keeler Jolson, her name appeared below that of Eddie Cantor. "How can you have a Jolson below Cantor?" he asked Ruby. He took her out of the cast the next day.

A few months later, Jolson and Ziegfeld met on a train. The big producer told Jolson, "I've got just the part for Ruby in my new Broadway show. Give her a chance." Al signed the contract for her soon after they arrived in New York. He had a new role as his wife's business manager.

Ruby came to New York to seize what was the biggest break she had ever had. She was to dance in *Show Girl,* the big new Gershwin show at the Ziegfeld Theatre, also featuring Jimmy Durante and his partners, Eddie Jackson and Lou Clayton.

Jolson was a paragon of magnanimity all the way. He liked his wife's role and he liked the deal he had made with Ziegfeld: not less than a thousand dollars a week. And he didn't want to turn the taps on his wife. After all, she was another Jolson and wherever she went, his name went, too.

Show Girl opened for a pre-Broadway run in Boston, with Ruby biting her nails alone in her dressing room. Unknown to Ruby, Al had followed her to Boston, stayed in another hotel and, as the orchestra struck up the overture, was waiting in the foyer of the Colonial Theatre.

When the lights went down and the curtain went up, Jolson walked down the center aisle with Ziegfeld at his elbow.

For him it was unbearable. Ruby now had a big role and he was merely sitting in the audience. Seeing his wife perform to a full house while he sat in the dark was torture. By the time the orchestra had struck up for Ruby's entrance and the chorus had begun the opening bars of the song, Jolson could contain himself no longer.

He stood up in his seat, raced down the aisle to the foot of the stage and joined in the chorus: "Liza, Liza, skies are gray. When you belong to me, all the clouds will roll away."

The audience went crazy. The great "Ziggy," who knew a show-stopper when he saw one, beamed. "Do that every night, Al, and you can have half the show," he told him.

When *Show Girl* moved to Broadway and the Ziegfeld Theater, Jolson moved, too. And when the orchestra struck up "Liza," Jolson came in on cue.

Ruby seemed pleased enough at first. But she didn't know her husband well enough to realize that the reaction of the ecstatic audience to Al was like a bell to a boxer. When she tried to tell Al that she didn't want him to upstage her, she didn't get very far. The next morning's papers made her task that much harder. The showstopper in *Show Girl* was Jolson's performance. That was all he needed to hear.

He phoned Jack Warner in Hollywood and told him to hold up work on his new film. "I'm stayin' on in New York for a couple of days—to keep Ruby company." For the whole week, Jolson was at every *Show Girl* performance, and when Ruby went into her "Liza" number, Jolson did too.

And as the performances went by, no one seemed more tickled with the continuous Jolson contribution than Flo Ziegfeld himself—even though *Show Girl* was roundly condemned by the critics as his weakest show in years.

No one bothered much about Clayton, Jackson, and Durante. The audience had probably heard better music from Gershwin and, although Ruby herself had a certain curiosity value, what the audiences really wanted to see and hear was Jolson. Al was in his element.

But he couldn't stay in Manhattan long. There was the small matter of his five-hundred-thousand-dollar new film for Warners at Burbank. Soon after his return to California, he had the telephone men at work setting up a direct line between his Encino home and Ruby's New York apartment.

One of the first calls he got, however, was not from Ruby but from Ziegfeld. His tap-dancing star had fallen from the top of the spiral staircase she used in her "Liza" number and had been rushed to the hospital with a broken ankle.

For Ziegfeld the accident was almost a blessing. Jolson was in California and who wanted to see *Show Girl* without him? The show closed and Ruby followed her husband West, her ankle in a plaster cast.

To most outsiders they seemed a happy couple. She went with him to the races, more than once adding her two cents' worth of advice and picking up enough winners to make Al happy. She followed him to the prizefights, which were becoming more and more a Jolson "thing" (on one occasion he had even sparred with Jack Dempsey).

But the important public occasions for Al and Ruby were the Hollywood premieres. Al enjoyed these occasions a lot more than he did other people's Broadway first nights. People wanted to see who was going to the cinema, not just who was actually on the screen. And going into a theatre was something Jolson did better than anyone else.

As he got out of his car, he had only to smile, tilt his silk hat at a jaunty angle, twirl his silver-topped cane, and the crowds became his audience.

Al bought Ruby fabulous presents—diamonds, fur coats, and cars. In one year, he ordered three of the latest Mercedes models imported for him from Germany, and gave one to Ruby.

But there was no getting away from the fact that the couple were from completely different backgrounds. Ruby may have been Abie's Irish Rose, but for all his fabulous success he was still Abie, with the Jewish mannerisms, the insatiable desire for gefilte fish, and the Yiddish phrases.

And Ruby was small-town Irish. Was there any conflict? No one said so at the time—but not long after the wedding, Jolson went to Chicago for a cosmetic operation to his Jewish nose. Some acquaintances noticed that Al really did seem to change. He may have been the big star on stage and on screen, but at home it was plain that Ruby was beginning to twist him around her little finger.

The gamblers on both Broadway and Sunset Boulevard were taking odds on the marriage's surviving six months. Soon after their first anniversary, Jolson gave a press conference in which he pointed to Ruby's finger. "Look," he said. "No matter what she's doing, that ring never comes off."

When *Show Girl*'s run was over and Ruby's leg had healed, the Hollywood columnists were saying Mrs. Jolson might well follow in her husband's footsteps. Al plainly didn't like the idea, until Warners assured him that a little tap dancer couldn't be much competition to a singer and personality like the Great Jolson.

When Jack Warner phoned Al to offer Ruby a part in his new picture, *Forty-second Street*, Jolson put on a hard business front. He and Darryl Zanuck discussed it in their ringside seats at the Hollywood Bowl during a boxing match.

"I want ten thousand dollars for her first picture just like I made in *The Jazz Singer* during its first weeks," Jolson said.

Ruby plainly could not believe her ears. "You really ought not to

130

ask so much," she whispered, tugging at his sleeve. "I'd do it for $250 a week. That's still a lot of money."

"Look," Jolson chided her. "Am I your manager or not?"

She didn't have to answer. Zanuck had a contract made out for ten thousand dollars. There was only one further stipulation. "Don't expect me to see yer work," Al said. "I don't want to watch any other guys kissin' yer."

For Jolson that would be as bad as hearing people applaud her. But now Ruby Keeler was in films and on the threshold of what seemed like a never-ending partnership with Dick Powell.

Every time Jolson saw the two together, he squirmed; he was more concerned about their success than about the possibility that they could be having an affair. That, in fact, was the one thing Jolson never alleged.

The money coming in persuaded him to like what was going on. Like everyone else in 1929, Jolson was money-crazy—although he rushed into nothing, bought stocks and made investments only on the basis of professional advice, and then frequently advised his advisers. Some said he knew the money market as well as he knew show business. There might have been some truth to that, for he was without much doubt the richest man his side of the footlights.

When everyone was putting money into the stock market, Jolson was, too. He speculated widely while others dabbled. But when Wall Street crashed in October 1929, Jolson was not one of those lining up to jump out of skyscraper windows.

He was reported to have lost four million the day the market crashed. But he had securities and investments worth at least another two million to fall back on and money invested in overseas bonds that were almost unaffected by the Wall Street crash. He also owned a great deal of real estate. When everyone else was selling at rock bottom prices, Jolson was carefully buying, knowing it was likely to recover.

When the dust finally settled on Wall Street, Al's stockbrokers and accountants began systematically calling his friends in show business, Eddie Cantor among others.

"Al said to offer you anything you want—fifty or a hundred thousand—whatever," said the voice. Why didn't Al make the calls himself? It might have made the offer seem more genuine had he done so, but it could be that he would have been too embarrassed to do it.

Some people said Jolson never did anything without a motive. It is difficult to see how he would have gained materially by this gesture. Another incident involving the two entertainers does seem rather more in character.

Al and Ruby were in Mexico with Cantor and his wife Ida. Cantor spent a few dollars more than he wanted to on some perfume for Ida. He saw the look on his wife's face when she heard how much he had paid.

"Don't worry, Ida," he said rolling his banjo eyes. "I'll win it back for you."

He tried to recover the money in a crap game that night, and ended up losing eleven thousand dollars. At the sight of this huge loss, Jolson collapsed in a fit of hysterical laughter. "Meet my friend, the business-man," he said, pointing to Cantor.

But then he always did like using Eddie as the foil for his jokes.

On one occasion, he phoned the Cantor residence, saying he was from the Beverly Hills Water Company. He advised that since the supply was going to be cut off for forty-eight hours the family ought to stock up. That evening he walked into Eddie's house to find it lined wall to wall with pots, pans, cups, plates, and bottles filled with water. "Can I have a glass of water, please?" he asked—and then admitted the joke.

When Al started work on his fourth picture, *Mammy,* he began to wonder himself whether Hollywood itself was such a good joke.

Another Jolson had come to Hollywood. Harry moved to the West Coast with Lillian in 1929 and took a full-page advertisement in *Variety* announcing he had signed a contract with the Universal Picture Corporation to make four films. He had the contract, but not the pictures.

One day Universal called to say that they were not picking up his option. Al had nothing to do with it. Harry just didn't have the talent.

Universal wanted a Jolson of their own, but by late 1929 the Jolson name was not enough. It wasn't enough for Al and it certainly wasn't enough for Harry.

Al starred in *Mammy* as the leading member of a minstrel troupe. He sang the Irving Berlin number, "Let Me Sing and I'm Happy," that became his epitaph. But that was not quite all he wanted. Now he demanded: Let me hear applause and I'm happy. And now he was quite clearly not hearing enough of it.

8

ALMOST LIKE BEING IN LOVE

THE 1930s proved to be a watershed in the Jolson career. Ruby and public taste were both having their effect on the way he saw life. And if the Jolson leopard wasn't going to change his spots himself, there were plenty of influences being brought to bear to try to change them for him.

But a lot of the old glory was still there. He entered the decade making the same sort of money that he had ten years before, and confident that nothing could knock him from his pedestal. Indeed, he was still being treated like a king.

When he made his one and only appearance at the Broadway temple of vaudeville, the Palace, in 1930, he was left in no doubt that this was the way show business still thought of him. He was sitting in the stalls when the emcee called him to the stage. He only sang one song, but for more than an hour, he held his audience spellbound with his ad-libbing.

For a time it seemed as though vaudeville was biting into Jolson. The man who had been the king of the legitimate musical stage was tempted by its illegitimate sister. New York's Capital Theatre booked him for just a week—for fifteen thousand dollars, with a contract stipulation that he would get half of everything over a gross of a hundred thousand.

The bets were on that Jolson would clean up another fortune. Broadway expected it. But for the first time in his meteoric career, in a stage life that didn't know the meaning of the word failure, things were going ever so slightly wrong.

The week's takings showed that Jolson—with Harry Akst at the piano—had made well under a hundred thousand. The writing did seem to be on the wall. And of all people, it was most painful for Al Jolson to see.

By anyone's reckoning, he was still a top entertainer. But being "top" was never really good enough for Al, he had to be supreme. And when he heard whispers that perhaps he wasn't that any more, he wondered whether they were true.

He made two films in 1930. *Mammy*, he told journalists proudly, was his best yet. The film was novel in many ways. For one thing, it featured a new score by Irving Berlin. In addition, its final reel was in Technicolor, another Jolson almost-first.

But the story was so trite it was embarrassing. Jolson played a man in a minstrel troupe who was being blamed for shooting his interlocutor, supposedly his rival in love. On the run, he hides in his mother's house in a scene reminiscent of the reunion sequence in *The Jazz Singer*, but not nearly so effective.

There were a few new songs for him to sing, but again, the limitations of the movie camera were as obvious as Al's discomfort. Only when he was singing in blackface in the minstrel line did a glimmer of the old Jolson come through.

The picture's theme song was "Let Me Sing and I'm Happy." He was not being allowed to sing enough to be happy enough.

In London, the great showman C. B. Cochrane remarked: "The Jolson I saw on the screen is not the Jolson I knew in the flesh. It was a Jolson without a soul."

Jolson could see what was happening, what he was doing to his career for a combination of money and the desire to entertain. He confessed to *Screenland* magazine, "I made two good pictures. I made *The Jazz Singer* and *The Singing Fool*. I showed 'em what I could do.

"Then they start tellin' me they can't find enough good pictures. 'All right, I'm reasonable. Can you find me two good pictures a year?' I asked them. 'No.' 'Can you find me one?' It seems they can't. So I take what they give me and live in hope. And I find that the pole is only greased one way—down."

Paramount Pictures tried to get into the Jolson act by offering him $6500 a week for a tour of their theatres in the Southwestern states. Jolson turned it down.

Later in 1930, Al made *Big Boy*, a filmed version of the Winter Garden success, complete with horse. One observer noted that his real horses seemed to be making more for him than the ones up on the screen.

Big Boy was a hodgepodge of a picture in which Al, as Gus, tries to remember some of the things his grandfather (Al again) used to say and sing. In the final scene, Al, in whiteface, appears on a theatre stage and sings "Sonny Boy." No producer ever let him forget that his name was Al Jolson and that he was to sing Jolson songs.

For three years, Jolson made no more films, and it was five years before he was back at work on the lot for Warner Brothers. The hot property had cooled.

"Sure I Miss the Stage," Jolson had written in a signed headline for *Theatre* magazine in July 1929. He told the magazine that he loved to be able to shout back at an applauding audience, "Keep it up, I love it," which he never could do from the screen. "I meant it. I still love it. I still love an audience. And if the making of talking pictures meant that there would be no more audience or offer no substitute, I would chuck them tomorrow—this very night."

He also said he sometimes felt "like one of those dolls whose strings are pulled to the right for a smile and to the left for a sad expression. I couldn't wait until evening came, when friends would be gathered around who would ask me to sing. I hungered for the live sound of actual people."

Those who now knew Al Jolson's face from his pictures didn't know how great he could be in the flesh or just how that doll on a string became a ball of fire as soon as the theatre curtain opened.

Abe Lastfogel of the William Morris Agency in Los Angeles recalled, "Jolson was a little man—until he got out onto a stage. Then he became a giant. When he left the stage at the end of the performance, he shrank to a little man again."

Al's desire to hear a real audience applaud again was satisfied in 1931. Back on Broadway, on March 17, he opened at the Nora Bayes Theatre in *The Wonder Bar,* his first Broadway opening since *Big Boy* at the Winter Garden in January 1925.

It is not remembered as Jolson's greatest show. For one thing, the book of this show was more difficult for Jolson to discard in his usual way. But he tried; and when he tried, he generally succeeded.

To demonstrate that his power over an audience was still intact, he told them four jokes, one after the other, without stopping, and jumbled the punch lines from one gag to the next. The audience roared. What Jolson had said was totally unimportant. It was the way he said it.

The Wonder Bar was the name of a restaurant-cum-nightclub in Paris run by Monsieur Al—Jolson himself. The music was by Irving Cesar and Rowland Leigh. The high spot of it all was a cabaret scene featuring Al.

He sang his own favorite song from *Der Heim*—the Yiddish term for the ghetto from which his music had really all sprung—about the cantor's audition for the tailor, the shoemaker, and the coach driver.

And he sang Irving Cesar's "Oh, Donna Clara" in English, German, and Russian—for which Cesar laboriously coached him. His Russian version of the song was so impressive that the great bass Fyodor Chaliapin heard about it, and came to see how this ghetto Jew from his own country had made out. He was singularly impressed.

The two Russian-born singers became close friends. Chaliapin would frequently phone Jolson during the day and say, "Arll, we both have no matinee today. Why not come around to my hotel and we have some wine and we have some caviar and perhaps a couple of girls?"

"Arll" was happy to accept. Girls were always an attraction, much to Ruby's regret. But Mrs. Jolson was in Hollywood pursuing her own career and did not always hear what was going on on the East Coast.

The friendship between Jolson and Chaliapin was a meeting of equals. Each admired the other's singing and since Chaliapin was in no way Jolson's rival, the entertainer was flattered that such a great name from opera should be interested in him.

It occurred to Jolson that it might be fun to work with Chaliapin. "I'm gonna do *The Jazz Singer* in grand opera," he told Eppy. "Chaliapin is gonna play my father—the cantor."

It never happened. And no one thought it would—no one except Jolson, who saw this as just the challenge his career needed.

But for as long as *Wonder Bar* played at the Bayes Theatre it seemed no challenge was necessary.

"The old Winter Garden's fair-haired boy has come home," noted the *New York Times*. And indeed he had. It became obvious during rehearsals that it was the same old Jolson.

He bounded backward and forward, brown bowler cocked on his head, to the back of the stage one moment, in the lap of the audience the next.

136

Wonder Bar was a revolutionary show. It had no curtain and the cafe staff moved back and forth on the stage throughout the performance to add a touch of realism no Jolson show had needed before.

Wonder Bar also cemented another friendship, one that several years later was to be sorely tried.

Walter Winchell, Broadway's legendary columnist, had Jolson to thank for being allowed back into the Shubert empire. The Shubert brothers, in one of their imperious bans on people they thought had crossed them, refused to allow Winchell into any of their theatres. Since the Shuberts owned more than half of Broadway's real estate, this was a considerable penance for anyone who regarded the theatre district as his beat.

On opening night, more than an hour after the advertised opening time, the performance of *Wonder Bar* still hadn't started. Jolson had heard about the exclusion of Winchell and refused to go on until the columnist had been admitted. As soon as he was shown through the front door, Jolson gave the word for the orchestra to play the overture and start the show.

Although the book was difficult to ignore, he managed to get away with some of his old tricks. One of them involved George Jessel.

When he first arrived in New York, he bumped into Jessel. "Come along to the theatre tonight and I'll introduce you from the stage," he said.

When Jessel showed up at the Bayes Theatre that night, Jolson was out front waiting to greet him.

"You know, there's a number later on with a lotta bales of straw lying around in the background. Hide behind one of those bales and I'll bring you out so that folks can clap you. You'll have a swell time."

When it came to the straw number, Jessel got down as he had been told and crouched uncomfortably as Jolson marched onto the stage for the big introduction for his guest.

At that moment, someone in the audience shouted for a song. It was more than Jolson could resist. He sang the number and the audience begged for more. And they got more. An hour and a half later, the guest straightened himself out, walked toward the singing Jolson, and told the audience: "This —— said he was going to introduce me to you tonight," and walked off.

Jolson got the laugh. Jessel took a cab home.

He fell for the same gag at a benefit show. Jolson had persuaded his arch-rival to join him on the stage "while I sing one or two songs."

The "one or two" songs became five or six, then nine or ten, and Jessel was still standing next to him. Finally when Al, completely oblivious to his guest, shouted, "Folks, you ain't heard nothin' yet," Jessel pushed his way to the front, dropped his trousers, and shouted, "And now you ain't *seen* nothin' yet," and hobbled into the wings with his trousers around his ankles.

Wonder Bar ran for seventy-six performances. When Jolson returned to Hollywood, there was a new hit for him to sing whenever he had the opportunity. "Brother, Can You Spare a Dime?" said all that needed to be said about the Depression.

"Depression" was a word Jolson didn't like. Early in 1932, he mounted a political soapbox to say so. In San Francisco, Jolson told a luncheon rally, "I've traveled all over, but here I haven't heard the word that I've heard in every other city. I see smiles on your faces because you think I'm going to say something funny. Well, I'm not. I ask you today to cut out that word and stop using it because it's hurting us more than anything else. Cut out that word 'Depression.' Will you do that from now on? Cut out that word 'Depression' and substitute 'panic.' You'll be nearer to it." The luncheon guests applauded wildly.

He said he had invested like everyone else. "I bought stocks that were supposed to be blue chip. We were told, 'Invest in the backbone of the nation!' Well, I bought the gizzard."

The guests laughed and patted Jolson on the back, and he left to sing "Brother, Can You Spare a Dime?" to the men waiting in the breadlines.

He sang it on the radio, too. Jolson had been slow to realize how big radio was. But after admitting to himself that pictures failed to show the true depth of his personality, he was reluctant to take on something that would rob him of yet another dimension.

He eventually succumbed when Chevrolet offered him his own show on the NBC network, for $7500 a performance. The half-hour shows went out weekly on Friday evenings with Al singing some of his old songs, some new ones, and some that others had made famous. He also introduced a galaxy of other performers.

It was a frustrating mixture, and the guests were the most frustrating part of the whole deal. He couldn't turn on the water taps now to drown the applause the other people received. And even when the studio audiences were applauding him, he realized that they were clapping for the cue cards rather than for the real Jolson.

Neither the network nor the sponsor would agree to vary the routine, as Jolson wanted. Al didn't want radio vaudeville; he wanted to be able to put his own version of the Winter Garden on the air. He wanted to be able to star in his own dramatized versions of famous plays and films.

"Al, we know what's right," the men from NBC and General Motors told him. Although no one said that what was good enough for General Motors was good enough for Jolson, they doubtless thought so. They also pointed out that Al's salary of $7500 a program wasn't peanuts. Kate Smith, the sensation of the airwaves at this time, was getting a mere fifty dollars for her regular fifteen-minute shows.

Al sang "Toot, Toot, Tootsie," "Dark Eyes," "The Cantor," "Avalon," "Sonny Boy," "Little Pal," and fifty or more other songs during the series. But he only completed fifteen of the twenty-six shows he was contracted to produce.

He wasn't happy with radio in 1932. He couldn't understand why everyone went crazy in the operations booth when he would throw away the script to ad-lib. Nor did they like the way he moved about. It brought back memories of his early recording experiences. Instead of a straightjacket, he was now given two microphones.

When Jolson went back to the Hollywood sound stages, he was again experimenting—but this time he was very much the victim of the experiment.

Hallelujah, I'm a Bum was the Big Experiment. Looking at it today, it is quite clearly the most adventurous Jolson film and artistically one of the best. But the Big Experiment became the Big Flop.

Lewis Milestone—undoubtedly the most imaginative director Jolson had ever had—was fresh from *All Quiet on the Western Front* and had a reputation that he wanted to preserve. Rodgers and Hart provided the music and lyrics for the new film. "You Are Too Beautiful," the love ballad of the picture, was one of the smoothest Jolson ever sang.

But he didn't put on blackface once and his dialogue was written entirely in rhyming couplets. It was a new Jolson, a Jolson whose acting had made great strides since the embarrassing days of "Mammy." But it was a Jolson no one seemed to like.

The story was about a gang of tramps in New York's Central Park and was panned by all the critics. The public stayed away.

The film cost more than a million and a quarter—a colossal sum in those days. And United Artists lost nearly every cent of it. Not that it was a lavish production. But it was beset by the sort of problems Jolson would never have allowed to interfere with him on Broadway.

Just before the picture was completed, for instance, Roland Young, who had the key role of the mayor of New York, fell ill. Since the mayor was in most of the scenes, nearly the whole film had to be reshot with another actor, Frank Morgan, in the mayor's role.

When it occurred to the producers that most of the essential slang words would be incomprehensible to people outside the United States, the scenes containing this dialogue had to be shot again, too.

There was also title trouble. "Bum," someone realized, had a completely different meaning in England—and a most impolite one at that. So the title was changed to *Hallelujah, I'm a Tramp*—for British distribution—and the title song had to be completely rerecorded.

The film had more titles than most pictures have had reviews. In turn it became *New York, Happy Go Lucky, The Heart of New York,* and even *The Optimist*—which anyone working on the film had to be.

The picture had been made by United Artists as part of a contract Jolson had signed with its studio head Joseph Shenck the year before—a contract that has since gone down in motion picture history. Al had agreed to do three pictures for United Artists for twenty-five thousand a week for forty weeks, a sum no one had even dared to contemplate before Jolson came on the scene. It was drafted and signed when both Jolson and Shenck were on vacation in Palm Springs. At the time the deal was first brought up, they had nothing to write on but a paper bag. They clinched the deal in a few minutes. It became known as the "banana-bag contract."

The next picture Al was due to make was *Sons o' Guns,* a Great War story based on the Broadway show that had starred Jack Donahue. Jolson decided the role was not for him, and it went to Joe E. Brown.

Al told the studio founded by Mary Pickford, Douglas Fairbanks, and Charlie Chaplin that if they wanted him to work he'd do it for nothing. No one asked. For the first time in twenty years, it was hinted that Jolson needn't bother to work. The other two pictures stipulated in the banana-bag contract were never made.

It was an excruciating time for Al. Just as his star seemed to be falling, Ruby's was rising like a rocket. Warners loved her in *Forty-second Street* and signed her for more pictures, including *Gold Diggers of 1933, Dames,* and *Flirtation Walk.* They were all hits.

"I'll be known as Mr. Ruby Keeler, yet," Al quipped. Certainly, she was no longer billed as Ruby Keeler Jolson.

Jolson told the world that Ruby was his, and that, he said, was all he really cared about.

"This one really *is* the perfect marriage," he told people over and over, but he seemed to tell it principally to convince himself.

The gossips in Hollywood had been hard on Al and Ruby, although probably no more so than they were on any other stars. When Walter Winchell wrote a few stinging words about Jolson in his column, the singer took the law into his own hands and the feathers began to fly.

At the Hollywood Bowl the crowd was thirsting for blood at a boxing match. They got their glimpse of blood—from ringside, not from the fight on the bill.

Winchell was on one side of the ring and Al and Ruby were on the other. When Jolson saw the columnist, he charged over from his seat to where Winchell was sitting.

"Hello, Al," the writer said, standing up and offering his hand. But he sat down again very quickly when Jolson punched him. He got up again, rubbing his jaw, but Al punched him again.

"That'll teach you," Jolson shouted. "Write things about my wife, will you?"

Al smiled. Suddenly there was a blow on his own head—from Mrs. Winchell's shoe.

Several stories circulated about the cause of the fight. According to one version, Al was angry about Winchell's film scenario for Twentieth Century Productions about a showgirl's relationship with a New York gang leader. Since Hollywood had never forgotten the stories about Ruby and Johnny Irish, and since other gangster names were mentioned whenever Ruby's name cropped up, Al immediately assumed that Winchell was referring to her.

After the fight, the newspapers dubbed Jolson The Hollywood Carnera.

"Funny," Al remarked. "You can sing *Mammy* songs for a hundred years, wear out your poor old kneecaps on splintery stages, and talk on the radio till you're as hoarse as a bullfrog—but you have to sock a columnist before you really become famous."

Tempers were frayed for days after the incident. "Winchell sent word he was going to get me like I got him," Jolson said with a note of triumph in his voice. "Well, I'll meet him in a room or in an alley in the daytime or in the night. I'll show him again how an old guy of sixty-two can lick a young guy of thirty-six."

It was the same old Al, never allowing the facts to interfere with a good story. Who's Who in the Theatre that year gave Jolson's age as forty-seven. He was probably not much more than forty-eight or forty-nine by any reckoning.

The fight with Winchell left Al with a permanently crooked little finger—and rumors of a five-hundred-dollar suit for damages brought by the columnist. But the two men made up again soon afterward.

As a friendly gesture, Al sent Winchell a jar of "the famous Jolson salve." And indeed it was famous. Al collected recipes for old wives' cures as avidly as he had formerly collected good notices. He had cures for diseases no one had ever heard of, let alone contracted. The World's Greatest Entertainer was still the World's Greatest Hypochondriac. He read the medicine section of *Time* magazine before the one on show business. When there was a new miracle drug on the market, he ordered it by the jarful, long before the neighborhood pharmacy had its supplies.

But he could put his hypochondria to good use. Jolson was always afraid that one day he would develop a worse case of tuberculosis than he had experienced as a boy. At the first sign of coughing, he consulted at least half a dozen doctors before he would accept their assurances that his lungs were not going to be seriously affected. And when he felt ill or likely to develop TB, he'd phone the William Morris Agency and ask them to book him into the Saranac Lake sanatorium—not for a treatment, but for a show.

He earned the sanatorium hundreds of thousands of dollars at the frequent benefit concerts he ran there.

Jolson was always available to raise money for show people and also for Jewish refugees, whose plight in Germany was becoming more apparent. He was no longer a religious Jew, but accusations against his lack of religious observance or about other Jews were likely to hit a raw nerve.

Some people said that the big fight with Winchell was not so much what he had written about a girl like Ruby but that he had mentioned in his column that Al had had to work on the Day of Atonement, the sacred Yom Kippur feast. And that he took as a personal affront, as he would any hint that he was not a practicing Jew.

Several years later, Al was to have a row with Joe E. Lewis over the comedian's decision to back Max Schmeling in his fight with Joe Louis, the American Brown Bomber.

Lewis was annoyed about the number of times his name was confused with the fighter's, and announced that every time Joe Louis was fighting, he'd back the other man in the ring.

Jolson was incensed that his friend could consider putting money on a man who had been lauded by Hitler and the Nazis.

"How can you bet on that kraut?" Jolson asked Lewis, who was at least as Jewish as he was himself. Lewis put his money on the German and lost. Jolson was delighted—so delighted in fact that he patched up the quarrel.

But he wasn't delighted with his own career.

Screen Book magazine had the temerity to ask, "Is Al Jolson Through?" They reported how Al looked the night *Hallelujah, I'm a Bum* premiered in New York.

Jolson had flown into the city from California especially for the occasion. He told startled reporters that his mind was finally made up: he was going to retire from the screen. That retirement lasted exactly twenty-four hours.

Jack Warner, who was in charge of production at the Warner studios, got him on the telephone the moment he read the news of Jolson's announcement and got Al's agreement to do three more pictures at his old home.

But Jolson spoke bitterly of the things that had happened on the set of *Hallelujah, I'm a Bum.*

"No director should expect a star to leap off a bridge into the water at sundown," Jolson declared. "I decided, picture or no picture, I wasn't going to do it and get double pneumonia."

He had tried wearing a rubber suit under his linen clothes. "It looked like a swell idea until I jumped in the water. Then I found that the suit kept me afloat. I bounced on the water like a rubber ball. So I had to come out. No more pictures like that for me!"

"Jolson appeared on the stage [at the Hallelujah premiere] deeply tanned by the sun," *Screen Book* reported. "There was the same outward confidence and poise as of yore. But to the observing there was something lacking. Cold-hearted Broadway thought it detected a note of apology in the Jolson voice, a tone of a valedictory in his manner.

"Maybe Jolson, as does Broadway, feels that he has had his brief day of success on the screen."

But Al did go back to Warner Brothers and made a film version of *Wonder Bar*. Was he finished on the screen? Again, the critics wondered. And with good cause: there had never been so little Jolson in a Jolson picture before.

A whole galaxy of talent—Dolores Del Rio, Dick Powell, Kay Francis, and Ricardo Cortez—surrounded Jolson as Monsieur Al. But there had never been a better Al on the screen.

He seemed more polished in every way. In one delightful tongue-twisting scene with a Russian aristocrat, the old magic returned. And in the final production number, "Going to Heaven on a Mule," there was Jolson as only Jolson could be. He finally seemed to be mastering the camera. But it was all too brief a glimpse. While still working on the *Wonder Bar* film, he had begun kidding about leaving the screen.

Between scenes, he broke into unscripted song. That was a novelty, but now he asked the people around him to take note of the lyrics, "Headin' for my last close-up," he'd warble. "Git along, little Jolson, git along." And he'd add: "Jolie doesn't work here any more. I'm sure that I've told you this before."

The trouble was, he said, Warner Brothers didn't understand.

"They all think I'm kidding," he told Jack Grant of *Movie Classic*. "I told one of you newspaper boys once before that I would never make another picture after this one. I tell you I'm through with movies. I'm quitting. I'm getting out."

He said he had no quarrels with the studio. "It's all of them put together and called Hollywood, the town where your personal—social life, I mean—is based on your success at the box office. If your most recent picture slips, so do your friends."

The truth was, Al noted angrily, people were removing the word "Hallelujah" from the title of *Hallelujah, I'm a Bum* when they wrote captions for his picture.

"The only reason I've filmed *Wonder Bar* is to make 'em change their minds. Word got around that it is going to be pretty good—pardon, colossal—and right away the same guys who a few months ago wouldn't speak to me are calling me old pal. It just isn't in the cards for me to be as popular as I have been in these last few weeks."

Jolson was plainly worried about the way his career was going. He was the third richest man in Hollywood, the experts guessed—after Charlie Chaplin and Harold Lloyd—but he was unhappy about his status in the world. He said that when he appeared at a benefit performance even his father, now eighty-six years old by his own reckoning, didn't bother to go to see him.

Most of all, though, he was worried about Ruby. She was doing better and better, and the more gushing her notices were, the harder Al took it. Warner Brothers, as a publicity gimmick, put out a story that she was receiving more fan mail than anyone else in the studio. Al reacted by calling his wife "big shot." It was the one phrase guaranteed to produce a row between them.

He'd made things difficult for her in company by reminding her how hard he'd worked to get her first contract with Zanuck. He'd proudly tell friends how he pushed up the studio from its $250 a week offer to $1250 for every full week before the cameras. "I don't know why Zanuck didn't hear her gasp," he repeated to Ruby's constant embarrassment.

Jolson now told everyone that as far as he was concerned he was saying goodbye to Hollywood. "And I mean goodbye," he added.

Before Al announced he was giving up films, he gave up records—without announcing it.

The man who had more discs made at one time than any of his contemporaries had done nothing since recording a selection of the Irving Berlin tunes for *Mammy* early in 1930. In 1932, he pressed another selection of the songs from *Hallelujah, I'm a Bum* for Brunswick. When they did no better than the picture, he gave up recording.

But he did decide to give radio another chance. On June 26, 1933, he launched the new NBC series *Kraft Music Hall*—a name he was to be connected with on and off until his death. At first, he was to be just the program's guest star, but on August 3 he became the permanent host for the show, which had the dual goal of projecting Jolson and selling Kraft cheese.

Al had grandiose plans for the series. Instead of just singing, he was going to star in the radio plays he had wanted to do when he first started broadcasting. But it began with the usual dull vaudeville routine—and with almost consistently disastrous results. Early in the series, one writer had headlined his piece, "Al Jolson—Don't Make Us Cry Again." Another wrote, "His show is getting too humid for comfort." But every writer noted that when Al sang "Brother, Can You Spare a Dime?" on the air, he brought the house down.

Radio had one very real advantage over the movies. It allowed him to hear applause as he sang—even if there was a glass wall separating him from his audience.

Comedy was always the sticky part of radio for him. "It becomes tiresome always being a song-and-gag man," he said. "After half a dozen broadcasts, I knew the comedy would have to go. There are just so many jokes in this world and radio is a Frankenstein in the way it devours material.

"It's far better for you to leave your audience than for them to leave you—and remember, it only takes a twist of the dial."

Radio was more exacting than the screen, "and ten times more exacting than the stage. In the broadcasting studios, you work with a stopwatch. The laughs are timed to the split second, and the pace is more rapid.

"In the theatre, you have the chance to ad-lib if the pace is slow. You have the chance to put your audience in a receptive mood by a few funny asides or an impromptu joke. But at the microphone, you stand or fall on your script—and as much of your personality as you're able to project over the ether. It's really pretty terrific."

Jolson got his way and started work on radio plays. It paid off. There was an adaptation of *The Jazz Singer*, *The Singing Fool*, and *Green Pastures*. He also starred in a radio version of *Porgy*, the Dubose Hayward play that was the sensation of the Broadway season.

When Jerome Kern heard about Al's radio success, he offered Al the lead in a new operetta he was planning on the *Porgy* story. "It's just what the doctor ordered, Jerry," Al told him. "Get to work. But why not make it an opera—an American grand opera?"

Kern said he would get to work on it. But by the time he had got something together for the Theatre Guild, George Gershwin had beaten him to it. He decided he wanted a real Negro for the part, not Jolson in blackface.

146

Porgy and Bess was a Gershwin triumph—if a belated one. Not until long after his death was it fully appreciated. While Gershwin was still alive, no one could decide whether it was a good musical comedy or a mediocre opera. As far as Jolson was concerned, it was just another idea that didn't come off.

9

WHAT'LL I DO?

IN 1934, observing life with the Jolsons was like watching a marathon Ping-Pong game. Neither had any intention of ruining their marriage, but for both there was a subconscious need to compete.

When Al called Ruby a big shot, she wanted to show him just how big she really was in her own right. For his part, Al was constantly trying to prove that the great Jolson was anything but a has-been. He didn't like radio, but he worked hard at it because it was the medium of the day.

Al had a regular prime-time radio spot whenever he wanted it. He had offers of pictures and he could have had a Broadway show any time he gave the word. Few people in show business would have asked for more, but Jolson was not like anyone else in show business.

He wanted more than just to be in the public eye. He needed to *shine* in their eyes. But in 1934, he had slipped a couple of places down on his pedestal and he didn't like it.

His radio reviews gave him constant heartache. On April 6, 1935, he opened a new series on the NBC network for Shell Oil, under the name *Shell Château.*

The first program, with Al singing, introducing guests, and taking part in the playlets for which he wanted to gain a new reputation as a serious actor, was received warmly, and he felt more encouraged than he had been at any time since he had first seen a microphone.

But the New York *Telegram* critic heard the second show and shook his head: "Dull to embarrassing. If our glossy reports of last week led you to listen to the second broadcast, we're sorry."

Al was sorry, too. But in spite of bad reviews, the show continued to get good ratings and became one of Jolson's most successful forays into radio. His only embarrassment was that he did not score on the air with the jokes he told. He didn't write them and sometimes he couldn't read them. Some of them were so bad that only the joke writers themselves knew what the punchlines meant. It was something entirely new to Jolson to tell a joke and hear it received in absolute silence. When he quite obviously hadn't scored, he would cough in an attempt to bridge through to the next item.

The writers gave Jolson, who could really appreciate a promising gag, stories that made him simmer with indignation, but no one took any notice. His contract specified that he had to tell them. Even his better jokes hardly elicited the audience response Jolson was used to getting.

Then Jack Warner suggested that Al and Ruby should work together on a film, instead of competing against each other.

When Al said yes, the big publicity machine went to work. It was in Warners' interest to stress just how happy the Jolson marriage was. The film was to be called *Go into Your Dance* and the publicity pictures made life a dance for them.

Al Jolson was still the World's Greatest Entertainer, they said, and his marriage to Ruby was the world's greatest show business match. The old poses of Al in semiprofile, captioned, "You ain't heard nothin' yet," now showed Ruby at his side. This wasn't going to be just another Jolson picture. Al and Ruby were getting equal billing and Al tried to accept it that way.

"It seems *Wonder Bar* was a hit," he told the New York *Sun.* "All of a sudden people wanted to see me again. It was like an attack of renewed youth." And he told the man from the *Sun* something he wouldn't have dared mention a few years before. "They are actually paying money to see me!" Not long ago that would have been taken for granted; now it was news. But Jolson was bubbling again and it was good to see.

The studio publicity department prepared new questionnaires about the Jolson career, listing his favorite pastimes (racing), his favorite food (gefilte fish), and his favorite film to date (*Wonder Bar*).

Go into Your Dance came just at the point at which Al's radio work hit a setback. Like all artists, he was caught in the midst of the row over music royalties initiated by ASCAP, the group of composers and publishers who decided how much money each was entitled to.

In 1936, the Music Publishers Holding Corporation, the licensee of all Warner Brothers songs, withdrew from ASCAP. They had had an arrangement whereby they received twenty percent of the ASCAP stake and now they wanted more. When ASCAP refused, MPH withdrew its songs and banned all Warner Brothers movie songs from the air.

When Al said he wanted to do "I Love to Sing" from *Go into Your Dance* on the air, he was told: "It'll cost Warner Brothers fifty thousand dollars to get one of its songs played on NBC." So he couldn't sing his own songs on his own program.

But he could talk about his new film. And he could say nice things about Ruby. Whenever he saw a newspaperman, he was full of the sort of praise for his wife he felt he was expected to offer.

"Maybe I'm prejudiced," he said. "Go ahead—sue me. But I'm honestly of the opinion that Ruby Keeler is the ten best women in pictures all rolled into one! Ruby has the faculty of bringing to the screen the sure sweet qualities she has in real life—charm, sweet sincerity, and winsomeness.

"I'm Ruby's most severe critic and her most devoted admirer."

Hollywood buzzed with the news of the picture and the husband-and-wife team starring in it.

A great deal was made of the theme song in the picture, "About a Quarter to Nine." The New York *Sun* announced that the picture would premiere at a quarter to nine.

The same paper reported the Jolson-Keeler marriage was "still a very genuine mutual admiration club [with] never a word of trouble."

Nevertheless, there were occasional glimpses of pain on Al's face when he saw Ruby getting the close-ups he thought were his due. From time to time he seemed to take over from director Archie Mayo.

"Sweetie," Al called to Ruby as she moved from one scene to another, "why not do it that way?" There was no doubt that he wanted to be in charge. "Honey! I think I'd do it like that if I were you," he'd add sweetly.

Not that Al was faultless. Many scenes had to be reshot because Al had called his wife "Ruby" on the set when he should have referred to her as "Dorothy."

Go into Your Dance was a big success. The public still wanted to see Jolson, but now it wanted Jolson as part of a team. The public cried for more Jolson-Keeler pictures, and it seemed sensible to fill the demand. The big number in *Go into Your Dance* had the couple walking arm in arm, with Al—in top hat, white tie, and tails—singing "About a Quarter to Nine" to Ruby in her flowing evening gown. The success of the picture, and particularly of that number, worried Al. "They don't want to see me any more. They want *us.*"

He decided there were to be no more films with Al and Ruby doing a double act. "I'm going back to radio," said Al. "At least there *I'm* the star."

And he was an expensive star, too. In one of his early broadcasts for *Shell Château* he welcomed golf professional Sam Parks, who had just become the national champion.

"What's the name of the place where you're instructor?" Al kidded, throwing aside the script in the old Winter Garden manner. "The Summit," said the pro proudly. "But that's a rotten hotel," Al rejoined—and the men behind the glass observation panel gaped in disbelief. They knew what to expect.

The next day a writ from the Summit Hotel Company arrived, demanding one hundred thousand dollars in damages.

Four years later the matter was finally settled. NBC was ordered to pay fifteen thousand. Al, meanwhile, had joined CBS.

Jolson was always slightly intemperate on the air. It was hardly surprising that a man who relied so much on his own personality on the stage should find it difficult to behave differently in front of a radio microphone. On one of his first radio interviews—he had just fled from D. W. Griffith—he sent shivers down the spines of refined old ladies who had tuned in to hear about the big star's return home from Europe.

"How's the beer in England, Al?" a radio reporter asked him. "Beer?" Al replied. "They drink it warm in England. Personally, I think they should have it put back into the horse."

A little later on, he got embroiled in a discussion about Clara Bow. "Oh, she's sleeping catercorned in bed," he quipped.

The protest flooded in from offended listeners.

In spite of such incidents—or perhaps because of them—Jolson became personally responsible for introducing censorship in all NBC broadcast scripts.

Early in the thirties he predicted great things for a new medium, television. The Bell Company had asked Jolson to try his hand at what they said was going to be the biggest thing in the history of entertainment.

They ran a pilot program starring Al from the Astor Hotel. He liked it. "It's like radio, movies, and the stage all put together," he said. "This really is going to be great."

151

But Bell decided they still had plenty of work to put into television before anyone could be asked to pay for air time or buy sets. And the first man to appear on the small screen in America never made another live TV appearance.

Early in 1935, he had another career to think of. Al was a father. He and Ruby were with George Jessel when they passed the Cradle Orphanage in Evanston, Illinois. Jessel knew the priest who ran the orphanage and introduced the Jolsons to him.

"Why don't we take one of these kids?" Al asked Ruby.

They had talked about having a family for most of the years of their marriage. Al was not going to be able to give Ruby a child of her own, so they had planned to adopt twins, a girl for him and a boy for her. But they settled for one, a seven-week-old boy. On May 7, 1935, in Chicago, they adopted Al Jolson, Jr.

The adoption agency stipulated that the Jolsons had to bring him up as a Catholic. When he made his next trip to Washington, Al didn't bother to tell Moses Yoelson. He knew it would hurt the old man and there was little point in doing that.

Al set about becoming a good father in every way he knew. He bought the biggest pedal cars, the biggest Teddy bears, and the best baby clothes for Al, Jr. When he and Ruby had a row over the boy, he'd shout at her, "He's my flesh and blood, isn't he?"

Two weeks after the baby was carried into the nursery at the Jolsons' Encino home, he became seriously ill. The child was rushed to the hospital and for two nights Ruby kept vigil by the bed. When the crisis passed and the baby came home again, Al was like a cat with two tails.

"Dat's my boy," he'd say when the youngster spoke his first words. "Father" seemed to be the best Jolson role yet. Here was an opportunity to give all the warmth he had previously given to his audiences to this one little boy, the boy he was convinced was going to become the World's Second Greatest Entertainer.

"Why not?" he'd say to friends who appeared a little skeptical. "He's my son, ain't he?"

He'd wheel the baby between the orange and grapefruit trees in the garden of the big house in Encino. Stopping to talk to the gardener, Al would ask him for some flowers for the child to hold. "Don't you think he looks like me?" he'd say.

The local community took full advantage of his presence among them and his absence from the studios. The Encino Chamber of Commerce elected him president. On December 28, 1935, Al Jolson became the town's mayor.

Al was genuinely happy now. He was a big shot in his town and in his family. With a son of his own, he was a big shot even to himself.

And he was taking an interest in other things. He bought the rights of the best-selling novel *Penny Arcade* and sold them to Warner Brothers on the condition that they star James Cagney in the lead.

In June 1936, he became vice-president of a mining company owned by one of Hollywood's ace showmen, Sid Grauman, the man behind the famous Chinese Theatre on Hollywood Boulevard. The company had been set up to dig for minerals in the Black Hills of South Dakota.

Jolson put in some money, but drew out no minerals. But he didn't seem unhappy; he had his Sonny Boy to take out, to play with, and to talk about on the radio. So many people wrote to hear more about Al, Jr., that his father once tried to persuade Ruby to allow him to bring the baby into the radio studio. She said no, and Al, Jr., stayed in the nursery.

All this wasn't doing Al's public image any harm, either. Early in 1936, he started work on another film, *The Singing Kid.* But that didn't go smoothly for either Jolson or Warner Brothers.

It was one of the most ambitious Jolson films to date, with a number of exterior shots that never failed to give problems. Jolson was once more behaving like the big star he had been six years before, and the people in the studio, who would have been delighted to execute his slightest whim back in 1930, were less willing in 1936.

When Al insisted on having his own way, rows were inevitable. For instance, Jolson was required in one scene to sing in the street, with traffic and pedestrians all around him. Jolson sang his heart out, but the big Jolson voice was drowned every time someone walked by or when a car appeared in the distance.

"Al, we'll have to dub your song in the studio," Director William Keighley told him.

"No dubbing," said Al. "I either sing it as it happens or I don't sing at all."

So to satisfy Al's demands for realism, the street had to be completely re-created on the studio lot.

The Singing Kid was about a first-rate entertainer who loses his voice. It began with Jolson singing a medley of some of his best known numbers, "Mammy," "Swanee," "Rockabye," "California, Here I Come," "April Showers," "A Quarter to Nine," and "Sonny Boy," all but the last in blackface.

What had seemed to be a Jolson vehicle turned out otherwise. His co-star Beverly Roberts had just as big a role as Ruby had had in *Go into Your Dance.* To make things worse, in the musical numbers "I Love to Sing-A" and "Save Me, Sister," Cab Calloway and the Four Yacht Club Boys seemed to be more prominent than Al.

Jolson was unhappy all the time he was on the set—and for the first time members of the crew could be heard talking about "cruel Jolson." The idolatry of the Winter Garden days was gone.

Beverly Roberts sparred with Jolson almost from the moment they met. She was introduced to him on the set just as she was about to be tested for the female lead. "I was rushed through by the makeup department so quickly that I went onto the set with my hair dripping wet," she recalled. "Jolson roared with laughter when he saw me and the director said, 'What are we wearing for hair this year, mouse's nests?' I was indignant—just like a firecracker. And I think that's how I got the part. Al admired how I reacted to the way I was being treated."

Jolson hated *The Singing Kid.* "That's it," he said when the filming was finished. "You can't treat Jolson like that. No more crummy pictures for me. *I'll* decide in the future what I'll play."

The film prompted another quarrel with his brother Harry. Early in the thirties, after Harry had come to Hollywood for a movie career which ended before it began, the elder Jolson brother had been involved in a disastrous business venture. He and Lillian had put all their savings into a restaurant they called Harry Jolson's Rendezvous. Not enough people chose it as their rendezvous, and when they did, too many of them escaped the formality of paying the bill.

Al came to the rescue and appointed Harry his personal agent. He sent him a telegram with the message, "With the salary I get, if I work one week, you'll live a year." Al arranged for Ruby to be one of Harry's clients, too.

Being Ruby's agent meant merely handing her the Warner Brothers and First National contracts. For Al, the contracts were few, far between, and not all to his liking. Radio producers mentioned Bing

Crosby and Rudy Vallee and suggested that Al start crooning their way if he wanted to be a success on radio.

It was more than Al Jolson's ego could stand.

In 1936, *Variety* printed an announcement from the William Morris Agency, "We are proud to announce that Al Jolson has exclusively authorized us to represent him for the negotiation of radio and theatre engagements. Any other person or persons purporting to represent Al Jolson in this connection do so without his authority."

The writing was on the wall for those "other persons," all of whom seemed to be Harry Jolson. A letter was sent from Harry's attorneys demanding seventy-five thousand dollars' damages. It never came to trial. When Al next saw Harry, he gave him a new car as compensation. "With my career in the shape it's in right now," Al told his elder brother, "I need an organization like William Morris to represent me."

The agency got Al a new CBS series for Lifebuoy Soap. Called *Cafe Trocadero,* it was to run for four years, although the title was dropped after the first two shows.

Here was Jolson again singing "April Showers," introducing guest stars, including Ruby, and fooling around with his regular sidekicks, Martha Raye and a very successful Greek-dialect comedian who called himself Parkyakarkus (his real name was Harry Einstein).

Meanwhile the Shell program had sponsored the radio debut of a bright child singer named Judy Garland.

Radio was no longer a challenge for Jolson, although when he wanted to do so, he could shine when the green light indicated he was on the air. On those occasions, he treated the microphone as one of his old live audiences. To listen to one of those Jolson performances was to be admitted to an enchanted land. But you had to turn the knob to take your choice and sometimes there was no enchantment, just the sound of a man bored with himself.

When he was bored, Jolson had to find new diversions. He bought more horses and told bigger stories about his successes. With George Raft, he bought a piece of prizefighter Harry Armstrong.

He also had his first really serious quarrels with Ruby, exploding at suggestions that his career was through, calling her names, and storming out of the house.

But every once in a while a columnist would do a piece on Jolson that encouraged him. In the mid-thirties *Metronome* magazine described him as "The First Salesman of Song."

"The Jolson pipes have been chipped by time of a bit of their platinum," the magazine said, "but you'll get the song and it will either thrill you or you will subconsciously feel that he is driving the song home. If you happen to have the latter reaction, class yourself in the minority. For Mr. and Mrs. Public like the way Jolson sings a song."

It did Al good to read things like that, even when he hardly believed it himself. But when he had a sympathetic audience, he was as much a star as he had ever been.

When he appeared on the Hollywood party circuit, he needed no agents to book him into celebrities' homes and he needed no persuasion to sing. Everyone at the party would sing or tell jokes, but if Jolson was there, he'd expect to be asked to go on last.

There was one party to which he and Ruby went, however, when the expected did not happen. George Burns and Gracie Allen were giving the party at their Beverly Hills home for Damon Runyon. The Burns and Allen parties were always special affairs. Burns liked telling stories that made him the life of his own party. He also liked to sing. "Why shouldn't I? I'm payin' for the piano player!"

Burns was just getting into the swing of things by the time his ninth or tenth number had ended; his guests all seemed to be enjoying themselves. All, that is, except Jolson.

After the eleventh Burns solo, Jolson did the unheard-of: he went up to his host and asked if he could sing.

"Sure, Jolie," said Burns, pointing the way to the piano with his cigar. "Go ahead."

Al told the accompanist to play "Rockabye Your Baby with a Dixie Melody," and had just got into the refrain when Burns sidled up to him and joined him.

Jolson bristled. He stopped singing, grabbed Ruby's arm, and marched them out to their car. Burns followed them, still singing, " . . . and when you croon, croon a tune from the heart of Dixie."

It was the sort of trick the Hollywood set loved to play, but Jolson didn't like it. A year passed before he and Burns teamed up again.

In 1937, Jolson and Sid Grauman got together again. This time, Grauman invited Jolson to preserve his hands and feet in the wet cement in front of the Chinese Theatre. Naturally Al went two better.

He held his fingers outstretched in his favorite "Mammy" pose and made an impression with his left knee at the same time.

Meanwhile his radio show continued. The *World-Telegram* wrote in 1936, "His air show is flimsy but his magnetism and vitality make it appealing." That criticism came at a time when people were saying he was completely washed up. By Jolson standards, he was, but that only proved how high those standards had been.

By 1939, Jolson was feeling restless. At the age of about fifty-four, he was regarded as the elder statesman of show business, a role he did not relish. He was still recognized wherever he went, but there was none of the adulation he had demanded—and received—in the past. Young girls lined up to see him enter the CBS studios, but he suspected they would have done so for any celebrity who was on the air every week.

He had his share of hangers-on, too—people who knew he was good for a dollar or two, and too big to turn them down.

On one occasion in Miami, he walked into the bar of the hotel where he was staying. At his entrance, the juke box played "Sonny Boy."

"I can't get enough of that song," said a woman at the bar, "lend me a couple of nickels."

Jolson gave the woman a quarter and said, "The next five are on me."

The woman recognized him. "You're Al Jolson," she stammered.

"Sure, and you knew it when I walked in," Jolson answered. "What's the idea of that corny routine?"

He knew what to expect. The woman was broke. Her husband had put a thousand dollars on a horse and lost. What was worse, it wasn't his money—it was Al's. The woman's husband was the desk clerk at the hotel. He had taken the money from the safe soon after Jolson checked in.

Jolson told the woman to get her husband and then took them both to the local greyhound racetrack. He gave the man five hundred dollars and instructed him to put it on a dog he believed to be a sure winner. The dog won, and the bet paid.

Al took his $1500 from the winnings and let the desk clerk have the other $1500. "Let this be a lesson to you," he warned. "Never bet the horses. If you've got to bet, bet the dogs."

But the fact that he could afford the time to play games with people like that worried Jolson. He asked William Morris to get him back into films. It was easier said than done. Warner Brothers did not want the man who had given them life. No one else did, either.

Eventually, Twentieth Century-Fox offered Jolson a movie role, not as the star, or even as the supporting role, but third billing with Alice Faye and Tyrone Power.

The film, *Rose of Washington Square,* was based on a story about a singer who falls for a good-for-nothing professional gambler. The rough plot outline was so reminiscent of the story of Fanny Brice that the old Ziegfeld star took Twentieth Century-Fox to court and collected on a libel suit.

Jolson was in it just to be Jolson. The character he played appeared on the same vaudeville bill as Alice Faye, became her friend, and warned her about what a double-dealer her husband (Tyrone Power) was becoming. But he also sang—in blackface—the old Jolson songs like "Rockabye Your Baby," "Toot, Toot, Tootsie," "California, Here I Come," and even "Mammy."

It was not so much a new Jolson as a recapturing of the old. He had never acted and sung as well on the screen before.

The film set no records when it was released. But people who saw it took notice.

In the New York *Herald Tribune*, John K. Hutchens reported, "It takes a motion picture—the one called *Rose of Washington Square*—to remind you of it and even then you didn't know whether it was pleasant or sad to reflect upon. A whole chapter of theatre flickering past you in the little while a film requires, and there in the middle of it was one who had been peerless in his field some twenty years and more ago.

"The other stars were in it, impersonating (after a pattern) characters suggested by real people of the same era. But the other, Al Jolson, was pretty clearly playing Al Jolson.

"In the picture, his name was something else, but no one would be taken in by that. Who but he had ever donned burnt cork, sunk to one knee and inquired lyrically after his celebrated Mammy in the Deep South? Indeed, his Mammy must have been copyrighted.

"The Wonder Bar wasn't a generally good show, but that didn't matter. It never had mattered. A lot of the Jolson shows hadn't been masterpieces of musical comedy writing. They hadn't needed to be. All they had needed was the tumultuous Jolson vigor and the smashing

Jolson style, unique and incomparable in the theatre of his prime and never equaled since by any popular singing star.

"Perhaps his style wouldn't do today, however painful such a notion may be to anyone who can remember even a few years into the past.

"At the performance of *Rose of Washington Square* attended by this department, the younger generation was somewhat less tolerant even of his trademark, the immortal 'Mammy.' You would never have thought it could happen.

"But since it did, you are glad that there are at least this and other film records of him, though they are the merest suggestion of what he once was. You will be very surprised if you ever see anyone else who was as good in the same way."

No other Jolson film since *The Singing Fool* had generated that sort of comment. It did Jolson as much good as a dozen blood transfusions. Later that year, Twentieth Century-Fox featured him in another supporting role in a Technicolor opus called *Hollywood Cavalcade* which also featured Alice Faye. Don Ameche played the main male lead.

Al's part was so small that he was billed at the end—"With special thanks to Al Jolson." It was a love story set around the story of the cinema. There were the Keystone Kops, custard pies, and Rin Tin Tin. Al just sang one song, "Kol Nidre," in a remake of the synagogue scene from *The Jazz Singer.*

He did it while working in the studio on another picture starring Dom Ameche. It was a smaller role than the one he had had in *Rose of Washington Square,* but somehow it was a more important one.

The picture, *Swanee River,* was supposedly based on the life of Stephen Foster. Jolson played E. P. Christie, the great minstrel who sang many of the Foster ballads for the first time.

But once again he was simply playing Jolson, an effervescent Jolson obviously delighted to be back at work. His rendition of "Old Folks at Home" was one of the most memorable performances of his screen life. People who had seen Jolson on the Winter Garden stage now felt that at last the studios were getting near the real Jolson, featuring him in just the sort of part he should have had ten years before.

Al's marriage to Ruby was having more than its share of problems. Every time they were seen together, they both looked morose. He was heard to shout at her in public. And if it was affecting their home life, the clearest victim was Al, Jr.

One day, when the child met Al at the airport after Al had been away for a weekend with George Jessel, Al had some indication how much the boy suffered because of his absence. Al raced down the steps of the aircraft, grabbed the child in his arms, lifted him up, and cried, "Who am I, sonny boy?"

"You're the Jew," said the child calmly. Even under his suntan, Al Jolson blanched.

"It was the only time I ever saw him humiliated," Jessel recalled.

10

ALL ALONE

FOR JOLSON, the hardest thing about being married to Ruby Keeler was trying to convince her how big a star he had once been. And that was never any harder than when he was working, doing the same kind of work his contemporaries were doing very happily, but without causing the sensation he had once regarded as his right.

In 1939, he did a radio broadcast from a new hotel run by the Paley brothers, controllers of the CBS network, for whom Jolson was then working. Mickey Rooney was on the bill with him for the show, which was broadcast only to the area covered by the local radio station. It wasn't even heard by the guests in the hotel.

The show was emceed by Rudy Vallee, who introduced Al with the tribute, "He's one of the greatest talents of all time," he said. "He's the man with the thrilling voice." Ruby, seated at a table at the back of the restaurant, couldn't hear the show presented on the stage at the other end of the room.

When the show was over, Jolson went over to Vallee's table. He asked him to tell Ruby "what you said about me on the air."

But even if he had convinced her about the throne he had once occupied on Broadway—and his scrapbook alone would have done that—it was not sufficient for him to save their marriage.

One evening, when Jolson was playing bridge at the home of his friend George Levy, Ruby phoned. Al didn't want to interrupt his game, but the butler insisted that it seemed important. When he came back to the game from the phone, his face was ashen. He took his seat and said nothing. But his friends looked at each other and knew what the phone call had been about days before it was in the papers.

When Jolson returned home the day *Swanee River* was completed,

161

Ruby was gone. She had packed her things in the Mercedes and driven with Al, Jr., to her parents' home.

Al was in tears. Eppy came over to try to comfort him. Finally, he telephoned Ruby's mother for Al, but she wouldn't allow them to talk. Al wrote to Ruby and made more telephone calls, begging her to come back to him.

The man who had made a profession out of crying on the stage and screen found it impossible to convince outsiders he was happy when he wasn't. On October 26, 1939, the New York *Herald Tribune* reported that the pair were parting.

"Jolson appeared brokenhearted," the paper noted. "I hope everything will work out all right," he told reporters. On learning that she had already consulted lawyers, he insisted, "These are family troubles, not important enough for divorce." Privately, he had little confidence that it would.

Later, he said he had decided to face the fact that they were apart and be generous. He offered her four hundred a week for life, fifty thousand in a lump sum if she married again, and a hundred-thousand-dollar trust fund for Al, Jr. Ruby's lawyers told him to forget it until it came to court.

Meanwhile, Al stayed alone in their Encino home and Ruby and Al, Jr., stayed on with her parents.

Every time Al thought about Ruby, his misery increased. In his own way, he loved her deeply. Their marriage had floundered, perhaps because Al had been unable to reconcile himself to the life of a soberly married man far from the spotlight, and then, when that wasn't possible, to face the even harder prospect of having a wife with a career more dazzling than his own.

When she had left, Al seemed to miss their verbal sparring as much as the more loving moments. He asked Harry Akst, his pianist, to spend the night with him so that they could just talk the hours away. Akst slept in the same room, in Ruby's old single bed, night after night. In the afternoons, he'd go to the racetrack with Al, and in the evenings, to the prizefights.

At the track Akst felt obliged to bet with Al and lose with him. At least, he assumed Al was losing with him. But Jolson never actually admitted it to him any more than he had to Jessel.

"You didn't have the winner, did you, Al?" Akst would ask incredulously. "I didn't have his sister," Jolson would reply. In those painful times, he needed small triumphs—even if he had to create them for himself.

In time, Ruby became much happier about her separation from Al than she was when she first appeared before the court, four days before the end of 1939. She had filed for divorce on grounds of extreme cruelty and physical suffering.

The court heard tales of Jolson's "publicly humiliating me. He would shout and call me names," she told the judge. "He called me stupid and kept me up all night calling me names. He would sit at the table and refuse to talk, and just leave me to keep up the conversation. Then he would go upstairs to bed and leave me to entertain our friends. Whenever I expressed an opinion, he would say, 'That's wonderful. Do you know about that, too? You are too smart.' "

When the judge asked, "Did he say that in front of friends?" she replied, "Oh, yes. He criticized the friends I brought into the house and at a restaurant, we had bitter quarrels. He would never agree with me about anything, and when I suggested things, he would fly into a rage. He never takes me anywhere."

Even after Ruby's appearance in court, Al hoped for a reconciliation. She had been given an interlocutory decree, but he hoped their marriage could be salvaged from the wreckage. "Who knows?" he told reporters. "It takes a year for a divorce to become final. And Ruby's a wonderful girl."

If there was a chance for a reconciliation, it would come through Al, Jr., who was in Ruby's custody. Al would see the youngster on Saturdays or Sundays and take him for long drives or on outings to baseball games.

But these afternoons were always painful. "The kid's growing away from me," Al confided to friends.

After a while it became too painful, and Al agreed not to see the boy again. Instead, he concentrated on his career. He had big plans; remarkably, Ruby still played a part in them.

Earlier in 1939, Al had made a deal with a stockbroker friend, George Hale, who had asked Jolson to look over a script he had been offered about a radio singer's dreams of the Wild West.

Originally, the show, with a score by Rodgers and Hart, was to be called *On the Line*. But by the time Jolson and Hale came to an agreement, Burton Lane and E. Y. ("Yip") Harburg had come up with a new score and the show was retitled *Hold On to Your Hats.*

For the first time in nine years—since *Wonder Bar* in 1931—Jolson was returning to Broadway as the star in his own show. Ruby was to be the lead dancer, and Al saw the show as a chance to recapture her, too. It was arranged that she would open at the Shubert Theatre in September 1940, after a six-week trial run in Chicago.

Al sent her roses every day of the first week and paid for her stay at an expensive hotel. She sent back the flowers and the jewelry he plied her with later.

On the stage, he acted as both star and producer—but not husband. When he found fault with Ruby's dancing, he'd tell her so. He'd shout and rave and Ruby would walk out. In the evening, there would be more roses and more gifts, all of which were returned to him.

Finally, during the Chicago run, Ruby walked out on him for the last time. She was replaced on the stage by Eunice Healey. And once again, he tried to fill Ruby's place in his mind by playing the horses.

Every spare moment, he'd drive to Arlington, Chicago's main track, to take his mind off his lost marriage. When the show hit a sticky patch in rehearsals, he could be heard muttering, "What's going on at Arlington? I gotta get there."

He was noticeably nervous, constantly walking up and down on the stage, seeking the nearest water cooler for a drink. Just as he had in the old days, he'd poke his head into the box office regularly to see how many tickets were being bought.

A reporter told him he was looking good. For the first time in weeks, he smiled. "Hollywood took it off," he said, rubbing his midriff. "But no more Hollywood for me. And no more marriage either. You can put *that* in caps. This is the life. Sure I'm tired. Never tireder. These rehearsals are costing me a hundred dollars a minute. A hundred. Hear that—a hundred. I'm going to the doctors."

But he didn't see a doctor. He found his way to the track at Arlington.

In the show that night, with Eunice dancing in Ruby's place, he seemed a different man. The *New York Times* noted that he stood in the spotlight "while the oldtimers out front sent a wave of applause that washed down from his shoulders all the loneliness for the stage

164

that Hollywood put there. He bounded around the stage and was all movement, and remained so for the next three hours."

On September 11, 1940, the curtains parted at the Shubert Theatre on Broadway. The prodigal son was welcomed home.

Brooks Atkinson of the *New York Times* was cheering with the rest of them. In his piece he wrote, "It's all right, folks. *Hold On to Your Hats* has arrived at the Shubert where it opened last evening, and the musical comedy season has begun with enormous gusto. This is the show that is bringing Al Jolson back to Broadway after an absence of nine years."

And then, coming right to the point, he went on, "If you think you have lost some of the old fondness for him during the interim, prepare for a pleasant surprise. He is a little older now, his hair is a little thinner. But none of the warmth has gone out of his singing and none of the gleam has departed from his storytelling.

"By great good fortune, he is also appearing in one of the funniest musical plays that have stumbled onto Broadway for years. Hold your sides as tightly as the title directs you to hold your hat."

He was pleased to welcome Martha Raye to the show with Jolson (a young lady named Joanne Dru, who was to do well in Hollywood a few years later, escaped his attention). Jolson and Raye, who were already working on the radio together, were, he said, a "just about perfect combination."

Jolson was "the magnetic minstrel who has a way with a song and the power to capture an audience instantly."

The New York *Post* joined in the rhapsodies.

"It took Al Jolson in person to remind us what an extraordinary entertainer he really is. His throaty hymns to Mammy may in memory have become easily resisted. But Mr. Jolson in person and in action is quite a different proposition. The people who can match his personality in our theatre are rare.

"He is at once host and performer, minstrel and crooner, hero and autobiographer."

Yes, Al had come home. Once more he was going to be the king. Once again he held his head up high when he walked down Broadway, as often as not with the show's new junior female lead, Jinx Falkenberg. There were rumors that they were about to marry, and Al was quite clearly flattered to be seen in public with her and the pack of dogs she usually had around her.

Once more, he enjoyed the tricks he had always played on Broadway. He threw away the book and managed to infuriate other people regularly.

He and Jessel crossed swords on the Shubert stage just as they had nine years before. This time it was over a chorus girl Jessel was taking out. Jessel had arranged to meet her after a performance of *Hold On to Your Hats*. He sat in the stalls and waited and waited.

While the rest of the audience ate up Jolson's onstage antics, and while everyone in the company was obviously delighted to just sit down at the back of the stage and listen, Jessel was going crazy. Finally, he marched onto the stage, took his girl by the hand, and walked out with her.

"I had a dame and Jolson was holding her up," he said. "What did he expect me to do?"

Jolson seemed generally happy. On December 28, 1940, a Los Angeles judge gave Ruby her final divorce decree and Al didn't mind any more. It had taken a year and two days. Jolson promised to pay her four hundred dollars a week for herself and Al, Jr.

Not long afterward, the financial settlement was changed to a lump sum payment of $50,000. Ruby had married a real estate magnate named John Lowe and Al, Jr.'s name was changed to John Lowe, Jr. Al did not want to fight it; he had been hurt too much already by the lack of affection from the boy. When he had asked the boy to come and see the show, his mother had forbidden him to do so.

To console himself, he took Jinx wherever he went—to the races, to Lindy's, to nightclubs. Rumors of romance proliferated and there was talk of a new Jolson marriage. But it never happened. *Hold On to Your Hats* was all the romance he wanted, and his loving audience appeared to be giving him all he needed.

He even managed to settle his own part of the suit with the Summit Hotel Company over the Shell broadcast by offering Leo Heyne, the proprietor, four tickets for the new show. As far as he was concerned, the radio libel had been forgotten, along with all the recent libels on his career.

Five months after the show's opening, Al caught a severe chill and

166

was rushed to the hospital with pneumonia. The show that had delighted him and thrilled Broadway had to close.

Jolson went to Florida in a state of acute depression. He insisted that Eppy stay with him, and talked to him night after night about his wasted life—just as he had with Harry Akst a year before.

"Success is great," said Al. "But does anyone love me?"

It floored Eppy. But it was a good question. In recent months, Al had felt the warmth of love from his audiences. But there was none for him in his own home.

In July 1941, *Hold On to Your Hats* was revived in Atlantic City. The local critics and the public loved the show. But Al thought his voice was leaving him. His old paranoia had returned. For the first time in his life, he installed microphones in a theatre in which he appeared.

He sang with all the old gusto—new songs like "Don't Let It Get You Down" and "She Came, She Saw, She Can-Canned," old ones like "Hello, My Baby" and "Alexander's Ragtime Band," and his own songs like "Mammy," "Sonny Boy," and "California, Here I Come." But if the will was there—and sometimes it wasn't—the ability was missing. Again he was taken ill and again the show was forced to close—this time for the last time.

Al was more unhappy than he had been for years. And to make things worse, Harry was suing him again. He claimed that back in 1934, Al had agreed to pay him $150 a week to keep him out of the theatre and away from the Jolson name. Al had paid for three years but had stopped in 1937.

Harry was down on his luck. He had been trying to sell insurance— with about as much success as he had had on the stage—and he needed the money. He claimed twenty-five thousand dollars.

Supreme Court Justice Samuel H. Hofstadter dismissed the claim summarily. He said it had been a verbal contract and was "repugnant to the statute of frauds, and could not be enforced in the courts."

But Al's victory did not make him any happier. Although the battle in the court was won, the fight in his family continued.

11

DON'T FORGET THE BOYS

THE WORLD'S Greatest Entertainer was fast becoming a subject for newspaper and magazine nostalgia columns.

He continued to go racing, make outrageous bets, and score incredible coups at the track. He was on the air regularly on his own show and as the guest attraction on other people's. But there were no more offers from Hollywood and when he suggested movie ideas to his friends in the big studios, no one took much notice. The only stage work offered to him was occasional benefit concerts, and these opportunities were fewer and further between, too.

What Jolson missed in idolatry from his theatre audiences he tried to make up for with his own bravado. He took it upon himself to be a father figure for other entertainers, some of whom appreciated it and some of whom did not.

He was once on a benefit bill with Cesar Romero when the Latin star's joke on stage fell completely flat. Jolson went up to him. "You didn't tell that story right, son," he said. "You should have had more feeling in it."

Ruby was never completely out of his mind, but he tried to find comfort in the pretty girls he always had around him. He always sent them flowers, booked a table at the best restaurant, and wore an immaculately pressed suit. The man who had been the toast of Broadway now looked like a thousand other successful businessmen. He gained a reputation as a charming escort. When he took a girl out more than once, he would tell her what dress to wear on their next date.

But out of the public eye, Jolson was miserable. At the Hillcrest Country Club, the predominantly Jewish haunt of the California show biz set, he would buttonhole the other members and engage them in conversation. But the club's regulars, like Jack Benny, noticed that he was frequently alone.

"You'd see him in a corner by himself, looking very dejected," Benny recalls. The Hillcrest and everyone else in the entertainment business was writing him off as a back number.

Early in December 1941, Al was in New York. He had some business plans, had seen his lawyer and talked to the people at CBS.

On Sunday mornings, he would go for long walks down Fifth Avenue, sometimes down Broadway, the scene of his old triumphs. He managed to believe it might be nice to be able to walk down Broadway on a peaceful morning, with few other people around and no one to bother him for an autograph.

On this particular Sunday morning, he asked Eppy to make him some coffee before he went out. While he waited, he turned on the radio in his hotel suite. He was just in time to hear the announcer break in with a news flash. Like everyone else listening to the radio that morning on December 7, 1941, he froze: The Japanese had attacked Pearl Harbor.

Al walked down the ghostly deserted streets and thought. He came back to the Sherry Netherlands Hotel and made the decision that was to profoundly affect his life. He picked up the telephone in his suite and called the White House.

Al Jolson was enlisting. And he was going to the top to do it. The operator put him through to Mr. Stephen Early, personal secretary to President Roosevelt.

"This is Al Jolson, Mr. Early," he said. "Those boys fighting the Japanese and Germans are going to need some entertaining. Well . . . I entertain better than anyone else. Get me to them."

At that point, Mr. Early was not able to offer much more than the familiar "Don't call us—we'll call you."

Al's agents, William Morris in New York and Abe Lastfogel in Los Angeles, were both given Mr. Jolson's personal instructions to get him overseas.

When Al made his annual visit to Washington to see his father—now in his late eighties—his stepmother and his halfsister and halfbrothers, they noticed how Al had changed. He was no longer the cocky success; he was visibly worried. They were also surprised to note just how frequently he came to Washington now.

But there were no gilt-edged invitations to the White House and he appeared more concerned with lobbying the congressmen than with seeing his family. On Capitol Hill, he talked to every senator who would see him. He called at all the Armed Services' headquarters, always with the same message: "My name's Jolson and I sing. Let me sing to the boys. I'll pay my own fare."

Finally, the War Department gave him the green light. A new group called the United Service Organizations (USO) had just been set up to send entertainers to the battle zones. Al would be the first to go under their plan.

One of the first places to which Jolson was shipped was Alaska. His old friend and accompanist Martin Fried went with him.

Jolson told *Variety* the broad facts of the trip: "We arrived in Anchorage at 9 P.M. Anchorage time and stayed at the Westward Hotel. When they told me to observe the blackout regulations and put my lights out, I had to laugh, for in this part of Alaska at midnight it is so light you can thread a needle on Main Street.

"We gave two performances in Anchorage—each to an audience of 1500 soldiers. Each show lasted an hour and I almost wore the knees out of my pants singing 'Mammy.' But 'Mammy' really got a workout the next day when Fried and I gave nine shows—each of an hour's duration."

What was missing from Jolson's own story of that Alaskan trip was the drama of this fifty-six-year-old in a private's uniform performing for over 1500 men at one sitting.

The troops had been told that a great star was coming to see them. Rumors swept the camp that it was going to be Lana Turner. Counter-rumors said it would be Dorothy Lamour. When Al Jolson was introduced the disappointment was practically audible. But he came on stage cheerfully enough. "Hello, boys—I'm Al Jolson," he called. "You'll see my name in the history books."

Someone laughed and then the laughter began to carry from seat to seat, from row to row. When he heard the troops laughing, Al laughed and proceeded to tell another joke—and then another. The jokes got dirtier, the laughter grew louder, and then someone called for a song.

Al gave them what they wanted. He chatted about home, told them what he thought of Hitler and Hirohito, and was rewarded with their whistling and applause.

For the first time in more than ten years, Al Jolson had found an audience. And the audience had discovered Al Jolson. Jolson had never had an audience quite like this one. As he joked, "You either stay here and listen to me or get buried by a hundred feet of snow. You've got no place else to go."

When the War Department heard how Jolson had gone over with the men, they asked the USO to provide more shows like it, and Al was asked to do as many of them as he could.

He had established a new relationship with his audiences. They liked him as much as he liked them. He appreciated it all the more because he thought he knew now, for the first time, what it meant to be unwanted. He refused to wear any insignia of rank, and insisted that at all his shows priority be given to enlisted men. "The officers can stand at the back—if there's room," he'd say.

He traveled from base to base by Jeep. In Europe, he would stop a couple of men in the street and say, "Hello, I'm Al Jolson from the USA. If you don't believe me, I'll sing for you." And he did. For two men on a street corner, there was a private performance of anything up to half a dozen numbers.

When General George Marshall heard about these performances, he decided that Al Jolson deserved campaign medals.

On that first Alaskan tour Jolson set a precedent he followed for the rest of the war. One young soldier called out to him, "Kiss my wife for me when you get back to New York, will you, Al?"

"I'll do better than that," Al called back. "I'll take her out to dinner. What's her name?"

The name was shouted and Al wrote it down with her telephone number. "Any more?" he called. And almost 1500 names and phone numbers were called out in chorus.

"I'll write down those I can—and I'll call them when I get back."

And he did. No sooner was he back in his New York hotel than he started his dialing operations: "Hello, Mrs. Schwartz? Sammy sends his love." "Oh, Mrs. Murphy? I was talking to your Michael yesterday. Yeh, in Alaska. My name? Oh, Al Jolson."

From Alaska he was sent to the steamy tropics of Trinidad to sing the same songs and tell the same jokes. He wore the same uniform all the time—although once he donned a tam o'shanter lent him by a Scottish soldier.

Al seemed happier than he had been for a long time. Harry Akst had joined him now as accompanist and it was clearly a happy arrangement. The two men had become fast friends in the prewar jungle of show business, and they had developed an almost telepathic relationship.

The two were in British Guiana when something happened to plunge Al into a deep depression. Akst was at the piano when Al called for requests at the first show. A Negro youngster with a Southern accent called out "Swanee!"

"You heard him, Professor," said Al. "Don't let's keep the man waitin'."

The piano sounded the first chords and Al got into the rhythm of the tune. He reached the chorus, "The folks up north will see me no more/When I get to that Swanee shore." But the word "shore" didn't sound right. Jolson did a second chorus just to convince himself—and the same thing happened. He just couldn't reach the high notes.

Back at the hotel where they were staying that night, Al decided it was all over. "I can't sing, Harry. And if I can't even sing 'Swanee' I'm finished."

"What yer talking?" Akst answered. "Sure you can sing—only the high notes are a bit difficult. So forget 'em. Who worries about high notes? Crosby doesn't—and he's doing all right. That sort of singing went out with vaudeville, anyway. Nobody wants high notes any more."

So Jolson decided to forget about the high notes and concentrate on a voice that was sounding decidedly better in the lower registers. His audiences didn't seem to mind at all.

Jolson and Akst toured all the U.S. bases in the Caribbean, getting hotter and stickier; but Al enjoyed every round of applause that came to him.

The USO flew him to England and Northern Ireland. Again the men were eating out of his hand. He told them what he had told their fathers about English beer—"it should have been put back into the horse"—and sang "Avalon," "April Showers," "Mammy," and whatever other songs they wanted to hear.

But he made it a practice never to sing "Sonny Boy"—unless he couldn't get away without singing it. "I found too many guys crying for their own Sonny Boys," he explained afterward. "And they've got enough to worry about."

But England was not the happiest place for Jolson during the war. The party of USO players of which he was a member also included Merle Oberon and Patricia Morrison. Before very long it was plain that they were not getting along too well together.

Also, London and the Savoy Hotel, where they were staying, were a bit too civilized for the new Jolson. By now he was used to living in a tin hut with just a bunk for a bed. In a luxury hotel, he liked to be mobbed by admirers. No one in England seemed to recognize him.

When he bumped into Ralph Reader and was able briefly to relive their days at the Winter Garden, his spirits picked up momentarily. "They were great days, English," Al said wistfully, "Great days." He feared he would never see their likes again.

Every evening, he could be seen pacing the floor of the hotel lobby, walking up and down, head bent down, hands in his pockets.

He entertained groups of civilians in an air-raid shelter. "You know why I'm in the shelter," he joked. "It's not that I'm scared—but I'd look awful silly singing 'Mammy' with just one arm."

The *New York Times* did a magazine piece about Jolson entertaining in England. He was always surrounded by cronies, the writer of the article, S. J. Woolf, noted. "It was as if he were on Broadway."

But "the Broadway atmosphere which pervaded the rooms did not dispel a feeling of nervous tension which surrounded the showman in khaki. 'The Jazz Singer' seemed more like a doughboy waiting the zero hour than a 'Sonny Boy' listening for the curtain call.

"There were few jokes in his talk. The comedian was playing a straight part. The lighter side of army life apparently had not made much of an impression upon him. For, like many other comedians, at heart, Jolson is serious and sentimental."

Jolson told Woolf why he had made the USO tours. "Some of the places where those fellows are stationed are not ideal summer or winter resorts," he said. "But the morale is great. As you go around you can't help comparing this bunch with the bunch in 1918.

"These fellows have their feet firmly on the ground. They aren't bluffing themselves. When I say this, I'm not handing out propaganda. I have run up against fellows who kicked because their food was not served on the finest china. I'd be lying if I said they were all as happy as larks. But all of them want to know how things are going at home and they all feel that it's the things at home that they are fighting for.

"When the war started, I felt it was up to me to do something, and the only thing I know is show business."

He went from England to Tunisia, from Tunisia to India, always with Harry Akst, always singing the same songs, and always making new friends. He seemed to spend his life overseas eating nothing but Spam. When he was home, he entertained Army, Navy, Marine, and Army Air Corps bases all over the country. Again the staple diet was Spam.

But on one occasion, the general hosting Jolson decided that Al couldn't be treated like that. He invited the entertainer to his house for a fried chicken dinner.

Before he left, he asked the general what his driver, Mickey Rosenberg, could expect. The general said that the driver would get the same as all the other men. "Spam?" Al asked. The general shrugged his shoulders. "I'm afraid, General," said Jolson, "Mickey has to have what I have." And he did.

In 1943, Jolson, who had been the first to go overseas and who had tried so hard to persuade other stars to follow him, was accused by an army newspaper of shying away from the China-Burma-India theatre of war. The paper, *CBI Roundup,* wrote that Jolson had avoided their area because "the going is too tough."

Jolson retorted, "It's a dirty lie. These guys don't know what they're talkin' about. I've just never been booked into that area."

But he came pretty close. He described Dakar as "the filthiest hole I have ever seen. Every known insect is there breeding with every known other insect."

Other places were cleaner, but not much easier on the Jolson constitution. He and Harry Akst flew into South Africa. In Natal they gave a series of concerts to military-hospital patients. Of the first of these, he said, "I sang all the songs in my repertoire—and then Harry played numbers requested by the sick kids—and how they liked it!" The concerts were long—but after a short break, he would repeat the performance for more patients.

"The dinner again with the men. Main dish—Spam! Oucha-ma-goucha! Awakened at 4 A.M. Raining cats and dogs. Ready to span the South Atlantic. But at the last minute the trip was canceled due to motor trouble. So I gave another show at the hospital for the shut-ins who missed yesterday's shows."

At dawn, Al and Harry finally took off for Dakar. "At 7 P.M., we had dinner. You guessed it—Spam. And for dessert, a substitute for quinine called Atalrin—little yellow pills which Akst mistook for soda mints. They gave him a bellyache, which so far is the only bellyaching he has done.

"Just had lunch—broiled Spam! We're going to do three shows tonight, one for the officers, one for the men, as well as a radio show. Yes, the work is tough and the going sometimes rough. But compared with the tremendous job the boys are doing, who are we to complain?"

When he was not singing, Jolson was buying war bonds. In 1942, he bought the first ticket for the premiere of *Yankee Doodle Dandy,* the George M. Cohan story with James Cagney—for twenty-five thousand dollars. Later in the year he bought another benefit ticket—this time for seventy thousand.

There could be little doubt of Al's devotion to the Allied cause. He regarded Hitler as the man who was personally exterminating not just the Jews, but the whole of civilization. He saw the Allied troops as knights in armor who were going to save humanity.

There wasn't a man he met who didn't want to win that war. This inspired him with the same infectious spirit that he himself had always conveyed to his Broadway audiences. He had never had a more reciprocal understanding with the people on the other side of the footlights. What he gave the people on Broadway was only a fraction of what he delivered in Dakar.

When he returned to the States between overseas tours, it became even clearer how successfully he was communicating with his audiences.

In October 1942, Colgate tooth powder launched a new *Al Jolson Show* on CBS. Jolson was decidedly unhappy about the series—but no more unhappy than the sponsors were about him. He constantly referred to the product he was supposed to plug as "toothpaste." He was being paid to publicize tooth powder; someone else had the toothpaste account. When he did name the cleansing agent correctly, he could sometimes be heard in off-mike—and certainly off-script—references to say other than the kindest things about it.

Carol Bruce, who provided the series with glamour and singing, also provided Jolson with company outside the studio. He gave her the full treatment. There were flowers and always a note telling her what to wear. But it never blossomed into a long-standing romance. Sometimes he was a little too fresh for her liking. Nor could he get Ruby out of his mind.

· Only when he was overseas was he visibly happy. He felt he had something in common with boys who had left their wives and sweethearts behind.

The day before Al flew out to Miami, where his plane was to leave for Algiers, he received an urgent message to telephone Mrs. Mamie Eisenhower. She had heard that Jolson was going to meet her husband and wondered if he would be kind enough to deliver a note for him.

"Sure, honey," he told her. "What do you want me to say?"

Mamie dictated the note, "Dear Ike: Al will give you this note and give you a sweet kiss from me—and also a swift kick, because you haven't written for so long."

When he arrived in Algiers, the singer was taken to the general's headquarters immediately.

"What do you know, Al?" asked Eisenhower.

"I've got a message for you, General," he replied, and showed him the note.

"Well," said Ike, "when you get back home give Mrs. Eisenhower back that kiss. As for the other. . . ." He bent down, lifted up the flap of his jacket, and instructed Jolson to carry out his wife's bidding.

On this trip, life was harder than it had ever been for Jolson. In Sicily and Italy, he followed the advancing Allied troops through "hell and mud." He made more tours of the other European bases. But he was warmly rewarded.

In 1943, the *New Yorker* magazine reported in its diary, "We've just heard from a soldier who was fortunate enough to be on hand at one of the entertainments presented before the troops in Ireland by Al Jolson and some of the other performers from the States. Jolson, our soldier reports, concluded the entertainment with what was obviously considered to be the best number in his repertoire.

"It was 'Brother, Can You Spare a Dime?'—and Jolson gave it, as the show people say, everything."

On Jolson's fourth overseas trip—this time he covered forty-two thousand miles and entertained over four hundred thousand American troops—he gave up to four shows a day.

He was the talk of the entertainment industry, much of which was content to keep him as far away from the home market as possible. The big money was in films, and films were definitely not being made with the men at the front in mind. Some of the younger singers, anxious to keep their reputations intact, went out on one short USO trip and came back quickly, before the people at home had forgotten them.

When one famous Hollywood actor had to be commissioned as a captain before he would leave to entertain at military bases, George Jessel quipped, "If that's the basis on which commissions are granted, then Al Jolson should be commissioned as a fort."

In the South Pacific, Jolson sang, "Is It True What They Say About Dixie?" and had boys from the Deep South begging for more. In New Guinea, he sang "Give My Regards to Broadway," and one of the soldiers in the audience wrote home, "As he sang, I felt as though I were back in New York. Only a short time ago, New York seemed as if it were a million miles away. Then along comes Al Jolson and he drops the city right into my lap—Empire State Building and all—boom!"

His audiences adored him. When he had first gone to a military camp he had been greeted with derision. Now, the men in the forward positions knew what to expect. For them, he did not even have to sing—although he did. Just being with him was enough.

In North Africa, the men out front begged for autographs. He signed everything: official passes and even the five-franc scrip notes.

The only thing one young soldier could find for Jolson to sign was an American ten-dollar bill. Al took it and then gave it back to the youngster unsigned. "Son, my autograph isn't worth tying up this much dough. Invest it in war bonds." He fished into his pocket, found a five-franc note, scribbled his name all over its face, and gave it to the soldier. "Here, Sergeant," he said. "This is on the house."

Jolson made speech after speech, begging the entertainers who had so far held back to come out and perform for the troops. "Quit the Battle of the Brown Derby," he implored, referring to the Beverly Hills restaurant where the stars would meet to discuss the war and their jobs.

There was a new respect for Jolson among everyone who knew of his work. When they joked about him, and particularly about his age, it was all in good spirits—and with no small measure of admiration.

On a brief trip home between his Far East tours, loneliness struck him again. Because he and Harry Akst shared the same hotel suite, they gave up the privacy both needed from time to time. Akst realized too late how much he needed this privacy. He was phoning his wife when he caught Jolson, sitting in a corner of the room looking out the window, with tears rolling down his cheeks.

"What's the matter, Jolie?" the pianist asked.

"Nothing," Al replied. "It's just that I realize you've got someone to come home to. Who've I got? Who cares whether I live or die? Not a soul in the world."

On occasions like that, Jolson realized how much he needed to get back to his audience as soon as possible.

Another trip was being planned when, in October 1943, Al stood in a hotel lobby in New York reading a newspaper. Suddenly, the type in front of him became blurred, the room started spinning, and everything went blank.

Several days later he woke up in a hospital, shielded from the rest of the room by the loose plastic covering of an oxygen tent.

He had picked up two bugs overseas. One was a recurrence of his old trouble—audience fever. The other was malaria. Malaria won out. Before long, it had turned into pneumonia, and for more than two weeks Al was on the danger list.

After being discharged from the hospital, he felt so shaky that he wondered if he would ever get up before an audience again. Eppy, Harry Akst, and Martin Fried were with him.

"Get me on the next plane to Europe," he shouted at them. "I've got to get back to my boys." They gave Al a glass of lemonade and told him to relax.

There weren't going to be any more overseas tours, they insisted, and Al had better accept it. What they didn't realize was that they were dealing with Jolson. He had discovered again what it was like to be worshiped by an audience, and it was a religion he didn't want to die out too quickly.

While it was quite clear that Al wanted to continue to work, it was equally clear that the old openings were not available to him any more. There was the occasional radio appearance, but no one was offering Al the chance to sing before live audiences, or even before the cameras. Hollywood just didn't want to know about him as a performer.

"Take it easy now," the studio bosses told him. "Enjoy yourself."

But that was something Al Jolson had never really learned how to do on his own, without an audience.

He became more and more unhappy. He knew he was weak, but he knew, too, that he would become even weaker if he didn't have a chance to recharge his batteries soon. The fact that he had no social life only made him feel doubly inadequate.

At the Hillcrest Country Club, he searched for new friends. Here the Jolson ingenuity succeeded where his jokes had failed. The club was in an uproar about the fact that the war had struck from the menus their principal delight, sturgeon. Most of the club members, like Benny, Burns, and Jessel, were sturgeon devotees. So was Jolson. But only Jolson knew how to break the embargo the State of California had imposed on the import of this delicacy.

Al had a friend in New York who could get sturgeon through to California. Every week, a parcel would arrive at the Hillcrest in a refrigerated truck addressed to Mr. Al Jolson.

"Want a piece of sturgeon?" Al would call and his friends would come running.

"We knew when Jolie was doing well again," Burns joked. "We didn't get any more sturgeon."

At last, Al found himself a job. An old admirer, Harry Cohn, head of Columbia studios, invited him to become a producer. At that point Columbia was making a fortune for itself with Rita Hayworth pictures.

Al was told he was to work on the new Hayworth picture, *Burlesque.* He was given the title producer and was advised that he was to supervise everything that went into the film. But before long, he realized he was producer in name only.

Columbia also hinted he was going to work on his own life story, but then were not ready to commit themselves.

Sometimes, he just sat alone in the studio, thinking. His depressions were frequently acute. At other times, he was able to laugh at his predicament.

"I had an office with couches and beds in it," he told a group at lunch at the Hillcrest. "For months, nobody called me. One day, the phone finally rang and I answered, all excited. A voice said, 'Is that Shapiro, the plumber?' "

With more than a touch of irony he told them about the big studio happening of the day. "One of the other producers liked his men to laugh at all the jokes he told. And every one of those employees always did. Except today, when one man didn't laugh. 'Why aren't you laughing?' the producer asked the man. 'Oh,' he replied, 'I'm leaving on Saturday.' "

If Jolson could have told Harry Cohn he was leaving Columbia that Saturday, he would have been equally delighted. The only trouble was that he had nowhere else to go.

He called the USO offices again and demanded that they find him more work. "I want to go overseas and I want to go soon," he thundered. But he had to agree he could never pass the rigorous medical inspections that were now compulsory for anyone who wanted to play at bases abroad.

"How about touring our hospitals?" he was finally asked. Al jumped at the chance.

For a start there would be a tour of the West and of the Deep South—and again, Al was happy. He was doing the only work he ever wanted to do—singing to an audience who really wanted to see and hear him.

He felt he was helping the sick boys more than their doctors were. And he was finding new admirers in the nursing and medical staff, too. At the army hospital in Hot Springs, Arkansas, he was mobbed by autograph hunters after his performance. There was nothing new in that.

But on this occasion, one of his admirers made a deep impression.

Twentieth Century Fox

Reliving memories—of his own childhood in the synagogue and of the film that made history. Singing Kol Nidre on the Day of Atonement. (From *Hollywood Cavalcade*, a 1939 re-enactment of the famous scene in *The Jazz Singer*.)

Top: He even had a sparring match with Jack Dempsey. *Bottom:* Charlie Chaplin with Jolson.

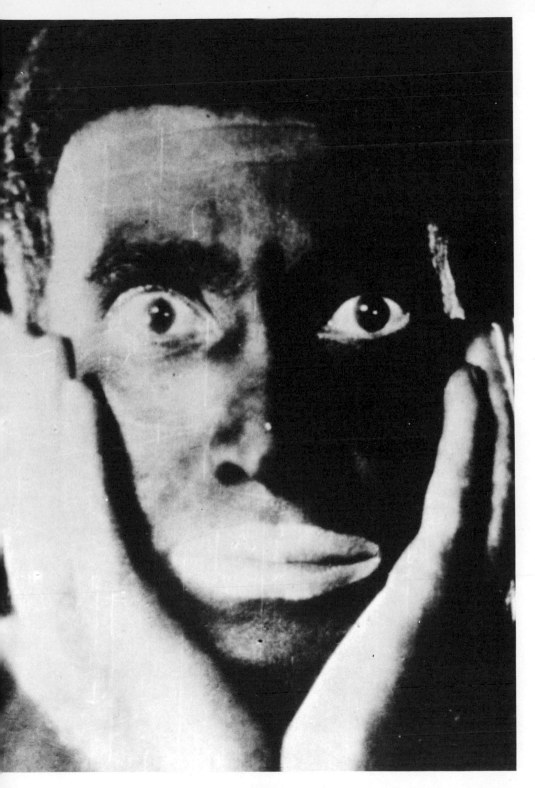

The Jolson the world remembers.

Larry Parks made up for the title role in *The Jolson Story*.

The two Jolsons: Al "Larry Parks" Jolson and Al "Asa Yoelson" Jolson.

Jolson the radio star. *Top left:* With Humphrey Bogart. *Top right:* With Decca Records chief, Jack Kapp, and Bing Crosby. *Bottom left:* With Peggy Lee. *Bottom right:* With Dinah Shore.

Jolson with Asa, Jr., 1949: "That's my boy!"

Top: The last month. Jolson in Korea, 1950. The GIs loved him—and so did the United Nations. As a tribute to his work, he is presented with a UN flag (bottom).

12

THAT WONDERFUL GIRL OF MINE

SHE WASN'T exactly petite. Nor was she tall. Her dark hair fell down to her shoulders. When she smiled in the crowd gathering around Jolson that night late in 1944, there was something about her that made Al smile back.

"That was a cute little one," Al told Harry Akst as they got into their khaki-colored staff car waiting outside the hospital.

"We'd better get some gas," said Akst, and directed the car toward the filling station just outside the hospital grounds. When the car stopped, Al got out to stretch his legs and get a breath of air.

The colonel in charge of the hospital was also at the filling station, and Jolson asked him to authorize a new batch of gasoline coupons to cover the next stage of the journey. As they talked, Al noticed the brunette he had seen in the crowd a few minutes earlier. She had an autograph book in her hand, as she came over to where the two men stood.

"Would you write your name for me, Mr. Jolson?" she asked.

It was as though she had asked him to sing "April Showers."

"Sure, honey," Jolson replied, and gave her the sort of big wink he usually reserved for his audiences.

"What shall I write?" he asked her.

"Oh, just say 'To Erle.' "

"How's that?"

"Erle—E-R-L-E."

Harry called from the driver's seat of their car, "We're ready, Al."

"Bye, honey," Jolson said as he walked to his car.

"Nice kid," said Harry as they drove off. "Sure was," Al mused. "Erle. . . ."

He talked about her all the way to Texas, the next stop on their tour. When he checked into his hotel, her image was still before him. He and Harry played cards but still he couldn't get her out of his mind. "Funny thing," he told his pianist friend. "I haven't thought about Ruby all day."

The two men went to bed about three o'clock in the morning, but Jolson couldn't sleep. Finally, after about an hour of tossing and turning, he switched on his bedside light, and dialed the long-distance operator.

"Get me the Eastman Hospital Annex at Hot Springs, Arkansas," he told her. "Personal call to the base commander."

A call from Al Jolson was important enough to be passed to the colonel at any time, even in the middle of the night.

"What is it, Mr. Jolson?" the colonel asked sleepily.

"Sorry to wake you, Colonel," Al replied. "But you see it's like this. That pretty gal we were talkin' to last night. Think I might have a job for her in pictures. What was her name?"

The colonel said he didn't know. "But I'll get it for you. Want to hang on?"

"Please," said Jolson.

Within a short time, the colonel had his answer.

"Mr. Jolson? The girl's name is Erle Galbraith. She's an X-ray technician out here. A civilian."

"Thanks, Colonel," Al said, jotting down her name on the pad beside his telephone. "Yes—Erle." At last Al was able to sleep.

When he awoke the next morning, Al hurried through dressing and eating his breakfast, and got to the writing desk in his hotel suite.

"Dear Erle," he wrote, "I think your face is a natural for the flickers." And he offered her a stock contract at one hundred dollars a week. Just to put the record straight, he emphasized he was not in love with her—which wasn't quite true.

He heard nothing for several days, although he still couldn't get Erle out of his mind. Then he received a call from a Los Angeles lawyer, asking if he could come and see Jolson.

An appointment was made at the Beverly Hills Hotel. When the lawyer arrived, he shook hands with Jolson and told him how much he had always admired his work.

"You haven't come here to tell me that, have you?" Al asked. "What do you want?"

The lawyer said he had some dear friends in Arkansas by the name of Galbraith. They had asked him to call on the singer to ask for more details about the offer he had made their daughter. They didn't know he had become a movie producer but, even if they had, it wouldn't have been enough. Old men who made that sort of proposition usually had a different course of action in mind.

"Of course I'm serious," Jolson told the lawyer.

"Well, Mr. Jolson," came the reply, "it would be *most* unfortunate if you were throwing a curve."

The language was more polite than Johnny Irish had used nearly twenty years before, but somehow the message seemed the same. It didn't worry Al any more now than it had then.

His mind was made up. He wrote to Erle and told her to come straight out to the West Coast. In the letter he told her exactly which train to catch. The train arrived in Los Angeles eight hours late, but Al was there to meet her.

A group of Columbia executives were hovering in the background at the same time. This girl, he had told them, was going to be the new Rita Hayworth—"and with a voice like an angel."

When she stepped down onto the station platform, Al was delighted. She was as beautiful as he had remembered her. The studio man next to him smiled appreciatively, as Al nudged him in the ribs.

"Hello, honey," Al said as he welcomed her and gave her a peck on the cheek. "How have you been?"

"Mistah Jolson," she replied, "Ah've been just fine."

The man from Columbia looked at Al and Al looked at him. Al hadn't remembered at all how this "angel's" voice sounded. Hearing it now, he knew what Harry Cohn would say when he heard it.

A screen test had been arranged for the following day and Cohn was waiting to see it. He respected Jolson's judgment and knew a man of his experience would be unlikely to sell him a lemon. The test turned out the way Al expected—Erle had a face made for the movies, and a voice that quite obviously wasn't.

"I was quite floored by that Southern drawl," Al said later. "But I had only to take one look at that kisser, that little face, and those big dark eyes. I knew with a dialect like that she would never stand a chance on the screen, though. So I thought I'd better marry the poor kid."

To make her feel better, Jolson used his influence to line up a couple of small nonspeaking parts at Twentieth Century-Fox. And then he popped the question.

"Sure, I'm old enough to be your grandfather," he told her. "But I love yer." Erle was twenty-one. Al was sixty.

As he expected, she turned him down. But she mentioned the proposal to her parents, who were prosperous, respected, conservative people in Little Rock. For their Erle to marry a singer who was older than they were themselves was quite out of the question.

While the Galbraiths were discussing the proposal, Al Jolson was being rushed to hospital. His malaria had struck again, this time more seriously than before.

The doctors decided there was only one way to save his life—although they were making no guarantees. They would have to cut out a large portion of his left lung. To reach the lung, two ribs had to be chopped away.

Recuperating several days later, Al pondered what effect the operation would have on his career as a singer.

"I'll never sing again," he told his nurse. He refused to see anyone. The thought that he would never sing again was worse than a death sentence. His doctor said he would pull through, but to Al it seemed a promise of living death.

He just lay in the big white hospital bed and thought about the past, about the future, and about what might have been. He decided not to think about Erle.

When he eventually condescended to allow visitors in his room, Eppy, Harry Akst, and his half brothers came to offer good cheer, but nothing any of them said could bring him out of his depression. Another visitor managed it.

Erle walked into the hospital room, sat by his bed, and gradually got him to smile. She also managed to bring him back to thinking about a future that perhaps would not be as cloudy as he had feared. Before she left the room, Al had proposed again—and this time, she had accepted.

There was still a drainage tube in his back and he had to have injections. "But I felt like a kid of sixteen," he recalled afterward. "I knew I was head over heels in love."

Al went to Palm Springs to convalesce. There, he wrote a letter to Mr. Galbraith asking for his daughter's hand in marriage. The father's letter came back by special delivery. "You are old enough to be my daughter's father," it said. The idea was preposterous.

Al told Erle what her father had written. "I'll go home and see him," she promised. "I can twist Dad around my finger."

On March 23, 1945, just as World War II was coming to an end, Al and Erle were married by a justice of the peace at Quartzite, Arizona. This time, Moses Yoelson was not told of his son's marriage. The cantor was ninety years old and his own health was failing rapidly.

The Jolsons took a bigger suite at the Palm Springs hotel where Al had been convalescing. But Erle wanted a real home. She heard about a ranch-style house on the market that might have been built especially for them, it was so beautiful.

"It was," said Al. The house, which was being vacated by Don Ameche, was the one Al had built after his marriage to Ruby. As Erle said, it was ideal for them—although the memories were at first painful for Al. But there was something about his new young wife that brought those memories into clearer perspective.

Ruby had had her own glittering career. Erle didn't want a career. She was only interested in being with Al by the swimming pool during the day, or knitting socks for him as he sang to her in the evenings.

"Why don't you sing again in the movies?" she asked him.

"But I can't sing any more—you know that."

"You're singing now, aren't you?"

"Yeh, but this isn't the sort of singing I used to do on the stage. I need strength for that."

She continued to knit and Al continued to hum. Could he have the strength to start singing professionally again?

Without Erle's knowing, he had been doing some experimenting with his voice. Somehow it wasn't the same voice he used to have. It wasn't just that he couldn't hit the high notes. After the operation, it had vanished. Now, though, it was coming back—at least four keys deeper than it had been before surgery. Although he wouldn't tell Erle this, he liked the sound of his "new" voice.

193

Milton Berle made Al the star guest on his weekly radio show and for the first time the new Jolson voice was heard in public—singing the old songs.

"I'm not too strong now," Al told his host, "but they've promised me when I'm feeling a little better they'll let me go to Tokyo to sit in Emperor Hirohito's palace. And there, I'll sing 'Mammy.'

"Of all the wonderful audiences I've played to in my whole life, the ones that gave me the biggest thrills were thousands of miles away from Broadway, in the jungles of the South Pacific and in the hell and mud of Italy."

He meant it and the audience knew he meant it. They liked what they heard and the way Jolson sang his songs.

When he returned home he asked Eppy to try to arrange some work for him—a picture or two and perhaps his own radio series again. Radio was just right, not too strenuous, just the kind of work he could do.

Erle agreed. "If you're well enough," she said, "do what you really like doin'."

But Eppy came back empty-handed. Kraft was looking for a new star for the Music Hall Jolson had introduced years ago, but they said politely they didn't think Al was the man for the job. He wasn't well and they didn't want to overtax him. Besides, Crosby and Sinatra and young Perry Como were the voices bringing in the money now.

It was all true. Every radio station broadcast the cool, gentle, crooning voices of these singers who had hardly been old enough to talk when Jolson was packing the crowds into the Winter Garden.

No one was giving Jolson the same chance. Every approach was rebuffed.

Eventually, however, Warner Brothers came to the rescue—but with something rather different from what Jolson was hoping for. They were planning a biographical picture based on the life of George Gershwin and wanted Al to play himself singing "Swanee."

He was happy to accept—and played the role with all the energy he could summon up. When it was all over, he refused to take a fee.

The film was called *Rhapsody in Blue*. Jolson's part was a cameo, and although it gave him a certain satisfaction to appear in blackface again, to stand before a camera once more, and to sing that song another time, it wasn't quite the same as being invited to take on a new challenge. He wanted to set the Mississippi on fire again and singing

"Swanee" in a biographical film about someone else wasn't really the way to do it.

Decca Records invited Al to record "Swanee" for them. On the flip side he recorded "April Showers." Although there was a lot of pep in the "Swanee" recording—possibly a little too much (it may have been deliberately speeded up by the engineers)—the arrangement of "April Showers" did neither Jolson nor the song very much good.

It was Al's first commercial recording in twelve years and it seemed destined to flop, even though he had been promised five cents for every copy sold.

No one wanted Al Jolson as a star in his own right, and it broke his heart. Even more disappointing, he wasn't showing Erle what he really could do.

"Tell her how great I was," he'd implore visitors to their home. But, although Erle constantly assured him that she did know just what a sensation he had been, he was convinced that she needed reconfirmation.

He couldn't even find a spot on a benefit bill—the kind of show producers would at one time have gone down on their hands and knees to ask him to appear in. By everyone's standards, Al Jolson was washed up. Erle tried to help but, all too often, to no avail.

Then, suddenly, everything changed. The renaissance came unexpectedly, just when Jolson seemed resigned to his life of obscurity.

13

ME AND MY SHADOW

IT WAS in 1943 that the idea first hit Sidney Skolsky.

Jolson saw the columnist sitting ringside at a boxing match. He walked over to where Skolsky sat and, before the columnist could say anything, hit him on the jaw. Al told him that was just the sort of treatment he could expect for printing such scandalous stories about him.

Skolsky insisted that someone else had written the item. It hadn't even appeared in any of the papers that carried his column. Al was deeply apologetic. It was, he agreed, a case of mistaken identity.

Oddly enough, the confrontation seemed only to increase Skolsky's long-standing idolatry of Jolson. He had always been known as one of those writers on the Hollywood scene who toyed with vague notions and turned them into wild extravaganzas. He didn't merely have an idea, he played with it, rolled it around, and shaped it.

His idea was to adapt the story of Al Jolson to the screen and produce a film that would create interest and enthusiasm all over the free world. The story of Jolson's life had everything a picture needed—color, escapism, and music. It was, Skolsky believed, his best idea to date.

There were also none of the problems one frequently met when filming the life of a living person. The kids who bought movie tickets knew no more about Jolson than they did about the private life of General Tojo, so all sorts of liberties could be taken with the facts without disturbing anyone.

Nor, he reasoned, could there be any problem about getting a younger actor to play the part. Jolson had not, after all, been seen on the screen for so many years.

So Skolsky—newspaper and magazine columnist and screenwriter—

started his determined effort to make his own idea a reality. Everywhere he met resistance: Metro, Warners, Twentieth Century-Fox, United Artists—all gave him the same answer: "Save your breath and we'll save our dollars."

The polite ones used a phrase Jolson himself had coined a generation before: "You're daffy." The less polite used altogether different language. Warner Brothers thought the suggestion was just about the most ridiculous idea that had yet been put on a desk in the executive suite.

Skolsky was not merely laughed off the Warner lot at Burbank; he was positively ridiculed. The moguls chuckled over their champagne glasses at the stupidity of the idea and secretaries spilled coffee on the memos that rejected it.

Working in the Warner studios as an assistant to veteran Broadway writer Mark Hellinger, Skolsky could see the Warner reaction at first hand. Jolson had just made his guest appearance in their own *Rhapsody in Blue;* as far as they were concerned, he was a has-been. An interesting has-been perhaps, but a has-been just the same.

Jolson went virtually unnoticed in *Rhapsody in Blue.* More than one theatre running the film billed him as "Al Johnson," and the record he had cut of "Swanee" sold barely enough at the music shops to cover the cost of waxing.

Only Columbia Pictures showed any initial interest at all in Skolsky's idea. And that was only when Jolson was a producer for them. When Skolsky came back to them with the idea, Harry Cohn did not laugh. He merely puffed at his huge cigar, muttered a few obscenities, and showed Skolsky the door. But that was just what the writer had expected.

Cohn was polite to no one. He was the man who had made Grace Moore an overnight hit with *One Night of Love,* and who had turned a seventeen-year-old dancer called Margarita Cansino into a star named Rita Hayworth. Hollywood respected him because of his undoubted know-how. Everyone at Columbia seemed to fear him; most hated him. He had the reputation for being the hardest man in a city that fed studio chiefs on the broken-down careers of lesser mortals. A onetime vaudeville singer who turned song plugger on the way to becoming a Hollywood producer, he was known to be able to reduce some of the toughest villains in town to tears. A smile from Cohn, said some, was worth more than a contract from anyone else.

What Skolsky did not realize was that Harry Cohn was also a Jolson devotee. In all his years in show business, there had been only one artist who could make Cohn sit back, smile, and occasionally cry—and that was Al Jolson. While underlings bowed and scraped to Cohn, Jolson was his idol.

He had liked Skolsky's idea more than he intended to let on when it was first brought to his notice. But there was one thing he had learned very quickly in business: never appear too eager.

Three months went by without word from Cohn. But then the phone on Skolsky's desk rang. What followed became one of the most celebrated conversations in Hollywood folklore. It was the unmistakable gruff Cohn tone, "Get your ass over here. You're working on the Jolson picture."

As Cohn hung up, Skolsky smiled. The fight was on between two men, columnist and studio boss, who shared only one thing—an admiration for Al Jolson.

Cohn's No. 2 man, Sidney Buchman, was also dedicated to Jolson as much as he was to the business of making films. Born in Duluth, Minnesota, educated at Oxford, Buchman had worked at the Old Vic in London. He had seen Jolson entertain and became a one-man fan club.

Buchman had written some of the big Hollywood money-makers like Frank Capra's *Mr. Smith Goes to Washington,* which made James Stewart a top name, and had been largely responsible for the success of the Cornel Wilde film about Chopin, *A Song to Remember.* He was to play no small part in making Jolson's tunes songs to remember, too.

Only one thing remained before the idea could really take off: they had to talk to Jolson himself. In the midst of their long negotiations, the man at the center of it all had been left almost totally in the dark.

Occasionally a rumor filtered through to his country retreat, but since it seemed to be no more than a rumor, it only fed his constant depression. Jolson knew that Hollywood manufactured rumors as efficiently as it made films—only a thousand times faster. And the movie capital's rumors were frequently a thousand times more extravagant than the plot of any picture.

Jolson was in New York when he found out it was more than a rumor. He had a call from Jack Cohn, the producer's older and generally estranged brother, who handled all the company's business deals in the East.

To Jolson it was as though it were 1912 again, with Jake Shubert asking him to play the lead in the Winter Garden's new show. Al was already choosing the costumes he was going to wear and the songs he was going to sing. He would be in Hollywood, he said, as soon as the reservations could be made.

Only once did he have doubts, when he began wondering whether any other living entertainer had ever had his life story filmed before. He remembered *Yankee Doodle Dandy* and breathed a sigh of relief. Yes, George M. Cohan had seen his film biography—and died a month later. Jolson swallowed and tried to forget that detail.

In the 1940s, there was only one comfortable way to travel to California from New York—train. Jolson had the best private compartment on the journey. The second best was booked by Jack Warner. The man who had turned down flat any possibility of Warner Brothers' handling the story of this "has-been" was furious that another studio had beat him to it.

Now he offered Jolson two hundred thousand dollars for the story rights and specified that he would put the whole production in the hands of Michael Curtiz, who had done such a brilliant job with *Yankee Doodle Dandy*.

Sure, Jolie could play the lead himself—after all, wasn't he a major stockholder in Warner Brothers? It was obviously the right thing to do. His company, he stressed, had a vested interest in a successful·film. And, Warner swore, there wasn't a grain of truth to the rumor that the project had once been offered to his studio and turned down.

When Jolson booked in at the Beverly Hills Hotel, Skolsky was there waiting for him. Despite his recent association with Columbia, the singer had only one word to describe Columbia—"crappy."

He was more and more attracted to the possibility of repeating the success of *The Jazz Singer* in the studio where both he and the film had made history.

Jolson and Skolsky discussed the idea of the new picture as they sat beside the hotel's swimming pool. Al had taken a small room at the hotel when he first arrived at Beverly Hills. Shortly after his first discussion with Skolsky, he and Erle had moved into a bungalow on the grounds. The idea was worth seeing through in comfort.

Jolson admitted that he liked Skolsky's approach when he first contacted Cohn. "Everybody's making biographical films," he told Cohn; "but no one's done one of the king."

199

He and Skolsky discussed the important parts of his life and which ones would make the best film story. From day to day, Jolson changed the stories, contradicting himself and complicating matters infinitely. As far as he was concerned, there was nothing particularly sacred about the truth.

Skolsky stressed Columbia's determination to make this the big picture of the year. There would be no risk of its being buried in a pile of celluloid and gathering dust as it probably would at a bigger studio like Warner Brothers. On Poverty Row, where Columbia was born and expanded into Sunset Boulevard, there was no such risk. For them, there was always one Big Picture, and that was going to be the Jolson film. Besides, Jolson could have half the film's profits.

It was that final clause which undoubtedly clinched things. "Jolson a failure?" Impossible. If anyone had any doubts, Jolson had none at all.

The Jazz Singer had made him a fortune in a deal that at the time had seemed no more certain. More important at this point, here was the chance to make everyone sit up and take notice, the chance he had been waiting for. Not only would he make good money, he would also be doing what he loved most: Jolson would be singing. A new public would be hearing the new Jolson voice.

He believed that that voice, with its individual sound, would be better received now than it had been before. When Jolson first sang in a high tenor, that was how the audiences wanted it. Even Rudy Vallee and Bing Crosby sang that way when they first stood before the public. But now Jolson had a more robust, deeper style that seemed to be what the bobby-soxers were asking for. And he believed he had something that the new generation had never heard before.

He began to build a new picture of the future. Here was the chance, at last, to sign autographs again—something which he never enjoyed but regarded as a necessary symbol of success; to meet youngsters at ballparks or in theatre lobbies without having to say, "Ask your parents if they remember me," and wonder if in fact any of them did remember.

But there was still more than a little of the old Jolson business sense left in him. He refused to sign his contract with Columbia until certain amendments had been made. In addition to half the film's profits, he wanted twenty-five thousand dollars for recording the songs in the picture.

Cohn balked, muttered more obscenities—and then imagined the scene in New York when his brother Jack heard the asking price. Jack, he knew, would say no. The thought of upstaging his brother and proving that he had the better business sense convinced Harry to agree to Al's terms. The twenty-five-thousand-dollar clause was added and the picture was on.

Cohn and Jolson had dinner together to celebrate and to talk about old times, the days when the man now known as King Cohn could hardly afford the price of a seat in a theatre where Jolson was playing. The shape the picture would take, or any idea of who was going to play the role, had not yet been discussed.

Rumors about the movie were spreading through Hollywood and the people who thought they counted on Sunset Boulevard were still laughing. And Jolson smiled as broadly as they laughed. But as the doubts multiplied, they caught up with him, and he started doubting, too.

The girl who had picked him up whenever he was down, who dearly wanted to see him on top the way he had told her he had once been, shuddered at the thought of a possible letdown.

"This is it, baby," he told Erle. "I'm going to be great again."

"Sure you are, Al," she promised. She had realized soon after their wedding that feeding his ego was going to be as important as feeding his stomach. Now the honeymoon was over. She saw his moments of depression and wanted to see him on top of the world again. Perhaps the time would come when he would not have to beg friends to tell her how great he had been.

Only a few days later, it looked as though everyone's doubts had turned out the way they either hoped or feared, depending on whether or not they were on Harry Cohn's payroll. Jolson's malaria returned with a vengeance. He was rushed to the Cedars of Lebanon Hospital and once more placed in an oxygen tent.

The news was withheld from Cohn by the people who knew they kept their jobs only as long as he kept his temper. When he did eventually hear of Jolson's illness, the patient was already a little better. Cohn and an aide rushed to the hospital—but not before Jolson had been warned that they were on their way.

When the men from Columbia walked through the door, Jolson was sitting up with a broad grin on his face and threw his arms out wide in a "Mammy" gesture.

Cohn walked straight up to him like a consulting surgeon—except that he did not bother to remove his big cigar. He took the Havana out of his mouth and, dripping ash on the bed sheets, looked deep into the patient's eyes. "You gonna die on me?" he asked. Even Jolson was speechless. "Can you still sing?"

That was all Al needed. He jumped out of bed, pushed aside a medicine chest, and sang "April Showers" as tunefully as his one lung would allow. He had never tried so hard with a song in his life.

Cohn left him, muttering, "The guy's gonna die, the guy's gonna die." For the next three days, Jolson was back in the oxygen tent. But the plans for the picture went ahead.

When he got home again, Jolson saw his work cut out for him; he had to show Harry Cohn and Sidney Buchman that he could still sing. Buchman, who had now taken over executive control of the picture, was the one who really counted.

Al suspected there were spies everywhere. He wondered if the postman was really a Columbia scout sent to check up on his voice. The delivery boy, he feared, might be one of Cohn's assistants, anxious for the break that would make his own career at the same time that it smashed Jolson's.

If these were just hallucinations, they had the right effect. Al began to sing wherever he went. He chanted the old numbers in the kitchen just as he always had in the bath. Every guest who came over for an evening drink was treated like a Winter Garden audience. There was a twinkle in his eye that seemed to say: "I'm not doing this just for you, you know. This is just a preview of how big I'm gonna be again. You see if I'm not."

When Skolsky first suggested the film idea, Jolson had not seemed too concerned that he might not be playing himself. As time went by, he grew more and more worried about the idea. Cohn, for whom a pretty girl or a handsome young man represented thousands and perhaps millions of dollars, was not prepared to entertain the idea of Jolson as Jolson in the film. Jolson had literally signed away his life, and there was not much he could do about it. The singer wished he had dealt with Warner Brothers and he told Cohn so.

Then Cohn amazed everyone around him by announcing that although Jolson couldn't play the part himself—that was final—he could have a say in who did play it. Al would not have a veto, but as an adviser to the production team, he would certainly have a say.

Hollywood wondered aloud: Who is going to play Jolson?

Day after day, actors came to be tested. Because they were to play Jolson, this could be no ordinary screen test. It was a matter of endurance as well as of acting ability. The chosen actor had to be able to walk like Jolson, dance like Jolson, and make love to an audience as Jolson had. He also had to look as though he were singing.

The first one to be tested for the role was a thirty-one-year-old actor who had been on the Columbia payroll since 1941. Jolson fidgeted in his seat before the lights in the projection room went down. When the fellow in blackface came out on the stage and tried to imitate him, he got up from his seat and stormed out of the room.

"You tryin' to kill me or somethin'?" he shouted to Cohn. "Fellers all over the world try to imitate Jolson. But are any of them like Jolson? Is that one a Jolson? He doesn't look right. He isn't right. Nobody can be right but Jolson himself."

Columbia began learning what a Jolson sulk was like. It got steadily worse with every subsequent test he saw. Well-established actors as well as newcomers who had done practically nothing came and went. Jolson hated them all, and made sure that everyone knew it.

The old Jolson habit of talking about himself in the third person was resurrected. "You can't do it," Harry Cohn was told. "There's only one Jolson."

But Cohn went on with the tests. More names were considered. There was Richard Conte, whose portrayals of hard-boiled gangsters were still to come. There was José Ferrer, who at that time had no more thought of playing Toulouse-Lautrec than he had of marrying Rosemary Clooney. And there was also Danny Thomas, a rising young performer who looked as though he could be more to Jolson's liking.

There was one drawback: Thomas, a Christian of Lebanese stock who looked more Jewish than Jolson, was advised to get his long nose shortened. "This nose has been in my family for generations and I'm not going to change it now," he thundered, and left—without the part. (Six years later, Danny Thomas played the lead role of the cantor's son in a Warner Brothers remake of *The Jazz Singer*—without changing his nose.)

While the casting traumas went on, Jolson continued to raise objections. "He doesn't stand right," he said of one promising performer. Or, "He moves his arms too much." Or, "That one looks like a penguin."

And always, "He doesn't look like Jolson." Time and again he stormed out of the casting sessions.

Cohn even suggested that he make a screen test himself. It would, he believed, prove that there wasn't a thing in the world that could make a man of more than sixty look like a twenty-year-old. Even Columbia's makeup department, which prided itself on being the most expert in Hollywood, couldn't.

When Jolson realized that nothing could persuade Cohn to change his mind, he suggested a compromise. "There's one guy who could do it," he said. "And that's Jimmy Cagney."

Jolson had always admired Cagney as an actor. He had been particularly thrilled by Cagney's performance in *Yankee Doodle Dandy* and secretly believed that Cagney had modeled his prancing technique in the film more on Jolson than on Cohan. He also had the same sort of build as Jolson.

Unfortunately, Cagney had had enough of being someone else's shadow and did not want to risk being typecast. He turned the offer down.

A youngster named Ross Hunter was tested—mainly because he was on the Columbia payroll—and rejected. Later, Mr. Hunter was to find it more profitable making his own pictures as a producer.

Finally, in desperation, Cohn called for a rerun of the first test he had seen. As he and Jolson watched a young man in blackface prance along the apron of the stage miming to a recording of "Toot, Toot, Tootsie," Cohn realized that the star of the picture had been there all along.

His name was Larry Parks.

Parks was perfect for the part for two reasons. He had made nine or ten "B" pictures with Columbia, none of which had done very well; he was therefore the sort of unknown who could carry conviction, without objecting to masquerading as someone else.

He was also good-looking enough to satisfy Cohn and he had shown that he was not going to be content merely to impersonate Jolson. He would give a performance that would be remembered for itself.

The day after the second screening of the Parks test, he was signed. Jolson was forced to accept the fact that someone else was going to play Jolson and he couldn't do a thing about it.

He objected that Parks was too tall, that his hair was too bushy.

Cohn had made up his mind, though, and no one—not even Jolson himself—could change it.

Resigned, he shook hands with "the other Jolson" and set about fulfilling his side of the bargain—singing the songs. The man who had once been called the King of Broadway and Emperor of Hollywood was not going to let anyone forget that there was no tale to tell without the songs. The Jolson voice was going to be heard again; the Jolson songs really were the vital part of the whole enterprise.

Morris Stoloff, Columbia's musical director, and arranger Saul Chaplin spent hours with Al, going over all the songs Jolson had sung through his long career. They agreed before they started that while they had to be the songs with which Jolson had been associated through the years, they also had to be numbers that would appeal to the more sophisticated postwar audiences of 1946.

It was up to Stoloff to test whether they could make the journey in time. Standard tunes that Jolson had made great were abandoned simply because no one could really be expected to take them seriously now. New arrangements had to be found that would provide a synthesis of the old songs and their period and of the demands of the current music-buying public. Stoloff changed the old arrangements and orchestrations and made old songs new again.

The film was to tell Jolson's story through the songs; Stoloff made sure that they would do so brilliantly. But the maestro admitted, "When I heard Jolson start to sing those songs, I turned to jelly. That man still had a magic that defied description."

The repertoire was reduced to some of Al's own favorites and, of course, the great songs: "Mammy," "April Showers," "Swanee," and "California, Here I Come." It excluded most of the comic numbers with which he had begun his assault on Broadway—except "The Spaniard That Blighted My Life"—and all of the old "pops" that he recorded in the early twenties.

There was also a new song, which became a hit in 1946. "The Anniversary Song" was written at about six hours' notice for a scene in the picture that was next on the shooting schedule. Buchman pointed out that a tune was desperately needed for a scene at the end of the picture in which Jolson's parents celebrated their wedding anniversary at a party at the Jolsons' California home.

Nothing came to mind until Al started to hum an old Viennese melody, long in the public domain. Saul Chaplin got to work on a lyric and new arrangements, and by the time he was finished, both he and Jolson had earned themselves a fortune. Both men have their name on the song's credits.

The story of the picture, never as important as the songs, loosely followed the life story of the man who, even when he was down, appeared to have done more in twenty minutes than most people do in twenty months. Sidney Buchman, who by now was the picture's godfather, is credited with working out the main story line.

He decided the basic theme of the story should be the man's insatiable need for the sound of people, sitting in plush velvet seats, applauding until their hands were sore and shouting for more until their voices were hoarse. When the "other woman" in the man's life turns out to be an audience, an incomparable love story emerges. It was too complicated, Buchman believed, to go into all Jolson's matrimonial troubles, so the decline and fall of the marriage with Ruby was chosen as representative enough.

As far as the story line was concerned, Jolson was not nearly as difficult to please as he had been about the casting. He sat in on the story conferences and agreed from the start that actual events and dates could be juggled around to fit the studio's needs.

The title of the picture came from Harry Cohn. At first, *Minstrel Boy* was considered; then, *April Showers*. The earliest publicity stills were captioned *The Story of Jolson*. But Cohn made the final decision. "There's only one name for this picture and you guys all ought to have thought of it," he said. "It's just gotta be *The Jolson Story*."

Long after the matters of story line, title, and songs had been settled, one vital character remained to be cast: Ruby Keeler. This was almost as difficult as finding a Jolson. Of all the actresses who came for tests, no one seemed quite right.

Cohn took some of the tests home and showed them to his wife Joan and their houseguests. Among them was a blond girl who had been on Columbia's payroll almost as long as Larry Parks and who, up to that time, had made just about as much of an impression as he had.

Her name was Evelyn Keyes. "Why can't I play the part?" she asked Cohn—at which point, Joan chimed in, "Don't be silly, Evelyn. You can't play that role. You know you aren't pretty."

"At that point," Evelyn recalls, "I was so determined to convince everyone that I was right that I yelled right back: 'All right, I know I'm not pretty. But I'm damned sure acting ability must have something to do with it.'

"I worked harder at getting that role than anything else in my life. I sent Cohn telegrams every day. I phoned him twice a day, three times, sometimes half a dozen times a day." Before long he gave in—she could have the role.

Now that that had been settled, the studio had to decide who would write the screenplay. A Hungarian writer named Bundy Salt was brought in first. Cohn asked him if he had ever heard of Jolson.

"I saw *The Jazz Singer* in Budapest," he replied.

"Anything else?" asked the studio boss.

"I hear he's washed up."

"Nothing else you know about him?"

"No."

"Good," said Cohn. "You're going to write the screenplay."

As it turned out, he didn't. Laurence Hazard was mentioned and rejected. Finally, Stephen Longstreet was brought in to do it.

Alfred E. Green, who had been involved in Hollywood musicals almost since the time Jolson showed the world that there could be such things, was appointed director. Sidney Skolsky was named producer.

One name which should have appeared among the credits, but did not, was that of Sidney Buchman. He wrote snatches of dialogue, coached dancers, supervised camera work—and helped keep peace between Jolson and Parks when it seemed that they were likely to have an argument. Buchman decided, with Jolson's help, which characters were to be kept, which were best discarded, and which were to be invented.

When Ruby Keeler heard she was going to be played on the screen by another actress, she threatened legal action. Amid widespread speculation around Hollywood, a financial settlement was made with her. Evelyn Keyes could play her part, and she could be seen starring in a musical called *Show Girl* and in films like *Gold Diggers, Flirtation Walk,* and *Forty-second Street.* But her name wouldn't be Ruby Keeler. She would be Julie Benson, Mrs. Al Jolson. Al didn't mind the use of this old Hollywood trick.

There were other, more fundamental, changes. Al's father was depicted as an indulgent, kindly gentleman, easily converted from strict

207

religious objections to show business to expertise on the theatre. A man who in the early scenes was never without his skullcap as a badge of religious orthodoxy somehow lost it as his hair thinned and his beard turned white. He was also portrayed as having no objections to his son marrying out of his own faith.

And as his real mother was pictured as having survived, there was no need to complicate the issue with half brothers and sisters. Even his full brother Harry and his sisters Rose and Etta didn't exist as far as the filmmakers were concerned.

Neither was there a James Francis Dooley, an Eddie Leonard, or an Eppy. A lovable character called Steve Martin—a complete figment of the imagination, although in many ways an amalgam of them all—took their places.

It was a sentimental story that could have been a success even without the music. Ludwig Donath was brilliant as Cantor Yoelson. His miming to the singing voice of Cantor Saul Silverman was masterly, and the home scenes with Mama Yoelson (Tamara Shayne) and their over-strong horseradish were full of the shmaltzy hokum that produced tears and laughs from the most hardbitten critics.

Steve Martin was played by one of Jolson's favorite actors, William Demarest, who a generation before *The Jolson Story* had shared scenes with Al in *The Jazz Singer.*

Harry Cohn saw the way things were progressing early on in production, before Jolson had spent much time on the set and before he had done any singing. Within two weeks of production beginning, he had lifted the budget ceiling of one and a half million dollars, imposed when the deal was first set up.

Now there could be more lavish sets, bigger orchestrations. What would Jolson make of them? It was obvious from the moment he first moved onto the sound stage and was shown into a soundproof glass booth where he was to record his songs while the orchestra played in the studio below.

As Jolson sang, a mysterious thing happened. Only Morris Stoloff could hear the songs through his own headphones, but the crowds gathered round for the performance just the same. They could see him move around just as he always had, and the old magnetism started working once more, even though they couldn't hear a note.

Evelyn Keyes recalled, "I remember just standing and staring, watching Jolson perform. It was uncanny. He was in the booth singing, but we could see him moving about and the people were just overwhelmed."

Jolson had been old business up to that point, and Columbia, a laughingstock. Now people in the business began to realize that he really was coming back.

The rumors continued just the same—rumors that Jolson couldn't manage a tune any more and that the engineers had to piece together a melody here, a chorus there, before they could come up with anything technically acceptable. There were other days, the stories said, when the Jolson voice wasn't usable at all.

Jolson put the lie to every such rumor. The truth was that from his first test recording, Jolson proved not only that he could still sing, but that he had never sung better in his life.

If the commercial recordings he made in the years after *The Jolson Story* cannot be considered proof (by then the tapes could have been doctored as easily as the soundtracks), the numerous extemporaneous performances on radio or at benefit shows that followed did demonstrate that those rumors were a slander on the Jolson talent.

For weeks after the recordings were made, it was impossible to walk on the set of *The Jolson Story* without seeing Larry Parks miming the old Jolson songs with the volume of his loudspeaker turned on as full as it would go. He would stand in front of the mirror and rehearse. He was not going to be satisfied with merely mouthing someone else's words. The secret of his success in this role would be that he sang at full volume the way Jolson had done.

Despite the resulting realism—the audiences saw Parks' lips move, his Adam's apple bob as the vocal cords vibrated, even the fur on his moving tongue, while Jolson sang—there were still criticisms from Jolson. He came onto the set more and more often as production advanced. "You don't move around enough, kid," he told Parks, and demonstrated exactly what he meant.

In Parks' dressing room, Jolson showed what his "easy approach" meant. He moved a lamp, then a chair, finally a bookcase. As he danced from one end of the room to the other, it seemed that a tornado had hit the Columbia studio. "See, kid," he said. "You gotta take it easy."

Parks embarked on a complete character-research program. He did more than read about Jolson; he practically lived Jolson's life. He asked his friends to find all the old Jolson records they could. These they delivered in boxes, by the truckload: old pressings of "Mammy," "Sonny Boy," still older versions of "The One I Love Belongs to Somebody Else" and "I'll Climb the Highest Mountain."

Parks could then appreciate how Jolson's voice had changed. He didn't sound the same and he took deeper breaths. So he had to rehearse the breaths as well as the vocal arrangements. He could hear that, although the Jolson voice had changed, the tremendous Jolson energy Al infused in his songs had not changed at all.

He raked up all the old Jolson movies, too. Warner Brothers was asked to supply prints of the early Jolson pictures. "Hell, no," said Jack Warner. But the films were found just the same and hour after hour, Parks would watch Jolson at work in the Columbia projection rooms. He saw scratched and faded copies of *Big Boy, Wonder Bar, Go into Your Dance, Swanee River* and—most useful of all—*Rose of Washington Square.*

Rose was seven years old when Larry Parks first saw the picture in the Columbia theatre. It had never been a great film, and Jolson very much played third fiddle to Alice Faye and Tyrone Power. But it provided several good lessons in projecting the Jolson style. Many years later, it is interesting to compare Jolson's performance of "California, Here I Come" in *Rose of Washington Square* and Larry Parks' imitation of him in *The Jolson Story.*

Almost every day Jolson was on the set advising Parks. To help him get into the spirit of things, he took him to the racetrack and to a synagogue. On the set, as Al told stories about the good old days, Erle sat at his side, knitting.

Once during rehearsals Jolson asked Parks to think twice about a certain gesture he had used in a song. "Don't you remember how I used to do that bit?" he asked.

The younger man admitted with embarrassment, "I've never seen you work at all before a live audience, Al."

"Wait a minute, wait a minute, son," Jolson replied gleefully. "You ain't heard nothin' yet." The next moment, he was on stage and was giving what turned out to be a two-hour show—just for Parks.

During the 107 days he spent before the cameras, Larry Parks lost eighteen pounds, trying to show how Jolson used to wow the audiences. In general Jolson was as happy as anyone with the way Parks was portraying him. He never admitted forgiving the studio for getting someone else to play his part, and he chided both Cohn and Parks from time to time. But deep down, he accepted what had to be accepted.

There was one scene that he was not at all happy with. And everyone knew it. It was a long-shot scene when Parks was meant to dance down the runway at the Winter Garden, singing "Swanee."

Al was distraught. "The kid just can't do it," he said emphatically. "And no one can do it—except me. Are you gonna have a film about me without 'Swanee'? Or are you gonna have a Jolson film without Jolson dancing—or without him whistling?" The answer to both questions had to be no.

So in this one scene, Jolson played Jolson. People who had seen the old Jolson said they recognized him. One woman writer said she recognized his overhanging paunch. When the film was shown in 1969 blown up seventy millimeter, this scene was enlarged to a close-up and there could be no further doubt. This was certainly not Larry Parks.

Probably the greatest problem that Parks or anyone else engaged in the musical side of *The Jolson Story* confronted was the fact that Jolson never sang the same song the same way twice.

When, for instance, he sang "Rosie, You Are My Posie," in one take for the film, the line ended " . . . don't be so captivating." In another, it concluded, "Don't be so aggravating." Parks was completely thrown. He already had enough trouble coping with the fact that Jolson never came in twice on the same beat.

The way Jolson did his songs caused one of the more legendary rows on the *Jolson Story* set. Al was recording "April Showers" for the sound track and, as usual, the growing audience around him applauded enthusiastically when he was finished. Everyone, that is, except Saul Chaplin.

"You left out something," said Chaplin innocently, and proceeded to show the way he remembered Al performing the tune on an old recording. Jolson was furious. Of course he couldn't give the song the old treatment, he fumed. He didn't have the breath any more. And, he said, pulling out a bundle of bank notes, "I made this in show business. What did you make?"

In the end, Jolson took Chaplin's advice and changed "April Showers" to something resembling his earliest version. It was clearly worth the effort.

Other recordings were made and then discarded for a variety of reasons. Two recordings were made of an old Jolson showstopper, "Rip Van Winkle"—one in German dialect, the other straight—but neither appeared in the film. A plan to interpolate "Caroline in the Morning" was left on the cutting-room floor (it was resurrected three years later in *Jolson Sings Again*). A scene in which Larry Parks mimes "Sonny Boy" in a reconstruction of the *Singing Fool* scene was dropped after the film's first public performance, not because Parks' portrayal was inadequate but because it seemed to stop the story dead in its tracks.

Another number, the song about the synagogue cantor's audition, was thrown out because it appeared to have the same effect in the cinema as it had had when Jolson first sang it in a smoke-filled nightclub. Jolson recorded it for a party scene and the cast was ecstatic about it. Larry Parks learned the Yiddish words phonetically and even Jolson admitted he gave a marvelous performance. But it had to be dropped. "Sidney Buchman decided that nothing, but nothing, could possibly follow that," Evelyn Keyes recalled.

It was difficult to follow Jolson when he was on the set at any time. On some occasions, the only person allowed near him was Cohn. And Jolson was the only man in Columbia's history ever to be allowed access to Cohn's own private office at any time of the day or night.

Any worry with regard to the business side of the operation had vanished from Cohn's mind soon after Jolson first appeared on the set. Hollywood's best musicians were pleading to be allowed to join Stoloff's orchestra. Cohn realized that his financial investment was secure, as long as Jolson survived the shooting of the picture.

Cohn cultivated a feeling of mutual confidence between them, producer and idol. When a cameraman stopped the shooting of "Swanee" because an arc lamp was flickering, Cohn flew into a rage. "No one stops a scene when Jolson is singing," he shouted at the cameraman. He was about to fire him, but cooled his temper when he was reminded that Technicolor film cost something like fifty cents a second and they were wasting time.

Things went well between Jolson and Cohn. But this was not always the case with Jolson and Parks. Rumors proliferated of a succession of rows between the two stars. At first Parks denied it.

In June 1951, he told *Picturegoer* magazine, "They were untrue.

Jolson and I were enthusiastic co-workers with a sound regard for one another. There was never a disagreement between us. I confess that, at the outset, I had no desire to be Jolson, but that was certainly not through any lack of admiration. I simply felt I was not the one to do the role justice."

Many years later, he clarified the situation. "Al Jolson didn't want me to portray him. He wanted to do it himself. I got the part and when the picture started, everybody called it 'Cohn's Folly.' They thought that Harry Cohn had taken leave of his senses. I had met Jolson but never broke bread with him.

"The big problem was that Jolson sang every song as if he was going to drop dead at the end of it—at full volume all the way—and my problem was to act out different emotions with Jolson singing at full pitch. It's very difficult to collapse in mid-song while the voice is at full throat."

No one had any doubts, however, that whether or not Jolson accepted Parks and wished him success, he somehow resented him—whether he told him so or not.

Evelyn Keyes remembered Jolson's behavior during the filming: "It's true, he was always performing. Wherever you went with him, he was on. You know, if you were sitting alone with him in a room, he was giving you a performance. He had this extraordinary energy. He would perform all the time—and you found yourself being grateful. He was absolutely charming."

The Jolson Story took six months to shoot from beginning to end. Sidney Buchman spent another six months in the cutting room, readying the picture for the first showing.

During those anxious months, Al and Harry Jolson met again for the first time in years. Harry called his brother to say there was an urgent message from Washington: their father was dangerously ill.

The brothers arrived at the small Washington apartment near the synagogue where he had helped conduct services for so long, in time for the old man, now ninety-four, to pronounce a final blessing on his sons. He told them that although their ways had not been his, he loved them still.

Harry had his wife Lillian to console him. Al had Erle. And at this moment, he needed her. Just when he was feeling on top of the world again, his past had caught up with him. The man against whom he had rebelled died without seeing his son's greatest moment.

By the time the film was finally in the can and sent off to Santa Barbara for a sneak preview, it had cost $2,800,000. Cohn had chosen the preview location because he was afraid too many people would know about the picture—and any unfortunate reactions from the audience would get too wide a hearing—if it were shown in Los Angeles.

As it was, everyone who was anyone did find out where the preview would be shown and was at the Santa Barbara Theatre that night. Al arrived with Erle and confessed it was like a Winter Garden opening all over again. He had a terrible case of nerves.

Erle sat on one side of him and Harry Cohn on the other. All the time, his legs shook so violently that a man sitting in front complained. "I feel as though I've been hit by an earthquake," said Jolson, and rushed out to the toilet at the rear of the theatre.

Cohn sent a young executive, Jonie Taps, to see how Al was feeling. Al said he was fine and would watch the film from the back of the house. But every time he heard his own voice he put his hand to his mouth and rushed back to the toilet. He saw the rest of the picture between the men's room and the manager's office, where he was persuaded to lie down halfway through the film.

When it was over, Cohn knew that, apart from the "Sonny Boy" number (which he decided to cut as he watched the preview), he had a winner. He thumped Jolson on the back. "It's great, Al."

Erle rushed to the back of the theatre to give her husband a big kiss. That seemed to be the most important thing: at last she could see not only how great he had been, but how great he still was.

As the audience filled in the comment cards on their way out of the theatre, Jolson stood behind a pillar and listened to the things some of them were saying to each other.

One comment he would never forget: "What a pity," said a little old lady, blinking into the strong glare of the foyer lights. "What a pity that he isn't alive to see it."

214

14

THERE'S A RAINBOW 'ROUND MY SHOULDER

THE OBITUARY to Jolson's career had been written and published many times in the years before *The Jolson Story* was released. When Jolson had the operation on his lung just over a year before work on the picture started, the Associated Press had circulated to their subscribers a full biographical obituary.

Suddenly, the ghost was walking, dancing, and singing. Reports of his imminent death had been grossly exaggerated.

No one could have predicted the amount of life the picture injected into Jolson's system, or the effect it would have on the entertainment industry, which had been so quick to show Al the door.

The picture opened at a world premiere at Radio City Music Hall in New York. Larry Parks was not present. The story at the time was that he couldn't afford the fare, although that seems unlikely. Probably, Columbia didn't see the need to get him to the East Coast until several days later.

Word that Jolson was back had spread through the film colony in Hollywood and Beverly Hills as soon as the curtain was down that first night. They knew it almost instinctively and they sensed that Jolson did, too.

From the moment "The End" flashed onto the screen, he was his old self again, behaving in the same old Jolson way. He was so excited that he put his arms around Stephen Longstreet, who had written the screenplay, and said, "Steve, I'm gonna give you a present to show how much I appreciate what you did." The next day, the gift arrived. It was a signed photograph inscribed "To Steve—who took my life."

"I hung it in the toilet," Longstreet recalls.

Al Jolson was now sixty-one. But he was behaving like a new

performer who had just been taken out of the second row of the chorus to receive the thunderous applause of an audience for the first time.

As proud as he was to show Erle that he could be on top again, he was equally glad to show his fellow entertainers what he could still do. The Hillcrest Country Club invited him to take part in their twenty-fifth anniversary benefit concert—at the top of the bill.

One by one emcee Jack Benny introduced Danny Kaye, Danny Thomas, Van Johnson, Frank Sinatra, Margaret O'Brien, Gene Kelly, Mickey Rooney, Red Skelton, José Iturbe, Xavier Cugat, Carmen Miranda, and George Burns.

Four hours later, another ten violin players came out to augment the regular orchestra of the evening. They played the opening bars of "Mammy" and Al Jolson, dressed in a smart, newly tailored dinner jacket, bounced onto the stage as if he were at least forty years younger.

"Danny Kaye said he was a young man when he came here tonight," Jolson gagged, "and that he was old by the time he got on."

"Well, Jolie's case is different. When I got here I was an old man already." As for his comeback, "That was no comeback. Until now I just couldn't get a job."

The show was expected to last no more than the four hours it had taken to reach Jolson. In the end, the proceedings lasted almost six hours.

Eight hundred people crowded in to hear Jolson sing, wisecrack, and reminisce about the days when being an entertainer meant more than a mere ability to hold the microphone properly.

Halfway through his performance, Jolson suddenly stopped to make a brief speech. "My biggest thrill is not seeing all you people here, but having my wife with me. All she knew about me as a performer was from my old scrapbooks or what Jack Benny and Groucho Marx told her. Tonight I've been showing off just to impress her."

There were few dry eyes in the house at that moment. Jolson was back—and in charge.

The Hollywood papers were full of it the next day. They were even more eager now to anticipate the sort of success *The Jolson Story* was likely to have. They expressed their feeling that a really great entertainer was back in their midst and what was more, the industry needed him.

Their sentiments represented more than nostalgia. A dinner in New York on October 1, 1946—just nine days before the scheduled world premiere of the film—substantiated this new enthusiasm.

The Motion Picture Chapter of the American War Veterans Committee gave a testimonial banquet for Jolson at the plush Hotel Astor, with the proceedings broadcast from coast to coast. In Los Angeles, Bob Hope and George Jessel paid tribute to Jolson between their own jokes and songs. Eddie Cantor joined in from San Francisco to sing "Toot, Toot, Tootsie"; Dinah Shore dedicated to Jolson her rendition of "You Made Me Love You"; Sinatra sang "Rock-A-Bye Your Baby with a Dixie Melody"; Hildegarde sang "April Showers"; Martha Raye was "Waiting for the Robert E. Lee"; and Perry Como performed "By the Light of the Silvery Moon."

In New York, the former mayor of the city, James J. Walker, in his final public performance (he died soon afterward), introduced Jolson.

"We are gathered to pay tribute to Al Jolson," he said. "We are saluting a great showman—and New York loves great showmen. The man whose very name means Broadway. . . ."

When Al came to the microphone, a thousand people clapped, cheered, and stood as James Walker announced, "The hearts of the American Veterans Committee and the microphone are all yours."

To Jolson, the tribute was quite clearly unexpected. "As a rule, ladies and gentlemen, I generally sing my speeches," he told the guests. "I am not a talker. Up to about eight o'clock tonight, I did not know I was going to have a dinner. I knew they were making a testimonial but I treated it, I'm ashamed to say, as a joke. I couldn't believe it.

"I am at an age in life when people quit. But then at about a quarter to eight I started to get nervous. I said to my wife, 'I've got to get dressed.' She said, 'What have you got to wear?' And I said, 'A blue suit and a tie.' I got dressed and came over here.

"There won't be any singing from me. There's been a lot of singing tonight and I don't think I could follow it. As usual, I'm not lost for words—but tonight all I can say is, to everyone, from the bottom of my heart, thank you."

The testimonial was a wonderful boost for *The Jolson Story*. But that was still an unknown quantity to most people. Jolson himself was at last being recognized as the man who had turned American entertainment into a national heritage.

To launch the film, Harry Cohn wanted to release an album of songs from the picture. But that was much easier said than done. In those days, no one conceived of using the actual film sound tracks on a record, and it was still two years away from the birth of the LP. And, despite the Hillcrest benefit, despite the dinner at the Astor, no one thought Al Jolson's voice would set the popular music market on fire.

Nevertheless, Cohn assigned Jonie Taps to the job of getting Jolson on records. Taps had just concluded a deal with Cohn to join Columbia as head of the music department. He was an executive with Shapiro Bernstein, the music publishers, and was still working out his six months' notice when Cohn phoned him with an SOS: he needed some Jolson records and no one would market them. Columbia had no recording setup of its own. Its namesake record company Columbia Graphaphone was not interested. RCA Victor and the other labels had said no, too.

And Jack Kapp, head of Decca, was equally unimpressed. But when Taps got Jolson's promise of ten percent of the deal as his agent if he could swing it, he decided to try again.

It seemed impossible to break through to Kapp. Jolson's "Swanee" and "April Showers" combination of the previous year had not done well for Decca, and Kapp was thinking of withdrawing the disc from the catalogue. "Look, I've got Sophie Tucker, Harry Richmond, and Ted Lewis under contract—and I can't give them away," he told Taps. "What do I need another one for? Crosby is the one who's making money for me now."

Eli Oberstein of RCA seemed to weaken. A special showing of *The Jolson Story* was arranged to convince him. It convinced him—that he should stay away from Jolson.

Taps decided to try the same tack with Kapp. "Come and see the picture," Taps pleaded with him. "Then you'll decide whether you're on to a good thing or not."

Kapp agreed to come and see the picture. He left the theatre in a daze.

"You make the pictures with Jolson," Kapp told Cohn, "I'll make his records."

By the time *The Jolson Story* opened at Radio City on October 10, a deal had been signed for an album of ten records featuring songs from the picture. When the first royalties from Decca reached Jolson a month after the records' release, he discovered he had earned four hundred thousand dollars.

The people who lined up for four blocks around the theatre to see the movie were also buying Jolson's music to take home with them. Long before the movie became an obvious success, Jolson had made a stupendous comeback on records.

In the recording studios at Decca, Morris Stoloff gave the Jolson numbers the same updated treatment that he had provided on the film set. He did for Jolson what Nelson Riddle was to do for Sinatra ten years later. He created the new Jolson sound.

Once again, Jolson's voice was heard on Broadway, blaring from the speakers outside the record stores scattered throughout the theatre district. Before, they had lived on a diet of Crosby, Sinatra, Como and Dinah Shore. Now it seemed that all the shops were playing on their machines were Jolson records.

You could hear him singing "Mammy" in one shop, "Toot, Toot, Tootsie" in another, "Swanee" next door, and "You Made Me Love You" two shops farther away. Everyone was playing Jolson—and everyone was buying Jolson.

Everyone should have been happy—but Jonie Taps wasn't. Jolson refused to give him the ten percent he had promised him. Taps never forgave Jolson.

"He tried to get Cohn to fire me before I started work," he remembered. "He thought I was proving too useful to Cohn and might prevent his getting near him himself. Cohn told him to leave the store alone!"

Jolson did not know what had hit him. As he lay back on his hammock as it swung on the patio of his house, he talked to Erle about the amazing change in his fortunes, and seemed completely unable to take it all in.

His house was once more plagued with sightseers. Day by day the fan mail poured in. But the fans were not the people who had seen him on Broadway or the ones who remembered seeing him on the screen with Ruby Keeler. This was a new generation of worshipers, the bobby-soxers and their boyfriends, who were just discovering this "hep new singer Al Jolson."

In spite of the excitement as his rating in the music business hit new heights daily, he could still walk through the streets unrecognized. The novelty of being successful again was too strong for that to concern him. More than once he admitted, "I never liked the idea of having leaking fountain pens thrust in front of my face."

To the average cinema fan, he was a gray-haired version of Larry Parks, the star they were now reading so much about in the newspapers and magazines. Few of them had yet seen the picture. It was doing such hot business at Radio City that the lines, blocks long, began forming as early as seven o'clock in the morning. Not since *Gone with the Wind* had there been such enthusiasm for a movie.

On the air, disc jockeys joined the Jolsonmania. The 1945 version of "April Showers" had been resurrected by Decca and transferred to the A side; "Swanee" was relegated to the B side. In the first week of its rerelease it had sold more than twice as many copies as when it was first issued.

Al Jolson's younger successors rode the wave of his enormous success. Bing Crosby, among many others, recorded "April Showers" and "The Anniversary Song." Jolson's "definitive" version sold a million copies in a month, many of them bought by people who had never even heard his name weeks earlier.

In Britain, too, "April Showers" was the most spectacular success. For five weeks, it topped the British music industry's hit parade. Everybody seemed to be singing it on BBC radio, and on the fledgling British television service the Jolson recording was being aired more than any other.

At home in California, Jolson sat back, read his mail, played his new records, and developed signs of a second childhood. He no longer walked anywhere—he ran. When he answered the telephone, he didn't merely say "Hello"; he sang it, usually to the tune of "Mammy."

He took up swimming. His doctor had told him that swimming was the perfect cure for ill health and old age, the two things Jolson feared most. He took the doctor's advice: every morning, he swam two lengths of the pool.

He also decided that ice cream was good for his voice. From the moment he started making records again he devoured two dishes of this "health food" every night before going to bed.

The press reported that Al was once more raising money for charity. At a United Jewish Appeal luncheon at the Hotel Astor in July 1947, the target set by the Greater New York division of the appeal— $1,750,000—was reached.

"Although governments of the world are callous and indifferent to the fate of one and a half million Jews of Europe," he told the luncheon guests, "we in America must rally our maximum resources to prevent the victims of Nazi persecution losing hope." Despite criticisms that Jolson was remote from his people, he had always responded to causes like this one.

In Denver, Jolson was presented with the Rose Award, named after Major General Maurice Rose, "for services to the Forces in the War."

The Jolson Story was building a real following, a special kind of fan loyalty. *The Jolson Story*'s appeal was international. In Britain in 1946, Jolson was hardly more than a memory to most people. Few of his earlier films had done well. Britain's rediscovery of the entertainer in *The Jolson Story* was even more tumultuous than America's.

It was bringing him a new fortune. More important, he was not simply working again—he was sought after as he had never been before.

By the end of 1947, it was clear that Jolson was back to stay. It wasn't just nostalgia, as some critics had suggested. Nor were his only fans soldiers returning from the front line, glad to welcome the man who had cheered them up when things were hot.

The Jolson Story was a spectacular success as a film and on records. The man who months before couldn't give away his services on radio was now the hottest property on the air—without a show of his own.

At three o'clock on the morning of October 27, 1946—seventeen days after *The Jolson Story*'s premiere—Al was invited to take part in a late-night radio talk show, the Barry Gray Show on WOR-Mutual. He was expected to talk for up to half an hour about his long career and his reactions to the picture. He brought Harry Akst along, found him a piano, and sang some of his favorite tunes from the picture. He finally went off the air eighty minutes later.

The reaction to the program, broadcast while most of New York was asleep, was astonishing. The next day the networks were knocking on his door.

But Jolson played it cool. He decided to confine himself to guest appearances. He had gotten out of the habit of driving himself hard on his own show.

In January 1947, Jolson was the guest star on Bing Crosby's *Philco Radio Time.* He was not just good on that show; he was as brilliant as he had ever been on Broadway. All his old reserve had left him and he was bubbling over with confidence.

As an experiment, he and Crosby did their very first duet together on "April Showers" and followed it with "Ma Blushin' Rosie." They left the studio audience shouting for more.

Philco liked it enough to sign Al for four more shows that year at ten thousand dollars each.

He appeared on the Crosby show two weeks in succession. The ratings were higher than they had ever been. If neither one had been successful as solo artists, they could have established themselves as the perfect comedy and singing team.

Even the commercial for Philco radios which the two clowned—to words and music by Jimmy Van Heusen and Johnny Burke—brought the house down. It seemed they could do nothing wrong.

Jolson had never been funnier. "What's that badge on your lapel?" Crosby asked him on one of his first appearances. "That's what you get for seeing *The Jolson Story* a hundred times," quipped Al.

Columbia Studios liked that idea. A publicity campaign was introduced offering real badges for people who had seen the picture ten times. The badges were gone almost as quickly as they could be manufactured.

Eddie Cantor, his arch rival of the old days, invited him to appear on his own radio program. They sang "Toot, Toot, Tootsie" together and Al sang "Ida"—dedicating it to Cantor's wife. As the program ended Cantor told Al, "Thank you, Al—you're still the world's greatest entertainer."

Al took the hint. The next time he appeared on the Crosby show he was wearing another badge bearing the letters AJTWGE. "What's that,

Al?" asked Crosby. "That, son, says 'Al Jolson, The World's Greatest Entertainer.'"

He now showed a new side to his character. The man who had been condemned for so long as cruel and uncharitable was generosity itself to the man who had done so much to help shape his new career, Morris Stoloff.

When he first received an invitation to appear on the Crosby show, Jolson asked whether he could bring Stoloff as his musical director. The producers ruled this out; Crosby had always worked with John Scott Trotter and it wouldn't be right to drop him just for Jolson.

"But I need him for my arrangements," Al argued. "Well," they told him, "bring him along as an adviser."

"Al did," Stoloff recalls. "I went to every session and never did a thing. But you ought to have seen those checks he gave me. I've never known a man more generous. I did absolutely nothing."

Al's last Crosby show in 1947 was in December—eight months after the one before. When the May show ended, Crosby's agents tried to sign Al for another ten programs that autumn. But the two singers couldn't agree on terms.

One report said that Bing and Al were at least a thousand dollars apart on what Jolson's guest appearance fee should be. The *New York Times* speculated that another, more likely, reason for the disagreement was that "Bing did not enjoy the publicity over the fact that his ratings went up on the show whenever Al was the guest."

Bing's brother Everett denied the rift and Al's press team said there had been hopes for a deal, but it had never materialized. Two years passed before Al appeared again on the Crosby program, although Bing did join Al on Al's program.

At the very beginning of their association Bing had wondered how the live studio audiences would take to Al appearing as himself. He thought they would be too amazed at the difference between Larry Parks on the screen and Jolson's real appearance. But it never seemed to matter. They loved Jolson as he was, and they loved the Crosby-Jolson team.

Decca cashed in on the situation. Since both artists were under contract to the label, Decca decided to issue a new version of one of the numbers Al and Bing had sung on the Philco show, "Alexander's Ragtime Band." The flip side was a novel version of "The Spaniard

That Blighted My Life." It was the only commercial recording Jolson and Crosby made together. Contractual difficulties prevented more.

Al continued to make records, but radio seemed to be the most interesting medium. The *New York Times* commented: "Thanks to radio, some of the brightest chapters in the Jolson story seem to lie still ahead." Jack Benny, Amos 'n Andy, Edgar Bergen, and Jimmy Durante all featured Al as their guest star.

Bob Hope asked him when he appeared on his show, "Tell me, Al, you're such a sensation on the radio now, why don't you get your own program?"

"What," Al tried to reply and was overwhelmed by a hysterical round of applause and cheers. "What?" Al tried again, and still the people out front wouldn't let him speak. Finally he managed it. "What—and be on the air only once a week?" This time the house collapsed.

He could tell his own jokes now; if he didn't like a subject, he didn't bother with it. And everyone seemed delighted.

Jolson and Eddie Cantor hit it off again on the Cantor radio show—acting out a routine Al devised himself. "How much do you want?" Eddie asked him.

"Don't talk about money," Al replied. "Forget it."

The day after the show, Cantor received a bill for fifteen hundred dollars from Jolson's tailors. Al had charged him with the cost of six suits he was having made at $250 each.

Early in April 1947, Al did star in his own program—a onetime feature in the Lux Radio Theatre series in which he was the narrator for a new version of the film *Alexander's Ragtime Band*.

He followed this in June with a version of *The Jazz Singer* hardly different from the one he did for Lux in the thirties. This time, though, his parents were played by Ludwig Donath and Tamara Shayne, the couple who played Papa and Mama Yoelson in *The Jolson Story*. The program did so well that copies were pressed and issued to American Forces radio stations.

Jolson had now come to terms with radio in a way he never had before. In October 1947, he once more headed the bill on NBC's *Kraft Music Hall*.

Maurice Chevalier had been provisionally booked to take over from Nelson Eddy, who had succeeded Crosby. But then came *The Jolson Story* and Chevalier was told politely that Al had the job instead.

Al was once again the host on the show he had founded so many years before.

Time magazine reported on Jolson's approaching Kraft soon after he heard Crosby was leaving the "Hall."

"I told the sponsor I'm the guy who can do it," he chuckled to the *Time* writer. "And what did they say? 'You're too old.' So I says to myself: 'Al, forgive them. They don't know what they're doin'.' But after *The Jolson Story* they did the Big Switcheroo. 'Please, Mr. Jolson, don't sign with anyone else—sign here, please.'

"Sign, ha! I didn't want to sign anything for nobody. So I tell 'em, 'All right—for seventy-five hundred a week.' They says yes and I almost drop dead."

The terms called for a four-year run, with thirty-nine shows a year. There was to be a regular format: Al singing his old songs and a few new ones, a female vocalist, and a new kind of "sidekick" for Al, Oscar Levant.

This brilliant pianist was regarded as one of the greatest living exponents of the work of George Gershwin, which set the stage for an easy rapport with Jolson, who naturally shared his enthusiasm. His caustic wit—he had been the star of the radio program *Information, Please*—rubbed Jolson the wrong way more than once, and there were the occasional rows on the air, but they seemed to get along famously most of the time.

Levant continually ribbed Jolson about his age. "Don't tell me you weren't around when Teddy Roosevelt led the charge of San Juan Hill?" Levant would chuckle. Or, "Weren't you there when Tchaikovsky first played his piano concerto?" "Of course not, Oscar," Jolson would reply, pretending to be hurt. "I was on tour at the time!"

Celebrity guests—not just singers like Bing Crosby and Dinah Shore, but also actors like Humphrey Bogart and Charles Laughton—all tried their own versions of "Mammy" and "Swanee" on the air.

Throughout the seventy-two Jolson Kraft radio programs the pattern hardly changed. He continued to sing the same songs and tell the same sort of jokes, which often had something to do with cheese.

"I saw a wonderful film last night, Oscar," he said on one program. "It was called *Cheese Every Saturday.*"

"You mean *Chicken Every Saturday,*" corrected Levant.

"Oscar," Al chided. "You just failed the Kraft loyalty test."

By the time the last show was aired (on May 26, 1949—Jolson's sixty-third birthday, by his reckoning), he had driven producers crazy and delighted thousands of listeners with his ad-libbing and repeating the songs he liked best two or three times.

Radio was the medium for Jolson now. There was talk of his starring in his own film, but he didn't appear to be interested.

The owner of New York's Roxy Theatre invited Jolson to appear live on the stage of his movie house. He offered Al forty thousand a week to do six shows a day. Al turned him down. "I don't need that sort of money—or to work that hard."

Meanwhile, many of the biggest American stars were appearing at the London Palladium, the only important variety theatre left in England. Danny Kaye, Jack Benny, and Bob Hope were attracting huge crowds. The invitations poured in to Jolson's home, to Columbia Studios, and to NBC—"Please come to the Palladium."

"Everyone's a sensation there," Al replied. "*I* like to set records."

The only live shows he wanted to do were benefit concerts. Every time word got out that Jolson was to appear, there was hardly room for the other people on the bill to get through the stage door.

When he sang for a benefit in honor of Bobe Hope at the Hollywood Friars Club, he demanded a full orchestra and a runway through the makeshift theatre created for the occasion in the main dining lounge. The Friars turned him down on the runway, so Al removed the vase of flowers in front of him and used the table as a stage. It was the usual Jolson performance.

Al Jolson was quite clearly happier now than he had ever been in his life. As far as anyone could see, he and Erle were happily married and although they had no children, it was quite startling, considering Al's past record, to see how well they got along. He was proud of his pretty wife and liked to be photographed kissing her goodbye in the mornings before leaving for a studio date.

When an ignorant waiter once asked him what his daughter wanted to choose from the menu, he pulled the man's sleeve and told him, "She's too young to be my daughter. That's my wife."

Since the movie had opened, several journalists had tried to contact Ruby Keeler to find out her views on the new Jolson success story. She repeatedly refused to comment. She did admit to one writer that she had not seen the film.

In 1948, Jolson donated the deeds of the seventy-five-thousand-dollar estate he owned on Mulholland Drive, Hollywood Hills, to the Cedars of Lebanon Hospital. He and Erle went to live in Palm Springs. He said he was grateful for the good health he now enjoyed.

"I may not be alive in ten seconds," he told a reporter, "but I feel better now than I have for twenty years."

Erle and Al decided to expand their family circle, so they adopted a baby boy and called him Asa, Jr. They had to wait months before the adoption agency approved them as prospective parents, but when Asa finally arrived, Al was a happy and proud father once again.

"Erle's crazy about kids," he explained. "Nuts about them—and so am I. I used to watch her with other people's kids. Why, I betcha if we hadn't found one of our own she'd be going into the babysitting business, just to be near kids."

The Jolsons converted a spare bedroom into a nursery, complete with a desert-air lamp to make sure that everything, including the air, would be just right.

"Look at him, honey. Just look at him," Al would call to Erle. "What a kid. What a sweetheart. Makes you want to sing or cry or something. He's just wrappin' those tiny fingers around my heart."

And he planned for the future expectantly. "Gonna send him to a good school," Al told reporters. "But a hard one. Want no spoilin' of this boy."

He told stories about Asa until the day he died. In one of his last broadcasts with Crosby he joked about the boy's amazing progress in arithmetic.

"You mean he can count all the way to ten?" Bing asked. "To ten?" Al replied. "Bing, don't be silly. He can go right up to the king."

Although Jolson was proving that he was once more a top name in the entertainment world, it bothered him to be thought old, even though he continually joked about it. He began painting his graying hair black. But he had to wear glasses to read and to walk down the street, too. If he saw someone he knew approaching, he'd make sure that the spectacles were back in his pocket before anyone noticed. He held his head high, as if to balance an invisible crown he believed was rightfully his.

At the Hillcrest Country Club he was his old brash self. He didn't

227

bother to get sturgeon for his friends any more. Occasionally, though, he still felt unsure of himself when he was about to do a benefit at the club.

"Al, put on the blackface and you'll feel better," Jack Benny advised him on one occasion.

"Somehow," Benny recalled, "he could lose himself under that makeup."

His age, as much as anything, could have been the real reason for Jolson's reluctance to face live audiences after his comeback. "I die every time I go on a stage." he confessed more than once. "What's the use of falling on my face now?"

But in the late 1940s, he wasn't likely to fall on his face.

Early in 1948, he went to Washington, saw his stepmother, and his half brothers and sisters, and called at the White House. President Truman welcomed him as an old fan. "I used to see you in Missouri," he told Al and asked how Al had managed to hold audiences spellbound over the years.

Jolson told him that he was thinking of retiring.

"I'll kiss sixty-two goodbye next May," he said, getting near to admitting his age. "And I'm trying to find a way to quit."

"Don't do it, Al," the President told him. "You might drop dead."

So Jolson announced he was going to keep on singing, and introduced a number on the radio especially for Asa, called "Nearest Thing to Heaven."

His records were selling everywhere, in Japan and Germany as well as in the United States, Britain, and Western Europe. Everything Jolson recorded sold in the tens of thousands. His radio program was getting higher ratings than any other. At the end of 1947, Jolson had been voted most popular male singer on the air—with Crosby second, Perry Como third, and Sinatra fourth.

In 1948, the musicians of America went on strike, and there were no orchestral backings for him. Decca got around the problem by recording two sides with the Mills Brothers and their guitar—"Down Among the Sheltering Palms" and "Is It True What They Say About Dixie?"— and another two sides with a mixed chorus.

Jack Kapp of Decca was responsible for the last two. He was

watching on television a rally at New York's Madison Square Garden celebrating the birth of the state of Israel when he got the idea.

"Al, you should have seen it," Kapp told him on the phone immediately after the broadcast. "It was the most moving thing I've ever seen. They sang 'Hatikvah'—you know, Israel's national anthem. Al, do me a favor. Record it for us."

Al recorded "Hatikvah" and an adaption of an old Jewish folk tune which he called "Israel." He donated the royalties to the United Jewish Appeal. "It's the most wonderful thing I've ever sung," he said. "I've never been so proud to sing a song in my life."

Jolson and *The Jolson Story* were so successful that Columbia made a decision that was absolutely unique for a film biography of this kind. They decided to film a sequel, and this time there was talk of Al's playing himself.

Al thought it wise not to pursue this suggestion after a pretty girl approached him with the greeting, "Gee, Mr. Jolson, you're much better-looking on the screen."

He may not have had the girls stopping in their tracks when they saw him, but he still had full control over the people to whom he sang. At a party given by Morris Stoloff, Jolson sang his heart out. When he finished, the entire gathering sat in rapturous silence. Stoloff approached another of the guests to sing.

"I can't follow that," replied Frank Sinatra, and walked away.

15

'N' EVERYTHING

JOLSON HAD more friends now than he had ever had before. A new generation of admirers found magic in the sound of his voice. Show business people wanted to share part of his spotlight or bask in the reflected glory. And there were the old-timers, for whom he still represented all that was brash, exciting, and pulsating about entertainment.

To them Al Jolson was the greatest thing that had ever happened. One man, shirt manufacturer Sammy Hamlin, phoned Jolson's California home regularly from his own house in New York. All he'd say was, "Al, I love you. Goodbye." He'd follow Al around the country, sometimes sleeping on the steps of the singer's hotel all night in order not to miss Jolson's early start to the day.

Another devotee was a New York dentist, Sam Lubalin. If Jolson called him from Los Angeles to say he had a toothache, Lubalin would cancel his appointments for two days and fly to California. For his devotion, Jolson gave the dentist a small percentage of the profits of *The Jolson Story*.

In his own way, Harry Cohn was just as devoted an admirer. In the days when *The Jolson Story* was still just an idea, his faith in the greatest entertainer he had ever seen had persuaded him to go ahead with the project. Now Cohn walked through the studio corridors with a look of triumph about him. He had told all the doubters that he would succeed and now he was determined not to let anyone forget it.

If *The Jolson Story* could succeed, he reasoned, so could a sequel. Cohn was willing to let the singer have virtually free rein this time. After all, it had been the soundtrack and Jolson's voice on that track that had been largely responsible for the triumph of *The Jolson Story*.

This time, Cohn felt he could afford to be magnanimous; if Al wanted to play himself, so be it.

He wasn't being very subtle. But neither was he betraying his real reason for the magnanimity: there were rumors that Jolson was moving to M-G-M, and that he had agreed that Gene Kelly should play him this time.

Predictably, though, Al was still slightly taken with the idea of playing himself. He even did a test shot singing "She's a Latin from Manhattan" to a group of soliders. But this time Jolson himself called a halt. Why risk sinking a ship that was very successfully floating along? *The Jolson Story* had been full of illusions that had proved exceedingly profitable. Why shatter those illusions now?

Larry Parks had done wonders with *The Jolson Story*. Let the people see the rest of that picture, he thought, as though they were picking up the tale where they had left it.

"This kid Larry Parks plays me better than I play myself," he said, only half joking.

In August 1949, the people saw the result: *Jolson Sings Again.* The preamble after the opening titles promised "the rest of the story of Jolson."

It began in the same night club where the earlier picture had ended. There was a quick flashback of Parks miming "Rockabye," dissolving quickly into the search at home for his missing wife.

Conveniently, the nightclub scene ended before Evelyn Keyes' departure, so there was no need to call her back to complete her side of the story. Just as Ruby had left Jolson's life in the early forties, Julie Benson ceased to exist on the screen.

The plot went through Jolson's fallow period, his triumphs in the war, and his meeting with a young brunette nurse named Ellen Clark (Ruby Keeler had another name in *The Jolson Story,* so Erle Galbraith had to have one in the sequel).

Barbara Hale played the new Mrs. Jolson. She had the same drawling Southern accent as Erle, the same penchant for teasing the man old enough to be her father, and the same addiction to knitting.

"This time she's really got to look like Erle," Al told Sidney Buchman, who was now officially writing and producing the picture.

Ludwig Donath played Cantor Yoelson again—this time, apart from the brief synagogue sequence, without his skullcap—but Tamara

Shayne's Mama Yoelson died just before Al's tour of the battle zones began.

There was the trauma of his losing part of a lung and the triumph of *The Jolson Story*, with no less than ten minutes of extracts from the original picture. They were not only entertaining; they were advertising a picture that Columbia had every intention of reissuing.

Once more, Parks was superb; once more, Al's voice was magnificent. It wasn't really the same voice as before. This time, it was even deeper and slightly more nasal. The old man of about sixty-four was singing better than ever.

Both Jonie Taps and Morris Stoloff had the same explanation: "He was so much more confident now. He couldn't help sounding better." And there were new Jolson hits to go with the picture. "Is It True What They Say About Dixie?" became as great a revival hit as "April Showers" had been three years before. "I Only Have Eyes for You" almost rivaled "The Anniversary Song"—although nothing could really do that.

Within five years, *Jolson Sings Again* took in five million and was listed among the ten most successful films of all time. It wasn't as successful as *The Jolson Story* had been—almost nothing could be—but it was successful enough for most people.

And it kept Jolson on top. Nothing, it seemed, could make him slip now. Everyone still appeared to want him. There were more Bing Crosby radio programs, more shows for Kraft. He started thinking seriously about the television offers he had been receiving.

He and Larry Parks made frequent radio appearances together and when his shadow wasn't around, Al joked about him on other people's shows.

"When I die," he said with a grin, "they'll bury Larry Parks."

As for Parks himself, a big row with Columbia robbed him of the parts he wanted to play. He complained of being type-cast. "That's just what I am," he told a columnist. "A shadow."

He was loaned to M-G-M for *Love Is Better Than Ever* with Elizabeth Taylor, and it was not only Miss Taylor's worst picture but almost the worst flop in that studio's history.

Jolson did not concern himself about Parks. Nor did he worry about Oscar Levant, who grumbled constantly about the Kraft show and its writers. "It's all above their heads," he told Jolson.

Al replied: "When things went above our heads when I was with Dockstader, everyone ducked."

As the money rolled in for the opening of *Jolson Sings Again,* and as he continued to draw a minimum of a thousand dollars a week from Decca for his records—in addition to the royalties—the pressure built for new Jolson enterprise.

For once he was taking television seriously and CBS believed they had just the deal to satisfy him. But the money still wasn't right and he wanted time to think. He was tempted to consider getting back to a live audience once more. Somehow now he felt ready for it again; he wanted to see the reaction on people's faces when he sang to them.

Columbia Pictures provided him with the means to do just that. They asked if he would agree to make a promotion tour of the East Coast for *Jolson Sings Again.* It turned into a nationwide tour by airplane, train, and car.

Once again, there was Jolson in the flesh, singing his great old songs. The man who had always known how to tailor his appeal to an audience hadn't lost his touch. In the Chinese district of New York, he sang "My Yellow Jacket Girl," and added a chorus of "Chinatown, My Chinatown" for good measure. In the Italian districts, he gave a sample of "Come Back to Sorrento" and his impersonation of Caruso.

But it was in the Bronx and Brooklyn that Al Jolson really felt he had come home. To the bearded men in wide-brimmed Homburg hats and their wives in head scarves he sang "The Cantor for the Sabbath." When he told them that his next song, "Hatikvah," had raised more than a hundred thousand dollars for the United Jewish Appeal, they shouted "Mazel tov!"

He told them stories in Yiddish and traded recipes for gefilte fish. The Yiddish press made certain there would always be a Jewish following for *Jolson Sings Again.* It praised the new picture lavishly.

While he was in the mood, he instructed the William Morris Agency to get busy on a tour of Israel, "just as soon as I get this television thing settled."

Television represented the sort of challenge he had never been able to turn down. But he was wary of the effect it had on performers. He was afraid it might be too intimate a medium for the kind of performance he usually gave. There were three or four sets in his own home—quite remarkable in those days—and he watched them, fascinated. He saw a youngster on the screen one evening and threw up his hands. "That fellow," he said in disgust, "proves that all you have to do to succeed on TV is to show up."

But on another occasion, he sat glued to the screen long after the star had left and the show had dissolved into the commercials. He had been watching Frankie Laine singing "Mule Train." Laine had the sort of technique he himself had employed. "No wonder they call that kid the Al Jolson of 1949," he murmured to Erle. "He's good—darn good." He didn't like admitting it.

Finally he and CBS came to terms. He would head a big television minstrel show, played with all the old ballyhoo, including the once familiar street parades.

Full-page advertisements of the new "find" in trade magazines showed a big hand clutched around the corner of the page, with the caption: "I'm coming." He was coming—to the tune of more than a million dollars over the next three years.

But he had other things on his mind before work on the series began. He and Erle had adopted a baby girl, Alicia, as a sister for Asa, Jr. They had big plans for the two children.

There were two film deals cooking, too. Harry Cohn was urging Jolson to do a third picture with Larry Parks and it was near the signature stage. But first he wanted to work on the other deal—one in which he was definitely going to play himself.

Jerry Wald and Norman Krasna of RKO Radio Pictures wanted to present a full flag-waving picture about the work of the USO during the war, centered around Jolson. He was going to play Al Jolson because he was never able to play anyone else. This time there would be no other stars to take the glory away from him. It was going to be a true story, but not a documentary. And there would be songs by the bundle.

Al was very excited about the picture, which had a working title of *The Stars and Stripes Forever*. Just as production was about to begin, the title was changed to *Let Me Sing*. The trade press announced that Jolson would begin work on the film as soon as he had finished a whirlwind tour of eight Midwest one-nighters.

New tunes had been written to go with the standard numbers, but Irving Berlin's song, which Al had first sung in *Mammy* and then used as the prelude to *The Jolson Story,* would be the title theme.

When he posed at the piano with Wald and Krasna for new pictures, doubts began to surface. Those publicity pictures told a story. Show business folk who had kidded Jolson about his age looked at them and were shocked. There was a worn look about him.

About this time, London *Daily Express* columnist Eve Perrick met Jolson at a party.

She wrote: "From his voice, from the stories of his triumphant renaissance into the entertainment world after *The Jolson Story* and *Jolson Sings Again,* you imagined he was someone of whom you would say 'Marvelous. He looks about fifty.' Jolson looked all of his sixty-four years."

But Al Jolson was not going to admit it.

People continued to joke about his age—and about his wealth. Bob Hope told an audience who had expected to see Jolson at a benefit, "He couldn't come tonight—because he couldn't get a sitter for the Bank of America."

It did the Jolson ego good to hear those stories, although it was easy to see that he enjoyed the jokes about his money more than those about his age. It was quite obvious, just to follow him down the street, that he was no longer a young man, but if he thought anyone recognized him, he would quicken his step and hold his head up high.

He was honored as *Variety*'s "Man of the Year" and in November 1949, the Variety Club of Washington named him their "Personality of the Year." That was the kind of praise he liked. The presentation was made by Secretary of Defense Stephen T. Early, the man he had bombarded with requests to be allowed to sing to the troops eight years earlier.

"This is presented to you in recognition of your outstanding contributions to the world of entertainment," he said. "The District of Columbia is happy to bring to the attention of its citizens the achievements of one of its own sons."

"Jolie's rarin' to go," Al replied.

Unlike the RKO publicity pictures, those released by Decca and the radio networks were usually at least ten years old—or doctored to look that way.

The pictures he had around his house, lining the staircase and the landing upstairs, were of an earlier vintage and mostly of Al in blackface. As always, he could hide from reality that way.

Remarkably, he needed no camouflage from the insurance companies. In 1949, at the age of (at least) sixty-three and after a rigorous medical checkup, he took out seventy-five thousand dollars' worth of life insurance.

By 1950 Al seemed more popular than ever. He had just recorded a number, with his name on the composer's credits, "No Sad Songs for Me." This song, based on the title of a hit film of the time, was the result of collaboration with Harry Akst, who was responsible for another of his big hits of this period, "Baby Face."

In Britain Jolson's name was featured in the country's first release of long-playing records, with a selection from *Jolson Sings Again.*

When Al met Harry Truman again, he asked the President if he intended to run for office once more. "I don't know," Truman told him. "They may not want me again. Maybe I should run on the slogan 'I need the job.' "

Al told him of the time he had been to Key West, and was shown to the same room that the President had occupied there.

"It was a room with two beds and I spent the night jumping from bed to bed. But I never did figure out which one the President slept in," he said.

Jolson always liked talking to the great—or the men he believed to be great. At the same time, he generally had a word of encouragement for new people who were just starting out on their show business careers.

He made a transatlantic telephone call from his Palm Springs home to Jean Simmons in London to tell her he believed her performance as Ophelia in the Laurence Olivier version of *Hamlet* was the most exciting thing he had seen in a nonmusical film.

Jolson seeing *Hamlet*? The cynics shuddered and Jolson laughed at their reaction. "I like to see a gal play romance and character parts," he said. "But then I haven't changed my style or my delivery for fifty years. It's your heart in it that matters."

And he could have added "your ego." He once said he thought Harry Lauder, W.C. Fields, and he were the only three really great showmen of his time.

In 1950, no one seemed to disagree.

After he had signed his new contract with CBS, the doubts about television recurred. Television, he predicted, would never take the place of radio.

"Television is eating talent and swallowing it wholesale," he said.

"You just can't get people to look at the same faces every week. But they'll listen to the same performer on the radio, unseen."

In the autumn of 1950, something happened to take his mind off his worries about TV.

Al and Erle had spent the previous Christmas in Honolulu, where Jolson had done a show for the troops stationed there—some twelve thousand of them. On the whole, it all looked very peaceful. But it rekindled the memories of the USO days and the magic of the audiences Al had often said were the ones he loved best.

In the summer of 1950 the flag was being carried by men who didn't look half as happy as the troops in Honolulu. They were in a far less happy place—Korea.

The politics of the situation—who fired first on whom—were of no interest to Al. As far as he was concerned, his country was always right. "His boys" needed him once again.

He phoned the White House again. "I'm gonna go to Korea," he told a startled official. "No one seems to know anything about the USO, and it's up to President Truman to get me there."

He was promised that President Truman and General MacArthur, who had taken command of the Korean front, would be told of his offer. But for four weeks, there was no response.

Finally, Louis Johnson, Secretary of Defense, sent Jolson a telegram. SORRY DELAY BUT REGRET NO FUNDS FOR ENTERTAINMENT STOP USO DISBANDED STOP. The message was as much an assault on the Jolson sense of patriotism as the crossing of the 38th parallel had been.

"What are they talkin' about," he thundered. "Funds! Who needs funds! I got my own mazuma, ain't I? I'll pay myself. Comin' too, Harry?"

Harry Akst was not as enthusiastic now as he had been about their World War II escapades. "No, Jolie," he said. "I've had enough—and so have you." He didn't think Jolson should make a trip of that kind.

Al tried to appear unconcerned about the refusal. "Okay," he said. "I'll get someone else."

Abe Lastfogel of the William Morris Agency called Akst the next day and requested that he change his mind. "I want you to go, Harry," he said. "Al wants you to go."

"If he wants me to go so bad, why didn't he ask me himself?" There

237

was no answer from Lastfogel. Two days later Akst put the same question to Jolson himself. "Because you're beautiful," he told his friend. In the thirty-odd years the two men had been together, Akst said he had never known Jolson to ask for anything.

Akst telephoned Erle to tell her he was going along for the ride. "It's Next-Town Reilly again," he said, recalling the character they had known on the racetrack circuit. Reilly was always losing, but certain that "in the next town, everything would be all right."

Erle was in tears when the military car called at their Palm Springs home to take her husband to the airport. She and Asa, Jr., came along for the ride. Al was all dressed up for his new part. He wore a ski cap, a hunting jacket, and a pair of riding boots left over from the second act of *Hold On to Your Hats*.

As they boarded the plane, Asa, Jr., called out, "Daddy, are you going to 'Okio?"

Okio it was. Tokyo, where years before, Al had vowed to sing "Mammy" in the shadow of Hirohito's palace, was to be the headquarters from which he would work. It was understood that he would take no outside engagements while there.

"Just imagine," he laughed, "outside engagements! That means we mustn't play at the Loewe's Theatre, Pusan."

Al laughed till it hurt—and it did hurt. He had to have eighteen shots of antibiotics and vaccine before the military authorities allowed him on the plane. It was much too painful to sit down.

Despite the discomfort, Al Jolson was like a little boy facing a new adventure. He looked very pleased with himself indeed.

But when the two veteran entertainers arrived in Tokyo, he wasn't feeling quite so happy. There had been an overnight stop at Wake Island after the Stratocruiser developed engine trouble, and the only place he and Harry could sleep was in a double bunk in a very cold, very damp hut. Both arrived in Tokyo suffering from streaming colds and irritating coughs.

As soon as they checked into their hotel, Al went down to the reception desk and asked for the nearest hospital. He was directed to an army dispensary, where he was immediately ordered to lie down.

"What are you here for, Mr. Jolson?" asked the young doctor who was examining him.

"To sing," said Al, and he croaked a few lines of "Mammy" to prove it.

"I'm afraid you won't be able to sing for weeks. Take it very easy. You're not a young man, you know."

That was the one thing Al didn't want to be reminded about.

"I gotta sing, son—so don't give me any of your nonsense."

He was obviously going to be a difficult patient. The doctor gave Al a towel to put over his head and a bowl of steaming menthol to put under his nose—and ordered him to inhale for thirty minutes. Jolson came out of the tent after thirty minutes and promised to repeat the dose every hour for the next week.

But what was he going to do, now that he had come all that way to Tokyo? "What do ya think I can do?" He turned to Harry Akst. "What do ya think I can do? Sing, that's what—if only my voice wasn't so rusty. Perhaps I'll just tell a few jokes.

A staff car came to his hotel to take him to the military hospital in the heart of the Japanese capital. "Just gonna tell your guys a few jokes," he told the commanding officer who came to meet him at the door. "My pipes are a bit bad. Hope they understand."

"Of course, Mr. Jolson," said the CO. "Of course, they'll understand."

But Jolson could see it wasn't really going to be enough.

"Look, Harry," said Al as he was being escorted down the hospital corridor. "I'll just sing 'em one song. Then it won't seem so bad. After all, look what some of these guys have got. Not just a little cold."

There was an uproarious welcome as Jolson entered the big hospital waiting hall, which had been turned into a temporary theatre. There were cheers, whistles, and thumps of wooden crutches on the tiled floor.

Harry Akst played the opening bars of "Mammy," and Al picked it up on the chorus. He coughed—but ordered Akst to play "Swanee." And then "April Showers." Then, "Some Enchanted Evening" and "There Is Nothing Like a Dame"—hit songs from *South Pacific.*

He sang for nearly an hour, joked for twenty minutes more, and then apologized for having to go. But he didn't go straight back to the hotel. His driver had to drop him off at the dispensary first for another menthol treatment.

The next day there was another hospital stop—followed by another dose of steam inhalation.

Jolson always had the people waiting to hear him sing and he always had a song especially for them. But there were some occasions when he had to work harder than others.

At Iwokuni, just before Al and Harry took off for Korea, he had trouble getting through to his audience. In fact, half of what should have been his audience wasn't even there.

"Where are these guys?" Jolson asked between songs, looking a good deal less hurt than he felt. This sort of thing had not happened to him for a long time. One man in front finally spoke up. "It's our wing commander," he said in a broad Australian accent. "He didn't come back from Korea today."

That was all Al had to hear. He left the platform, walked out into the airfield, and pushed the men outside into the mess hall. "Now," he said, "You gotta hear me. The CO warned that you'll all be in trouble if you don't listen to my songs. Now what'll it be?"

Once finished, Jolson rushed back to the dispensary for more inhalations. But now they weren't helping him as much as they had before.

The next day Al, Harry and the "purple latrine on wheels"—Akst's piano—were loaded on a plane for Pusan, Korea.

At Eighth Army headquarters, Jolson was introduced to the commanding general, Walton Walker. Al sang his heart out in Pusan, entertaining thousands of men. "I don't feel so good," he told them. "But maybe after listening to me, you'll feel worse!"

The Jolson-Akst show moved on to Chinghai, Miryan, and Masan. The sound of continuous rifle fire interjected itself between his songs.

"If they don't like my show, why don't these guys go away," Jolson joked, and brought the house down.

In a hospital ward, a nurse caught a soldier bandaged from head to foot, applauding wildly while his hands were supposed to be suspended in traction.

"Don't do that," she scolded. "That could be very dangerous for you."

"I don't care," answered the soldier. "This guy's good."

But there was no menthol in the hospital for Jolson. He had to make do with a gargle of antiseptic solution. It really wasn't enough.

"Al's going on nothing but nerve now," said Harry. At times, he was

240

so exhausted he had hardly enough energy to use the gargle. But he had enough to feel angry. It was obvious that other entertainers were taking their time in following him to Korea.

A tired and very shaken Al Jolson was heard live by short wave from Pusan on Louella Parsons' Los Angeles radio show. "You know, honey," he told her, "I performed for fighting men on battle fronts all over the world in World War II. But there's never been anything to compare with this. This is no borderline skirmish. This is war with all the hell, death, and destruction that only war can bring.

"I'd like to see some of you senators and congressmen come over here and live under the horrible conditions these kids—and believe me, they are just kids—are living under. They'd find out that this Korean thing is the worst ever. The mud, the stench, the filth everywhere are unbelievable.

"Louella, listen, honey, I want you to do me a big favor—and don't fail me on this—tell all the Bob Hopes, Jack Bennys, Bing Crosbys, Tony Martins, Eddie Cantors, Danny Thomases, George Jessels, and all the others, 'If you don't come to Korea to entertain these kids immediately, and do your part, you'll be sorry for the rest of your lives'—and I mean that.

"Oh, what a ham I am," he added for good measure. But no Jolson message got through louder or clearer—despite the static on the line.

Before Al had left Korea, the first USO troupe had arrived. In the meantime, there were many more Jolson concerts, more songs, and more coughs.

General Douglas MacArthur, not yet in disgrace with President Truman for wanting to extend the conflict into China, invited Al to his home. While waiting for the general to arrive, Mrs. MacArthur entertained Al and Harry with small talk about her family. Finally, she got around to Jolson's singing. " 'Sonny Boy' was always my favorite," she said.

That was enough—cough or no cough. Al motioned Harry to the piano in the MacArthur lounge—and sang "Sonny Boy" for his hostess.

The general arrived while Al was still singing. He spent the next two hours talking to Al about the fighting, about life back home, and about Jolson's singing. Al told reporters later, "I think the general is one of the greatest men there is."

That evening, a military policeman arrived at Jolson's hotel with a brown envelope. Excited, Al opened it with trembling fingers. Inside, he found a large photograph bearing the inscription, "To Al Jolson with gratitude and admiration. Douglas MacArthur, Japan 1950."

On Al's last night in Tokyo before returning home, Brigadier General Paul Kelly gave him a surprise dinner, complete with geisha girls. The girls had been especially coached to sing "April Showers,"the song he had sung for the last time in Korea the day before.

Jolson told Harry he was feeling better now. Harry thought otherwise. As far as he could see, it was just another form of self-deception on Al's part to prime himself for his reunion with Erle.

At the airport, Al was bubbling with jokes. His face was still deeply suntanned. On the aircraft, he chatted with newspapermen all anxious for a story on how he had managed in Korea after forty-two shows.

Every time the stewardess came around with the drinks, All pulled out a couple of dollar bills. During the whole journey to Hawaii, he paid for the drinks and refused to allow anyone else to spend a thing.

He talked as fast as the words would come out. "They're the greatest guys the world has ever seen. And Mrs. MacArthur, would you believe it, she's a baseball fan. Keeps talking about batting averages. Imagine!"

The plane arrived at Hawaii two hours too late to catch the connecting flight to Los Angeles. "Never mind," said Al. "We'll go to the Royal Hawaiian. And I'm paying. I paid my own way out to Korea, didn't I? So this won't make too much difference."

Jolson had found himself an audience again. He could afford to be generous, it was true. But now he wanted to be. In September 1950, he felt he had a lot to be thankful for and he didn't want anyone to even have to buy him a glass of whiskey. It was Jolson's party.

"Forty-two shows, eh, Jolie?" asked one newspaperman. "Whatda ya mean, forty-two shows?" the singer replied. "One forty-two, ain't it?"

Whether it was or not, Harry Akst had to agree that it had certainly seemed like one forty-two.

All the way to Los Angeles, Jolson told stories about his life, about Broadway, about Hollywood and about Korea.

"I wouldn't take a penny or a million dollars for the chance to sing for those guys. Believe me, 150 shows just wasn't enough."

By the time the plane landed at Los Angeles, Jolson had done 160 shows in Korea—and one reporter said he had told him he did 165. It didn't matter. On the Korean tour, Al Jolson sang out not just his heart, but every inch of his flesh and spirit, too.

Erle was waiting for Al at the L.A. airport with little Asa. Al gave them both a great big hug and handed Asa a sombrero he had picked up in his travels. With a cigarette in his mouth, he posed for the expected picture.

But the interviews he gave were unlike any he had given before.

"I'm not interested in anything," he told reporters. "I'm really two shakes ahead of a fit. My pulse is fast, I don't sleep good. So I think I'll go up to someplace, maybe Palm Springs, I don't know. Maybe a week will do it—if I can sleep.

"And I'm a little nervous."

"What of the future?" he was asked. "Well," he said, "the Morris Agency wants me to do a television spot around Thanksgiving, but I want them to find me somethin' to do for nothing.

"One of the first things I've got to do is to go around to Columbia to tell Harry Cohn that maybe I won't do a third picture."

Still wearing his overalls with an Air Force badge on the pocket, he took Erle and the boy to their car and drove off to Palm Springs.

He didn't rest. He spoke on the telephone, met friends, and "danced around." But he looked tired and ill.

There was one promise he had to fulfill before thinking about resting. His records were still being played on every radio station, and Bing Crosby had begged him to appear on his show, which was being taped in San Francisco. Crosby wanted to be the one who officially welcomed him back to the United States.

On October 23, 1950, Al kissed Erle and Asa, Jr., goodbye, got in his car and drove to Los Angeles Airport. The San Francisco flight was held up for the arrival of his party: Al, Harry Akst, Eppy, and Martin Fried.

16

WHEN I LEAVE THE WORLD BEHIND

THE CAR waiting at San Francisco's International Airport took less than half an hour to complete the journey to downtown San Francisco. Up and down the hills, following the rattling cable cars, to the St. Francis Hotel, where celebrities always stayed while visiting the Golden Gate city.

Al jumped out of the car, rolled his eyes for the cameraman, patted the doorman on the back, and walked into the lobby.

"What ya want to do, Harry?" Al asked Akst as soon as they got to their room.

"Well, maybe we should discuss the show."

"Sure, but let's go down to Fisherman's Wharf first and have some of that seafood everyone talks about. Haven't been in Frisco for a long time."

It was as though he were expecting a new earthquake. And in a way he was.

A car was waiting for the party outside the hotel. Al decided to sweat out his fatigue in the hotel's Turkish bath before doing anything else. After the steam session, Al said he felt tired, but very refreshed— and told his friends to get ready to leave. He bounced out of the lobby and into the car, followed by Eppy and Akst.

Martin Fried stayed in the hotel to work on the musical arrangements for the Crosby show while they were still fresh in his mind. He had a new version of "I'm Just Wild About Harry," dedicated to President Truman, that he wanted to try out on the piano.

At the Wharf, Al ate a hearty supper of clam chowder, prawns, and all the things his doctors, his father, and his religion had warned him against. At one stage during the meal, Al seemed to be searching for a belch that wouldn't come. But he passed off the momentary discomfort.

He had had the same feeling a week earlier, during a boxing match he and Harry Akst were watching in Los Angeles. Just as the fight reached its climax, Al put his hand to his chest.

"What's the matter, Al?" Harry asked. "I should never have had that Spanish food on the way here," Al said, looking pale. "I can't resist the stuff—but it always has the same effect."

Akst drove him back to Erle's mother's home in Beverly Hills, where Erle was waiting for him.

"Make him see a doctor, honey," Akst advised.

The next day, the Jolsons went to a doctor, who advised Al to start taking it easy. "No more Koreas, Mr. Jolson," he said. "Your heart isn't quite the same as it used to be."

"What da ya mean, it ain't the same?" he growled. "I'm goin' to Frisco next week to appear with Bing and I'm gonna make a couple of films."

"Do all the films and the radio shows you want to do," said the doctor. "But no more Koreas."

Al promptly went to two more doctors—and heard the same advice.

He could not help thinking about that advice now as he sat in the restaurant overlooking the bay. But there was a lot of satisfaction in being there. People were coming up to him, shaking his hand, telling him how great he was on the stage, in the films, and how much they admired his work in Korea.

On the journey back to the hotel, Al seemed content. "They like me, don't they?" he said to Akst. "Yep. Jolson still has them in his hand."

Back in his room, Al undressed and put on a bathrobe. Martin Fried was writing a letter and wasn't in the mood to discuss the show the next day.

"Let's play some gin rummy," said Jolson. It was the sort of suggestion his friends were delighted to accept.

They played two games—and Al won them both. "Another game, Al?" asked Eppy and began to deal the cards again.

"No," said Jolson. "I'm feeling a bit tired. Think I'll just have a lie down." He turned to Martin Fried. "Do Julie a favor, will you?" he called. "Go call room service and get me some bicarbonate of soda."

Fried dialed room service and then went in to check on Al, who was now lying on his small single bed. He looked pale; Fried decided to make another call—to the house doctor.

"There are two," said the operator. "But both are out on calls. Would you like the nurse?"

"Yes," said Fried. "And ask her to hurry."

Nurse Anne Murchison was there in moments.

Al knew what was going on. But he made no protest.

"I heard about a doctor here called Kerr," he said. "Why not get him."

It took some time for Akst to find the doctor—he wasn't listed in the telephone directory. But the hotel nurse knew him and found the number. She took Al's pulse and told him it was nothing to worry about. "I really think it's just indigestion," she said. "But try Dr. Kerr."

The doctor wasn't very happy about being called at that late hour. "It'll take me some time to get there," he said.

"But this is for Al Jolson," said Akst.

"Al Jolson? Is he in San Francisco? All right, I'll be straight down. But until I get there, call the house physician again."

Jolson picked up the extension phone. "Don't worry, Doc," he said, "I don't want to read in the papers tomorrow that Al Jolson called a big shot doctor out for a dose of indigestion."

"Don't worry, Mr. Jolson. I'm coming. You don't worry about the papers. I won't tell anyone."

When he arrived in Al's room, Dr. Walter Bech, the house physician, was already there with the patient. He heard Al joke, "You know, President Truman only had an hour with General MacArthur. I had two."

While Dr. Kerr went into the bathroom to wash his hands, Anne Murchison took a look at the patient.

"Don't worry, Mr. Jolson," she said. "You're going to be all right."

"All right?" said Al. "Who yer kiddin'? I've got no pulse."

The two doctors went to the bedside. "Pull up some chairs," Al instructed, lifting his head. "I've got some stories to tell you."

Al reached for his pulse again just as Eppy, Harry Akst, and Martin Fried came over to his bed.

Again, he seemed to be pulling himself up. "Well, boys," he said faintly. "This is it . . . I'm going . . . I'm going."

The men around the bed looked at each other. Dr. Kerr reached for Jolson's pulse. There wasn't one. Dr. Bech put his stethoscope to the patient's chest. It was quiet.

Jolson had gone. The entertainer was dead. No applause for his final exit—only tears and curtains.

17

YOU AIN'T HEARD NOTHIN' YET

NEWS OF Al Jolson's death hit the front pages of newspapers throughout the world.

In his home city of Los Angeles, the *Times* brought out a special extra edition with three-inch banner headlines, "AL JOLSON DIES—Heart Attack Claims Famed Jazz Singer in SF Hotel."

The *New York World-Telegram* printed a simple cartoon, a pair of white gloves outstretched with the caption, "The Song is Ended."

But the song was by no means ended. Even as Al Jolson's body was being taken into Temple Israel on Hollywood Boulevard to lie in state, stores throughout the United States, Canada, Britain, Australia, and New Zealand reported an unprecedented demand for Jolson records.

Jolson films were shown on television. Movie theatres throughout the world had Jolson festivals.

Neither the record buyers nor the moviegoers could know then that, far from disappearing from the scene, Jolson—now on records and in films—would be around for years to come.

But in October 1950, there was just an overwhelming feeling of sadness among both the people who had been paying money to see and hear him and his contemporaries in show business. Men, women, and children by the hundreds filed past Al's open coffin, paying their last respects.

It was a fitting end for a king. He wore a blue suit with the Jewish prayer shawl draped around his shoulders. In his lapel was a decoration he had been awarded by the Italian government for his work in entertaining the troops during the war.

Many of America's great showmen came to pay homage at the

funeral. Jack Benny and George Burns were among the pallbearers, as were Eddie Cantor and George Jessel. Larry Parks, Harry Cohn, Sidney Skolsky, William Demarest, and Louis B. Mayer were all there.

Erle, who had collapsed on hearing the news of Al's death, had to be helped into the temple by her brother, an army sergeant.

Harry Jolson and his half brothers were also at the service. For Harry, the past was forgiven but not forgotten. The bitter hatred that Harry had had for Al at times couldn't blind him to the impact his younger brother had made. Whatever one felt about Jolson as a person, one had to admire the way he had been able to dominate both the audience and the business.

When Al died, a British newspaper columnist said that even in death, Jolson had shown a trouper's timing. He had gone while still on top.

Daily *Variety* put it more poetically:

"An institution and an era of the show business stopped breathing Monday night in a St. Francis Hotel suite in San Francisco. A legend now begins to live.

"Al Jolson, the greatest musical comedy star of his time and perhaps of all time, died at the age of sixty-four. The end came suddenly and dramatically. It came at the height of his career, with the cheers of the GIs in Korea fresh in his ears—and a new fabulous picture contract to afford him sweet knowledge that he was still a top star. . . .

"He had a record to be envied, both for his war work and as a star. He hit the top in every medium he tried."

As the writer of that piece intimated, Al Jolson left behind a legend.

Jolson's published will showed he was worth $3,236,000, practically all of which went to charity. It was to be equally divided between Jewish, Catholic, and Protestant institutions, with three hundred thousand dollars earmarked for the college education of poor boys and girls.

He had made private arrangements for Erle and the children, and left his brother Harry ten thousand dollars.

Harry Akst and Lou Epstein were left nothing more than their memories. Al had made it clear that he believed he had looked after them more than enough when he was alive.

Jolson himself lives on in memories, in legend, and in voice. When

Asa, Jr., was ten years old, he was handed the keys to a vault in a Hollywood bank. It contained a real treasure—the tapes of the Jolson radio shows, many of which were transcribed onto records by Decca.

General George Marshall, Secretary of Defense at the time of Al's death, pinned onto the breast of Asa, Jr., the Medal of Merit, awarded posthumously to Al. The citation reads that, as much as any service man on the battlefield, Jolson had given his life in Korea.

At the Hillcrest Country Club, old-timers gather around the famous Round Table and talk about Jolson. The years have not erased all the jealousies or the honest resentments.

More than twenty years have gone by since George Jessel stared at the thousands waiting outside Temple Israel for Jolson's funeral and said, "Al's turned them away again." Much of the gilt has faded from the phrases he used in his magnificent funeral eulogy. Today Jessel sees Jolson in a different perspective. "He was a no-good son of a bitch," he has said. "But he was the greatest entertainer I've ever seen."

The members of the Hillcrest no longer complain about Jolson doing them out of their sturgeon or beating them to the final spot on a benefit bill. Most of them would give their not inconsiderable fortunes for one more chance to see that slightly corpulent figure roll his eyes, throw out his arms, and shout, "You ain't heard nothin' yet!"

INDEX

"About a Quarter to Nine," 150
Abrahams, Maurice, 69
Actors Equity, 79
Adler, Larry, 95
Akst, Harry, 95, 124, 133, 162-63, 177-78, 189-90, 192, 221, 237; and Jolson's death, 244ff., 249; on troop tours, 172ff., 237-38ff.
Alexander, Tsar, 19
"Alexander's Ragtime Band," 52, 223
Alexander's Ragtime Band (film), 224
Allen, Gracie, 156
Ameche, Don, 159, 193
American Mercury, 83-84
American Red Cross, 84
American War Veterans Committee, 217
Amos 'n Andy, 224
"Anniversary Song, The," 205-6, 220, 232
"April Showers," 83, 88, 113, 202, 205, 211, 218, 220, 222, 239, 242
Armstrong, Harry, 155
Artists and Models, 108
ASCAP, 149-50
Associated Press, 215
Atkinson, Brooks, 165
Atteridge, Harold, 65, 72, 84
"Avalon," 79

"Baby Face," 236
Bacon, Lloyd, 120
Bayes, Nora, 52
Bayes, Nora, Theatre, 135-37
Beatty, Admiral Lord, 84
Bech, Dr. Walter, 246, 247
Beeler, Aggie, 34, 35
Bell Company, 151-52
Belle Paree, La, 54-59
Benchley, Robert, 91
Benny, Jack, 16, 169, 179, 224, 226, 228, 249
Bergen, Edgar, 224
Berle, Milton, 194

Berlin, Irving, 16, 43, 52, 61, 134. *See also* specific songs
Bernie, Ben, 95, 96
Besinger, R. F., 109
Besserer, Eugenie, 117
Big Boy, 90, 91-94, 108; film, 134-35
Billboard, 87
Bombo, 82-84
Bow, Clara, 151
"Brass Band Ephraim Jones," 61
Brice, Fanny, 66, 110, 124, 158
Brigadiers, The, 40
"Brother, Can You Spare a Dime?", 138, 146, 176
Brown, Joe E., 140
Brown, Lew, 121, 122
Bruce, Carol, 175-76
Brunswick Records, 109
Buchman, Sidney, 198, 202, 205ff., 212, 213, 231
Burke, Johnny, 222
Burlesque, 179
Burns, George, 16, 76, 107, 156, 179, 249
Bijou Theatre (Washington), 33-34

Cafe Trocadero, 155
Cagney, James, 153, 175, 204
"California, Here I Come," 83, 158, 205, 210
Calloway, Cab, 154
Cantor, Asa, 20, 21, 22
Cantor, Eddie, 89-90, 91, 106, 114, 123, 127, 128, 131, 132, 217; as pallbearer, 249; radio show, 222, 224
Cantor, Ida, 132
"Cantor for the Sabbath, The," 233
Capone, Al, 88-89
Caruso, Enrico, 45, 76
"Carolina in the Morning," 212
Casey, Dan, 40
CBI Roundup, 174
CBS, 151, 157, 161, 233, 234, 236. *See also* specific shows

251

Caesar, Irving, 74, 75, 136
Chaliapin, Fyodor, 136
Chaplin, Charlie, 116, 120
Chaplin, Saul, 206, 211
Chevalier, Maurice, 224
Chevrolet, 138
Chicago *American*, 96
Chicago *Sunday Recorder-Herald*, 64-65
Children of the Ghetto, 36
"Chloe," 74
Christie, E. P., 159
Clayton, Lou, 128, 129
Cochrane, C. B., 134
Cohan, George M., 78, 175, 199
Cohn, Harry, 15, 179, 180, 191, 197-98ff.,
    211ff., 218-19, 230-31, 234; as pall-
    bearer, 249
Cohn, Jack, 198, 201
Colgate, 175
Collins, Josie, 59, 61
Colonial Theatre (Boston), 128
Colonial Theatre (New York), 51
Colony Theatre (New York), 113
Columbia Pictures, 179-80, 191, 197-214,
    215, 222, 229, 232, 233. *See also* Cohn,
    Harry
Columbia Records, 108-9
"Come Back to Sorrento," 233
"Come Along, My Mandy," 52
Como, Perry, 194, 217, 228
Conte, Richard, 203
Coolidge, Calvin, 105
Cooper, Al, 109-10
Cortez, Ricardo, 144
Costello, Johnny Irish, 124, 125
Crosby, Bing, 194, 200, 218, 220, 222-24ff.,
    232, 242
Crosby, Everett, 223
Crosland, Alan, 117, 118
Curtiz, Michael, 199

Dames, 141
Dancing Around, 68, 69-71
Dean, Barnie, 15
Decca Records, 195, 218-19, 223, 228-29,
    233, 235, 250
Del Rio, Dolores, 144
Demarest, William, 208, 249
Dempsey, Jack, 129
Dennis, J. S., 75
De Pinna's, 121-22
Deslys, Gaby, 59-60, 65, 66
De Sylva, Buddy, 73, 74, 83, 84, 121, 122
Dexter, Charles E., 85
*Dixon and Bernstein's Turkey Burlesque
    Show*, 40
Dockstader's, Lew, Minstrels, 48-51, 52, 54
Don Juan (film), 116
Donahue, Jack, 140
Donaldson, Walter, 75

Donath, Ludwig, 118, 208, 224, 231
Dooley, James Francis, 43
"Down Among the Sheltering Palms," 228
"Down By the O-hio," 81
"Down Where the Tennessee Flows," 67
Dru, Joanne, 165
Durante, Jimmy, 128, 129, 224

"E Lucevan le Stelle," 79
Early, Stephen, 169, 235
Eddy, Nelson, 224
Edwards, Big Bill, 79
Eisenhower, Dwight D., 176
Eisenhower, Mamie, 176
Ellis, Melville, 62
Epstein, Louis "Eppy," 76-77, 80-81, 95, 107,
    124, 167, 169, 178, 192, 194, 243; and
    girls, 111, 112; and Jolson's death, 249
"Everybody Rag with Me," 69
Exhibition Trade Review, 86

Fairbanks, Douglas, 116
Falkenberg, Jinx, 165-66
Faye, Alice, 158, 159, 210
Ferrer, José, 203
Fields, W. C., 236
Fifth Avenue Theatre (New York), 50
Flirtation Walk, 141
Forty-second Street, 130-31, 141
Foster, Stephen, 72, 159
Fox, Harry, 66-67
Francis, Kay, 144
Friars Club, 75, 226
Fried, Martin, 170, 178, 243, 244ff.

Garland, Judy, 16
General Motors, 139
Gerry Society, 31, 39
Gershwin, George, 16, 74-75, 88, 110, 128,
    146-47, 194, 225
"Give My Regards to Broadway," 177
Go into Your Dance, 149, 150-51
"Going to Heaven on a Mule," 144
Gold Diggers of 1933, 141
Gordon, Vera, 114
Goodman, Al, 75
Grand Opera House (New York), 50-51
Grant, Jack, 144
Grauman, Sid, 153, 156
Grauman's Chinese Theatre, 156-57
Gray, Barry, 221-22
Green, Alfred E., 207
Green Book, 79
Griffith, David Wark, 84-86, 87
Guinan, Texas, 123-24

Hale, Barbara, 231
Hale, George, 163-64
Hallelujah, I'm a Bum, 139-40, 143-44, 145
Hamlet, 236

Hamlin, Sammy, 230
Hammerstein, Oscar, 51
Harburg, E. Y. "Yip," 164
Harding, Warren G., 81
"Harding, You're the Man for Us," 81
Harold, Orville, 94
Harold, Patti, 95
Hart, Lorenz, 139
Hastings, Charles, 61
"Hatikvah," 299, 233
Hayworth, Rita, 179, 197
Hayward, Dubose, 146
"He Had to Get Out and Get Under," 56
Healey, Eunice, 164
"Hello, My Baby," 51
Henderson, Ray, 121, 122
Hess, Julius, 47
Hesselson, Hirsch, 18
Heyne, Leo, 166
Hildegarde, 217
Hillcrest Country Club, 168-69, 179, 216,
    227-28, 250
Hofstadter, Samuel H., 167
Hold On to Your Hats, 164-67
Holmes, Frank, 77
Hollywood Bowl, 141
Hollywood Cavalcade, 159
Honeymoon Express, The, 65-67
Hope, Bob, 217, 224, 226, 235
Horses, 90-91
Hunter, Ross, 204
Hutchens, John K., 158

"I Love to Sing-A," 154
"I Only Have Eyes for You," 232
"I Want Something New," 60
"Ida, Sweet as Apple Cider," 33
"If You Knew Susie," 91-92
"I'll Say She Does," 74
"I'm Glad My Wife's in Europe," 69
"I'm Sitting on Top of the World," 121
"Is It True What They Say About Dixie?",
    177, 228, 232
"Israel," 229
"It All Depends on You," 121
"It's a Long Way Back to Dear Old Mam-
    my's Knee," 50
"It's a Long Way to Tipperary," 69

Jackson, Eddie, 128, 129
Jazz Singer: film, 114-15, 116-19, 120, 122,
    126, 134, 204, 224; play, 113, 114
Jessel, George, 16, 110, 112ff., 137-38, 152,
    166, 177, 179, 217, 250; as pallbearer,
    249
Johnson, Louis, 237
Jolson, Al (See also specific relationships,
    shows, etc.): death; funeral, 15, 16,
    244-47, 248-50; family background;
    early childhood; move to U.S.; 18-35;

family members (See Yoelson); and
films, 72, 84-86, 87, 113-15, 116-23
(See also specific films); first status
symbols, 59; gets down on one knee,
67; and norseracing, 90-91; illnesses and
remedies, 32, 46, 51, 94, 142, 167, 177,
192, 201, 238-39ff., 245-47; marriages
(See specific wives); name change, 29;
and radio, 113, 138-39, 145-47, 221-26
(See also specific networks, programs);
and records (See specific companies,
songs); as runaway, 29-32; and runway,
62-63; and Spanish-American war, 33;
and Sunday performances, 61-62, 107-8;
and stock market, 131-32; and television, 151-52, 233-34, 236-37; and troop
tours, 169-75, 176-77, 237-43; whistles,
38, 52, 56; and World War I, 75-76;
and World War II, 169-75, 176-77
Jolson, Al, Jr. See Lowe, John, Jr.
Jolson, Alicia, 234
Jolson, Asa, Jr., 227, 228, 238, 243, 250
Jolson, Erle Galbraith, 189-92, 193, 195,
    199, 201, 210, 213-14, 226, 2237, 234,
    245; and Jolson's death, 249; and Jol-
    son's troop tours, 238, 243; portrayed
    in film, 231
Jolson, Ethel Delmar, 82, 86ff.
Jolson, Harry (Hirsch), 36, 46, 47, 67-68,
    69, 72-73, 77, 78, 90, 167; and Al's
    death, 249; birth; early childhood, 22ff.;
    boyhood in U.S.; move to N.Y., 26ff.,
    34, 35; due with Al, 38-44; and father's
    death, 213; movie contract, 132
Jolson, Henrietta Keller, 45-46, 51-52, 58,
    61, 63-64, 68-69, 70; divorced, 77, 78
Jolson, Lillian (Mrs. Harry), 47, 72, 77, 90,
    132, 154, 213
Jolson, Ruby Keeler. See Keeler, Ruby
Jolson Sings Again, 212, 231-32, 233
Jolson, Show, Al, 175-76
Jolson Story, The, 15, 31, 49, 118, 196-214,
    215ff., 221, 222, 229, 230ff.
Jolson's Fifty-ninth Street Theatre, 82-83

Kahn, Gus, 69, 74, 83
Kapp, Jack, 218-19, 228-29
Kaye, Danny, 216, 226
Keeler, Ruby, 130-31, 132, 150, 156, 159-60,
    168, 176, 226; and Al, Jr., 152, 153,
    160, 162; career, 128-29, 130-31, 148,
    149, 154, 155, 164; depicted in film,
    206, 207; leaves Al; divorce, 161-62,
    163, 166; meets Al; marries, 124-26, 127
"Keep Cool with Coolidge," 105
"Keep Smiling at Trouble," 90, 121
Keighley, William, 153
Keith-Orpheum circuit, 119
Kelly, Gene, 109
Kelly, PJaul, 242

Kern, Jerome, 54, 146
Kerr, Dr., 246, 247
Keyes, Evelyn, 206-7, 208-9, 212, 213
Klauber, Adolph, 56
Klein, Art, 48, 52-53, 54, 57, 59, 69, 72, 76, 77
"Kol Nidre," 159
Korea, 237-42, 250
Kraft Music Hall, 145-46, 194, 224-26, 232
Krasna, Norman, 234

Laine, Frankie, 234
Lane, Burton, 164
Lastfogel, Abe, 135, 169, 237
Lauder, Harry, 236
Le Boy, Grace, 69
Lee, Davy, 120-21
Leigh, Rowland, 136
Leonard, Eddie, 33-34, 47
Leslie, Edgar, 69
Let Me Sing, 234-35
"Let Me Sing and I'm Happy," 132, 134, 234
Levant, Oscar, 57, 225, 232
Levy, George, 161
Lewis, Joe E., 143
Lewis, Sam, 75
Life, 91
Lifebuoy Soap, 155
Little Egypt Burlesque Show, The, 39
Little of Everything, A, 43
"Little Pal," 122
Little Rock, Ark., 48
"Liza," 128-29
London *Daily Sketch,* 126
Longstreet, Stephen, 207, 215
Los Angeles *Times,* 248
Louis, Joe, 143
Love Is Better Than Ever, 232
Lowe, John, 166
Lowe, John, Jr. (Al Jolson, Jr.), 152, 153, 160, 162, 163, 166
Lubalin, Sam, 230
Lux Radio Theatre, 224

"Ma Blushin' Rosie" ("Rosie, You Are My Posie"), 30, 211, 222
MacArthur, Douglas, 237, 241, 242
MacArthur, Mrs. Douglas, 241, 242
McCree, Junie, 66
McGirk's, 30
McKinley, William, 39
Main's, Walter L., Travelling Circus, 33
"Mammy," 75, 83, 119, 158, 170, 205, 225, 239
Mammy (film), 126, 132, 134
Marshall, George, 171, 250
Mayer, Louis B., 249
Mayflowers, The, 39
Mayhew, Stella, 56, 60, 61
Mayo, Archie, 150

Medal of Merit, 250
Merson, Billy, 65
Metronome, 156
Metropolitan Opera House, 76
Milestone, Lewis, 139
Miller, Marilyn, 123
Mills, Isaac N., 93
Mills Brothers, 228
Mistah Jolson, 69
Moore, Fred E., 36-37, 46
Moore, Grace, 197
Morgan, Frank, 140
Morris, William, Agency, 106, 125, 142, 155, 157-58, 169, 233
Morris, William, Circuit, 47
Morrison, Patricia, 173
Motion Picture, 61
Motion Picture Academy, 119
Motion Picture Classic, 123
Movie Classic, 144
Movie Weekly, 85
Murchison, Anne, 246
Murray, George, 95-96
Music Publishers Holding Corporation, 149-50
"My Mammy." *See* "Mammy"
"My Sumurun Girl," 61
"My Yellow Jacket Girl," 65, 233

" 'N' Everything," 73, 74
Nathan, George Jean, 83-84
NBC, 113, 138, 139, 145, 148, 151, 224
"Nearest Thing to Heaven," 228
Nellie (press agent), 64-65
New York *Herald Tribune,* 158-59, 162
New York *Post,* 165
New York *Sun,* 68, 149, 150
New York *Telegram,* 148
New York Times, 56, 59, 75, 93, 94, 108, 136, 164-65, 173-74, 223, 224
New York *Tribune,* 87
New York *World-Telegram,* 248
New Yorker, 176
"Night Boat to Albany," 76
Night in Spain, A, 123
"No Sad Songs for Me," 236
Norworth, Jack, 52

Oakland, Will, 48
Oberon, Merle, 173
Oberstein, Eli, 218
O'Brien, Neil, 50
Odeon Theatre (Baltimore), 40-41
"Oh, Donna Clara," 136
Oland, Warner, 117-18
"Old Folks at Homes," 71-72, 159
"On the Mississippi," 61
Osterman, Jack, 107-8

Palace Theatre (N.Y.), 133
Paley brothers, 161
Palmer, Joe, 42, 43-44
Paramount Pictures, 134
Parks, Larry, 204, 209-11, 212-13, 215, 231, 232; as pallbearer, 249
Parks, Sam, 151
Parkyakarkus, 155
Parsons, Louella, 241
Pastor, Tony, 43
Patsy Bolivar Revue, 40
Penny Arcade, 153
Perrick, Eve, 235
Philco Radio Time, 222-23
Piccadilly Theatre, 126
Picturegoer, 212-13
Ponselle, Rosa, 107
Porgy, 146
Porgy and Bess, 147
Powell, Dick, 131, 144
Power, Tyrone, 158, 210
Price, Georgie, 72-73, 86-87, 110
Puccini, Giacomo, 79
Radin, Oscar, 57

Radio City Music Hall, 215, 219, 220
Riado Corporation, 119
Radio Corporation, 119
Raft, George, 155
"Ragtime Sextette," 61
Raphaelson, Samson, 114
Raye, Martha, 155, 165, 217
Reader, Ralph, 92, 173
Reece, Bonesetter, 109
Review of Reviews, 67-68
Rhapsody in Blue, 194-95, 197
Rhinelander, Leonard and Alice Jones, 93-94
Rice and Hoppe's Big Company of Fun Makers, 34
Richman, Harry, 110
RKO, 119, 234
Roberts, Beverly, 154
Robinson, Bill "Bojangles," 31
Robinson Crusoe Junior, 71
"Rockabye Your Baby ith a Dixie Melody," 74, 76, 113, 156, 158, 231
Rodgers, Richard, 139
Romberg, Lillian Harris, 84
Romberg, Sigmund, 69, 72, 83, 84
Romero, Cesar, 168
Rooney, Mickey, 161
Roosevelt, Franklin D., 169
Rose, Vincent, 79
Rose Award, 221
Rose of Washington Square, 158-59, 210
Rosenberg, Mickey, 174
"Rosie, You Are My Posie." *See* "Ma Blushin' Rosie"
"Rum-Tum-Tiddle," 59, 60

Runyon, Damon, 156
Ruth, Babe, 31

St. Mary's Industrial Home for Boys, 31-32
Santa Barbara Theatre, 214
"Save Me, Sister," 154
Say It with Songs, 122, 127
Scharf's, Lew, Restaurant, 41
Schenck, Joseph, 140
Schmeling, Max, 143
Schumann, Robert, 57
Schwartz, Jean, 65
Screen Book, 143-44
Screenland, 134
Shayne, Tamara, 208, 224, 231-32
Shell Château, 148ff., 155, 166
Shell Oil, 148
Shields, Ren, 41-42
Shore, Dinah, 217
Show Girl, 128-29, 130
Shreiber, Louis, 106, 107
Shubert brothers (Jake and Lee), 53, 54, 56fl,. 61ff., 66, 67-68, 71, 72, 81, 82, 86ff., 92, 123
Shubert Theatre (N.Y.), 165
Silvers, Lou, 83, 117
Sime (columnist), 50, 62
Simmons, Jean, 236
Sinatra, Frank, 16, 194, 217, 228, 229
Sinbad, 73-74, 75, 80-81
Singing Fool, The, 120-22, 134
Singing Kid, The, 153-54
Skolsky, Sidney, 196-97ff., 207, 249
Smith, Kate, 139
"Snap Your Fingers," 61
"Some Enchanted Evening," 239
"Sonny Boy," 121, 172, 212, 214, 241
Sons o' Guns, 140
"Spaniard Who Blighted My Life, The," 62, 65, 205, 224
Spanish-American War, 32-33
Stanwyck, Barbara (Ruby Stephens), 112-13
Stewart, James, 198
Stoloff, Morris, 205, 208, 212, 219, 223, 229, 232
Sullivan and Considine Circuit, 47
Summit Hotel Company, 151, 166
"Swanee," 74-75, 172, 194-95, 197, 205, 211, 218, 220, 225
Swanee River, 159
"Sweet Sixteen," 41, 50
Synon, Katherine, 64-65

"Take Away the Gun from Every Mother's Son," 81
Taps, Jonie, 16, 214, 218, 219, 232
Taylor, Billee, 57
Taylor, Elizabeth, 232

Templeton, Fay, 30
"That Develin' Rag," 57
"That Haunting Melody," 60
"That Lovin' Traumerei," 57
Theatre (magazine), 65-66, 135
"There Is Nothing Like a Dame," 239
Thomas, Danny, 203
Thornton, Jim, 41
Time, 225
"Toot, Toot, Tootsie," 83, 117, 158, 222
Truman, Harry, 59, 228, 236, 237
Twentieth Century-Fox, 158, 159

United Artists, 140
United Jewish Appeal, 221
USO, 170-77, 180, 241

Valentino, Rudolph, 66
Vallee, Rudy, 161, 200
Van, Billy B., 39-40
Vanderbilt, bets on horse, 91
Van Heusen, Jimmy, 222
Variety, 44, 50, 51, 57, 60, 62, 107, 155
170, 235, 249
Vera Violetta, 59-60
Victoria Theatre (N.Y.), 51
Villanova Touring Burlesque Company, 34-35
Vitagraph Company, 72
Vitaphone Company, 113-15. *See also*
Warner Brothers

Wald, Jerry, 234
Walker, James J., 217
Walker, Walton, 240
Wall Street crash, 131-32
War Department, 170, 171
Warner, Harry, 113, 116, 120
Warner, Jack, 113, 120, 129, 130, 143, 149,
199, 210
Warner, Sam, 116, 120
Warner Brothers, 113-15, 116ff., 127, 129,
135, 144, 158, 197, 199, 210 (*See also*
Warner, Jack; specific films); and music
royalty row, 149-50; and Ruby Keeler,
141, 145, 154
Warner Theatre (N.Y.), 122
West, Mae, 60
Westchester Biltmore Country Club, 110
"When the Grown-up Ladies Act Like
Babies," 69
"When the Red, Red Robin Comes Bob,
Bob, Bobbin' Along," 113

"Where the Black-Eyed Susans Grow," 71,
76
"Where Did Robinson Crusoe Go with Fri-
day on Saturday Night?," 71
Whirl of Society, The, 60-61, 62-63, 64
White Rats, the, 47
"Who Cares?," 88
"Who Paid the Rent for Mrs. Rip Van
Winkle?," 66
Whoopee, 127-28
"Why Adam Sinned," 52
Williams, Bert, 52
Wilson, Woodrow, 69-70
Winchell, Walter, 137, 141-42, 142-43
Winchell, Mrs. Walter, 141
Winter Garden (N.Y.), 53, 54-58ff. *See also*
specific productions
Wonder Bar, The, 135-38; film, 144-45, 149,
158
Woolf, S. J., 173
World War I, 73, 75-76, 84
World War II, 169-80
Wynn (columnist), 62

"Yaaka Hula Hickey Dula," 71
Yankee Doodle Dandy, 175, 199, 204
Yoels, Perri, 28
Yoelson, Emil, 106
Yoelson, Etta, 22, 23, 28, 31, 41
Yoelson, George, 106
Yoelson, Gertrude, 106
Yoelson, Hessi (stepmother), 28-29, 32, 38,
Yoelson, Hirsch. *See* Jolson, Harry
Yoelson, Moses (father), 18-27, 28, 34, 35,
38, 41, 70, 96, 106, 110, 145, 152, 169;
and Al's marriages, 46, 63-64, 125, 193;
death, 213-14; depicted in film, 207-8;
and runaway Al, 31, 32; visits New
York, 64
Yoelson, Myer, 106
Yoelson, Naomi, 21ff.
Yoelson, Rose, 21, 23, 28, 41
Yossi, Hayim, 25
"You Are My Jersey Lily," 34
"You Are Too Beautiful," 139
"You Made Me Love You," 70
Young, Joe, 69, 75
Young, Richard, 140

Zangwill, Israel, 36
Zanuck, Darryl F., 113, 114, 116, 130-31,
145
Ziegfeld, Florenz, 53, 127, 128, 129
Ziegfeld Theatre (N.Y.), 128-29